TRẦN QUANG HẢI

50 Years of Research in Vietnamese Traditional Music and Overtone Singing

Tran Quang Hai, Ph.D.

TỦ SÁCH KHAI TRÍ

2018

Cover photo: Le Phuc
Book Design: Thai H. Pham
Production Team: NHAN VAN NGHE THUAT
Published by TU SACH KHAI TRI
Copyright by NHAN VAN NGHE THUAT

ISBN: 9781794125674

My heartfelt thanks to my father (Prof. Trần Văn Khê) for all I have learnt from his teaching of Vietnamese music and Oriental ethnomusicology.

To my dearest wife Bạch Yến for her constant support and efficient contribution to the development of Vietnamese music performance.

PREFACE

Professor Tran Quang Hai asked me to write an **introduction** to this book about his Life and his Work.

Not an easy task since his life is not a mere portrait hung on a wall for anyone to look at and describe, if one can.

Professor Hai's life is a long road.

A long road that is.

A road which brings back the scenery of so many byways and highways this amazing man had covered in his memorable and outstanding life. They are the embodiment of the multifacet talents of an amazing artist and scholar.

Being a friend of Professor Hai does not make the task of introducing this book to the reader an easier task. There is always this concern that the writer, being a friend may be skewed to his favor and overstate the facts. Or on the contrary, for that same reason, being concerned of a perception of favoritism, the writer may try to minimize the facts. But should it be a concern? For a man of such talent and integrity, and a body of work which cannot be less than a rare precious jewel, under- or overstatement becomes an irrelevant issue.

To summarize it, the life of Professor Tran Quang Hai is a great but challenging road well-traveled.

And it is traveled by a traveler who, not only is not afraid to conquer it, he has been eager to make it fuller, better, more captivating, albeit more challenging not only for himself, but also for people and future generations who are going to travel this same road.

The Road is Musicology.

Not just from Vietnam where Professor Hai came from. Being born one day in May, 1944, in the Province of Dong Nai, South Viet Nam – a region blessed by its beauty and peaceful life, and also by its inspiring richness in resources and popular culture – the soul of this magnificent scholar and artist as Resourceful and Inspiring as the region he comes from. A soul being shaped by many generations of illustrious ancestors, giants in the field of Vietnamese Musicology with his father Tran Van Khe being an accomplished scholar of Vietnamese and World Musicology.

Professor Hai's road of musicology practice and musicology research goes beyond the confines of his country of origin.

It covers Vietnamese/Oriental Music, from traditional Vietnamese Music of all genres, to the musical background of the Montagnards in the Vietnamese Highlands. It went on beyond borders to address the wonderful aspects of the Musical Heritage of different countries spanning from Southeast Asia to Central Asia to reach as far as Israel, Central Europe to Western Europe.

Professor Hai has been working for the National Center for Scientific Research (CNRS) in France since 1968, and is now retired after working for 41 years at the Department of Ethnomusicology of the Musée de l'Homme (Paris). He was a lecturer on South East Asian music at the University of Paris X - Nanterre (1988-1995).

He plays 15 musical instruments from Vietnam, China, India, Iran, Indonesia and Europe. Since 1966, he has given over 3,000 concerts in 70 countries, and has taken part in a hundred or so international traditional music festivals. He has taken part in radio and television broadcasts in Europe, America, Asia, Africa, and Australia.

Professor Hai has perfected and made us understand more the Jew's Harp, the Song of Harmonics, he is the greatest specialist in overtone singing.

Apart from his artistic activities, he is also interested in musical research. He has improved the technique of spoons playing and of the Jew's harp. In 1970 he found the key to the technique of overtone singing. The film "Le Chant des Harmoniques " (The Song of Harmonics) which he co-produced with Hugo Zemp, and in which he was the principal actor and composer of the film music, won four awards at international scientific film festivals in Estonia (1990), France (1990), and Canada (1991). He is considered as the greatest specialist in overtone singing in the world.

Dr. Tran has written numerous articles on Vietnamese and Asian music (New Grove Dictionary of Music and Musicians, New Grove Dictionary of Musical Instruments, Algemeine Muziekencyclopedia, Encyclopaedia Universalis). He has also recorded 15 LPs and 2 CDs (one of which obtained the Grand Prix de l'Academie de Disque Charles Cros in 1983). He has composed hundreds of popular songs. His musical experience is very varied: contemporary music, electro-acoustical music, improvisation, film music. He continues to preserve and develop traditional Vietnamese music (numerous new compositions for the 16 stringed zither Đàn tranh).

He has received a Gold Medal for music from the Asian Cultural Academy, and honorary doctorates from the International University Foundation (USA), and the Albert Einstein International Academy (USA).

Along with multiple international awards, in June 2002, he received the medal of Knight of the Legion of Honor from the French President Jacques Chirac. In 2009, he was the recipient of the Medal of Honor, category Great Gold for his 41 years as a public servant of France.

He is the only Vietnamese to have taken part as a performer or composer in such great historical events as the Australia's Bicentenary celebrations (1988), the Bicentenary of the French Revolution in Paris (1989), the 700th Anniversary of the Birth of Switzerland (1991), the 350th Anniversary of the Founding of Montreal (1992), the 500th anniversary of the discovery of America (1992), the 600 Years of Seoul-Korea (1994), the Jubilee of the King of Thailand (1996), the 1,000 Years of Trondheim in Norway (1997).

As I have said. Dr. Hai's life is a long Road. A long Road indeed – not only for its length, but also for what has been left behind it.

For the two countries, Viet Nam and France, which are so dear to Professor Hai, his life will always be one of a model scholar for future generations to learn from, a symbol of pride never to fade away no matter the months and years.

For the World, Professor Tran Quang Hai will be remembered as a talented scholar with unparalleled character. Humble and compassionate. But call him simply a World Artist.

This book does render justice, if in part, to this Great Man and his Life. Well deserving to read with time well spent.

For me, Tran Quang Hai will always be, simply, My Friend. And the Honor is mine and the joy well shared.

Dr. Son Vi Nguyen, M.D.

Former Assistant Professor of Psychiatry
- The University of Texas, School of Medicine at Houston.
- Texas Tech University

Contents

Tran Quang Hai's Biography

Tran Quang Hai was born on 13 May 1944 in Vietnam. He is a talented and renowned musician. He comes from a family of five generations of musicians. He studied at the National Conservatory of Music in Saigon before coming to France in 1961 where he studied the theory and practice of Oriental music with his father, Prof.Dr. Trân Van Khê at the Center of Studies for Oriental Music in Paris.

He obtained his MA and Ph. D at the School of High Studies for Social Sciences, where he also attended seminars on ethnomusicology and acoustics with Professor Emile Leipp.

He has played over 15 musical instruments from all across Vietnam, China, India, Iran, Indonesia and Europe. Since 1966, he has performed in over 3,000 concerts in 70 countries, and has taken part in more than a hundred international traditional music festivals. He has taken part in radio and television broadcasts in Europe, America, Asia, Africa, and Australia. He has been working for the National Center for Scientific Research (CNRS) in France since 1968, and is now retired after working for 41 years at the Department of Ethnomusicology of the Musée de l'Homme (Paris). He was a lecturer on South East Asian music at the University of Paris X - Nanterre (1988-1995).

Apart from his artistic activities, he is also interested in musical research. He has improved the technique of spoons playing and of the Jew's harp. In 1970 he found the key to the technique of overtone singing. The film "Le Chant des Harmoniques " (The Song of Harmonics) which he co-produced with Hugo Zemp, and in which he was the principal actor and composer of the film music, won four awards at international scientific film festivals in Estonia (1990), France (1990), and Canada (1991). He is considered as the greatest specialist in overtone singing in the world. He has written numerous articles on Vietnamese and Asian music (New Grove Dictionary of Music and Musicians, New Grove Dictionary of Musical Instruments, Algemeine Musikencyclopedie, Encyclopaedia Universalis). He has also recorded 15 LPs and 2 CDs (one of which

2

obtained the Grand Prix de l'Academie de Disque Charles Cros in 1983). He has composed hundreds of popular songs. His musical experience is very varied: contemporary music, electro-acoustical music, improvisation, film music. He continues to preserve and develop traditional Vietnamese music (numerous new compositions for the 16 stringed zither dàn tranh).

He has received a Gold Medal for music from the Asian Cultural Academy, and honorary doctorates from the International University Foundation (USA), and the Albert Einstein International Academy (USA). Trân Quang Hai works with his wife Bach Yên who is a Vietnamese great folk singer. He has obtained more than 20 prizes and international awards. He was nominated President of the Jury of the Khoomei Throat Singing Festival (Tuva, 1995) He obtained the Cristal Medal of the National Center for Scientific Research (France, 1996). He was also President of Honor of the Festival d'Auch: Eclats de Voix (1999) and the Festival de Perouges / Au Fil de la Voix (2000). He was member of the Jury of the Song Contest 2000 "A Song for Peace in the World" in Roma (2000). And in June 2002, he received the medal of Knight of the Legion of Honor from the French President Jacques Chirac. In 2009, he was the recipient of the Medal of Honor, category Great Gold for his 41 years as a public servant of France.

He is the only Vietnamese to have taken part as a performer or composer in such great historical events as the Australia's Bicentenary celebrations (1988), the Bicentenary of the French Revolution in Paris (1989), the 700th Anniversary of the Birth of Switzerland (1991), the 350th Anniversary of the Founding of Montreal (1992), the 500th anniversary of the discovery of America (1992), the 600 Years of Seoul-Korea (1994), the Jubilee of the King of Thailand (1996), the 1,000 Years of Trondheim in Norway (1997).

Discography

1. Vietnam: Tran Quang Hai & Bach Yen PLAYASOUND PS 33514, Paris 1979, col. Musiques de l'Asie Traditionnelle, vol.10.

2. Cithare et chants populaires du Vietnam Tran Quang Hai & Bach Yen, Paris, 1979.

3. Music of Vietnam. LYRICHORD LLST 7337, New York, 1980.

4. Vietnam/ Tran Quang Hai & Bach Yen. Studio SM 3311.97, Paris, 1983. Grand Prix du Disque de l'Academie Charles Cros 1983.

5. Vietnamese Dan Tranh Music Tran Quang Hai. LYRICHORD LLST 7375, New York, 1983.

6. MUSAICA: chansons d'enfants des emigres. DEVA RIC 1-2, Paris,1984.

5 Compact Discs

"Reves et Realite- Tran Quang Hai & Bach Yen " edited by Playasound PS 65020, Paris, 1988.

"Bach Yen - Souvenir ", edited by William Arthur, Los Angeles, 1994.

"Cithare Vietnamienne - Tran Quang Hai", edited by Playasound PS 65103, Paris, 1993.

"Landscape of the Highlands - Tran Quang Hai", edited by Music of the World, Chapell Hill, USA, 1997.

"Les Guimbardes du Monde - Tran Quang Hai", edited by Playasound, Paris,1997.

5 commercialized cassettes on pop and folk music of Vietnam

1 videocassette on Vietnamese Music (1984)

1 videocassette "Music of Vietnam " produced by Ministry of Education in Perth (Australia) (1989)

4 DVDs

« Le Chant diphonique », CRDP, Co-authors : Tran Quang Hai & luc souvet, 27 minutes, Saint Denis, Ile de la Réunion, 2002.

« Le Chant des harmoniques » CNRS Audiovisuel, co authors : tran quang hai & hugo zemp, 38 minutes, (French version) Paris, 2005

« The Song of Harmonics », CNRSS Audiovisuel, Co Authors: Tran Quang Hai & Hugo Zemp, 38 minutes, (English version), Paris, 2006.

"La Voix", Lugdivine editions, author: Patrick Kersalé, with the cooperation of Tran Quang Hai, 100 minutes, Lyon, 2006.

1 film on Tran Quang Hai

"HAI: parcours d"un musician vietnamien" (HAI : path of a Vietnamese musician), author: Pierre Ravach, 52 minutes, Brussels, 2005.

Participation to these CDs

"Voices of the World", 3 CD, booklet in French/English (188pages), edited by Le Chant du Monde, collection CNRS/Musée de l'Homme, Paris, 1996. Grand Prix du Disque de l'Académie Charles Cros 1997, Le Diapason d'Or de l'Année1997, Le CHOC de l'Année 1997.

"Vietnam: Musics of the Montagnards", 2 CD, booklet in French/English (124pages), edited by Le Chant du Monde, collection CNRS/Musée de l'Homme,Paris, 1997. Le Diapason d'Or, Le CHOC.

"Phillip Peris - Didjeridu", edited by Les Cinq Planètes, Paris, 1997.

"Klangfarben der Kulturen", edited by Staatliche Museen zu Berlin, Berlin, 1998.

"World Festival of Jew's Harp in Molln", 2CDs edited by Molln Jew's Harp Ass., Austria, 1999.

Performer of more than 3,000 concerts in 70 countries around the world since 1966.

Performer of more than 1,000 school music concerts organized by JMF (Jeunesses Musicales de France), JMB (Jeunesses Musicales de Belgique), JMS (Jeunesses Musicales de Suisse), Rikskonsertene of Norway and Sweden.

Performer at more 100 International Music Festivals.

1970: International Sound Festival, Paris, France

Festival of Arts Chiraz-Persepolis, Iran.

1971: Cinq Journées de Rencontre avec le Groupe de Recherches Musicales (GRM), Paris.

Indochinese Cultural Week, Geneva, Switzerland

Oriental Music Festival, Berlin, Germany.

Ajaccio Music Festival, Ajaccio, Corsica, France

15 Days of Folk Music with the Bourdon Folkclub, Geneva, Switzerland.

1972: Pamplona Music Festival, Pamplona, Spain.

"La Geolette d'or", Knokke le Zoute, Belgium.

Traditional Music Festival, Vesdun, France.

SIGMA 8: Contemporary Music Festival, Bordeaux, France

1973: Music Festival of Royan, Royan, France.

International Folk Music Festival, Le Havre, France.

International Festival of Culture and Youth, Presles, France.

1974: Folk Music Festival, Bezons, France.

International Folk Music Festival, Colombes, France.

Music Festival of Haut Var, Haut Var, France.

Musicultura, Breukelen, The Netherlands.

1975: Three Days of Folk Music, Conflans Sainte Honorine, France.

Vth Contemporary Music Festival, Bourges, France.

"La Geolette d'Or", Knokke le Zoute, Belgium.

Festival of Unwritten and Traditional Music, Châlon sur Saône, France.

International Folk Festival, Olivet, France.

1976: The Spring of Present Peoples, Paris, France

Summer Music Festival, Chailles, France

Festival of Marais, Paris, France

International Musical Days, Vernou, France.

A Month of Asian Arts, Alençon, France,

Durham Oriental Music Festival, Durham, United Kingdom.

South East Asian Music Festival, Laon, France.

1977: International Musical Days, Vernou, France

World Music Festival, Berkeley, USA.

1978: International Musical Days, Vernou, France

Traditional Music Festival, Lugano, Switzerland.

Saint Jean Music Festivities, Dieppe, France.

1979: Durham Oriental Music Festival, Durham, United Kingdom.

International Contemporary Music Festival, Clichy, France.

1980: Autum Festival, Paris, France.

International Folk Music Festival, Sarajevo, Yugoslavia.

1981: Asian Music Festival, Seoul, Republic of Korea.

1982: Kuhmo Chamber Music Festival, Kuhmo, Finland

Polyphonix: Poetry and Music Festival, Paris, France.

1983: First Third World Music Festival, Rio de Janeiro, Brazil.

1984: Polyphonix: Poetry and Music Festival, New York, USA. (May)

Kaustinen Folk Music Festival, Kaustinen, Finland. (June)

Vitaasarii New Music Festival, Vitaasarii, Finland. (June)

Kuhmo Chamber Music Festival, Kuhmo, Finland. (June)

Festival of World Musical Cultures, Cape Town, South Africa. (July)

1985: First World Music Festival, Belfast, Northern Ireland, United Kingdom. (April)

International Music Festival, Langeais, France. (June)

Estival Festival, Paris, France. (July)

1986: Music Festival of Three Continents, Nice, France. (June)

Traditional Music Festival - North-South, Paris, France. (September)

Festival of Immigrant Musics, Paris, France. (September)

1987: Polyphonix: Poetry and Music Festival, Paris, France. (April)

Folk Music Festival, Ris Orangis, France. (May)

1988: First Meetings of Vocal Expressions, Abbaye de Fontevraud, France. (April)

Festival of World Music, Melbourne, Australia. (200 Years of Australia) (August)

Peoples Music Festival, Milan, Italy. (May)

Asian Music Festival, Etampes, France. (June)

1989: Bicentennial of the French Revolution, Paris, France. (July)

Intercultural Festival, Saint Herblain, France. (July)

1990: Music Festival: "Blossoming Sounds, Floating Songs", Osaka, Japan. (July)

First Forum of Asian and Pacific Performing Arts, Kobe, Japan. (July)

Asian Music Festival, Tamba, Japan. (July)

Traditional Music Festival, Arzila, Morocco. (August)

Berlin Music Festival, Berlin, Germany. (September)

Vox Populi, Brussels, Belgium (October)

1991: 700 years of Switzerland, Lausanne, Switzerland. (June)

Saint Denis Music Festival, Saint Denis, France. (June)

String Music Festival, Berlin, Germany. (September)

Vox Festival, Rotterdam, The Netherlands (February)

1992: 4th Meetings of Polyphonic Songs, Calvi, Corsica, France.

Festival around the Voice, Argenteuil, France

Festival about the Spirit of Voices, Perigueux, France.

Music Festival, Montreal, Canada (350 years of Montreal).

1993: Folk Music Festival / Ris Orangis, France. (May)

Voice Festival, Volterra, Italy. (June)

1994: Traditional Music Festival, Azilah, Morocco (August)

World Music Festival, Nantes, France. (September)

First Festival and Conference of the Asian / Pacific Society for Ethnomusicology, Seoul, Korea (November)

1995: Giving Voice: A Geography of the Voice, Cardiff, Wales, United Kingdom. (April)

2nd International Festival of Throat Singing, Kyzyl, Tuva, Russia. (June)

International Festival of Choir, Musica Choralis, Luxembourg. (September)

1996: International Symposium of Vietnamese Music, Saint Paul, Minnesota, USA. (March)

Giving Voice: An Archeology of the Voice, Cardiff, Wales, United Kingdom. (April)

Festival of Oriental Music, Les Courmettes, France (June)

4th World Symposium of Choir, Sydney, Australia (August)

Stuttgarter Stimmtage 96, Stuttgart, Germany (September)

International Symposium on Ethnomusicology, Minsk, Belarus. (October)

3rd International Conference and Music Festival of the Asia/Pacific Society for Ethnomusicology, Mahasarakham, Thailand. (December)

1997: International Symposium: An Archeology of the Voice, Wales. (April) International Conference of the ICTM, Nitra, Slovaquia. (June) International Symposium and World Music Festival, Cape Town, South Africa. (July)

Mediteria - Festival of Traditional Music, Montpellier, France. (October)

Festival of World Music, Montigny, France. (November)

International Symposium of Ethnomusicology, Vilnius, Lithuania. (December)

UNESCO-International Seminar on bamboo, Ho Chi Minh City, Vietnam (December)

1998: Tokker Festival, Amsterdam, The Netherlands. (February 7-8)

Festival of Mediterranean Musics, Genova, Italy. (March 10-12)

Transcendant Asia: A Celebration of Asian Music in Europe, London, England (April 23-24)

Vietnamese Spring Festival, Paris, France. (April/May)

Voice Festival, Auch, France. (May)

3rd International Jew's Harp Festival, Molln, Austria. (June 22-28)

Bartok Music Festival, Hungary. (July 4-11)

23rd Saint Chartier/ Rencontres Internationales de Luthiers et Maîtres Sonneurs. (July 11-14)

Autres Rivages/World Music Festival, Uzes, France. (1-2 August)

International Music Festival, Bergamo, Italy. (19-20 September)

Asian Music Festival, Firenza, Italy. (October)

International Festival of Voice, Rio de Janeiro, Brazil. (November)

1999: Voice Festival: Between Heaven and Earth, Chartreuse de Valbonne, France (12 March)

Symposium: Culture and Mathematics, Venise, Italy. (26-28 March)

Voice Festival: Eclats de Voix, Auch, France. (30 March and 29 May)

Symposium: A Divinity of the Voice, Aberystwith, Wales. (1-11 April)

Festival of Voices of the World, Bruxelles, Belgique. (1-5 June)

Festival Bela Bartok, Sombathely, Hongrie. (14-19 July)

World Conference ICTM, Hiroshima, Japon. (18-24 August)

Yoga International Congress, Montélimar, France. (29-31 October)

2000: SCONTRI - Festival of Corsican Culture, Paris, France. (12-13 February)

2ème Congrès annuel des Professtionnels de la Voix, Enghien les Bains. (26-27 February)

Printemps musical de Pérouges / Au Fil de la Voix, Pérouges, France. (May-June)

Tanz & Folk Fest Rudolstadt 2000, Rudolstadt, Allemagne. (4-7 July)

Congrès international sur l'enseignement de la voix, VASTA, Virginia, USA. (6-9 August)

6th Annual CHIME Conference, Leiden, Pays-Bas. (23-27 August)

Festival de Voix d'homme, Bretagne, France. (15-17 September)

Congrès sur la Voix parlée, Stuttgart, Allemagne. (21-24 September)

Annual Congress of Acousticians, Kumamoto, Japon. (3-5 October)

International Congress of Traditional Music, Taipei, Taiwan. (6-15 October)

2001: Symposium of Voice, Lyon, France. (February)

Festival of Traditional Music, Denain, France. (May)

City of London Festival, London, U.K. (June)

Festival " Performato ", Rio de Janeiro, Brazil. (July)

International Festival of Choral Music, Singapore. (August)

Festival " 1000 faces of Voice, France. (September)

2002: World Music Festival, Rennes, France. (February)

International Voice Festival, Genoa, Italy. (May)

13th Vivonne World Music Festival, Vivonne, France. (may)

Music Day Festival, Beyrouth, Lebanon, (21 June)

6th World Symposium of Choral Music, Minneapolis, Minnesota, USA. (August)

World Festival of Jew's Harps, Raudal, Norway (September)

International Congress of Polyphony, Tbilissi, Georgia. (October)

2003: Making New Waves Contemporary Music Festival, Budapest, Hungary. (February)

International Seminar of Shamanism, Genoa, Italy (June)

Telemark Folk Music Festival, Bo, Norvay (August)

International Congress of Psychotherapy, Hannover, Germany. (September)

Suoni di Mondo Festival, Bologna, Italy. (November)
2004
World Conference of the ICTM, Fushou, China. (January)

International Festival « Making New Waves », Budapest, Hungary. (February)

International Congress of Musical Acoustics, Nara, Japan. (April)

International Congress of Acoustics, Kyoto, Japan. (April)

International Congress of Yoga, Vogue, France. (May)

3rd Festival « Le Rêve de l'Aborigène », Poitiers, France. (July)
International Congress of Shamanism, University of Donau, Krems, Austria. (July)

Manifestations scientifiques et musicales dans le cadre « Lille, Ville européenne culturelle 2004, Lille, France (July)

International Seminar on Voice, University of Reading, Reading, United Kingdom. (July)

International Symposium of Sung and Spoken Voice, Stuttgart, Germany. (September)

2005

International Festival of Avant Garde Music « Making New Waves Â», Budapest, Hungary. (February)

International Festival of Choral Music, Arnhem, The Netherlands. (April)

International Festival of Mediterranean Music, Genova, Italy. (June)

Sunplash Festival of Reggae music, Italy. (June)

World Conference of the ICTM, Sheffield, United Kingdom. (August)

MELA Festival, Oslo, Norway. (August)

1st World Festival of Marranzanu, Cantania, Sicily, Italy. (September)

International Symposium of Voice, Stuttgart, Germany. (September)

« 30 ans d'existence de l'Université en Haute Alsace Â», Mulhouse, France. (October)
International Festival of Traditional Music, Limerick, Ireland. (October)

2006
Têt in Seattle, Seattle, USA. (January)

2ème Rencontre sur la parole chantée, Rio de Janeiro, Brazil. (May)

Festival « La Semaine du Son », Châlon sur Saône, France. (June)

International Seminar on Ca Trù, Hanoi, Viet Nam (June)
Festival international des Musiques sacrées, Fribourg, Switzerland. (July)

5th International Jew's Harp Festival, Amsterdam, The Netherlands. (July)

MELA festival, Oslo, Norway. (August)

International Meeting of the ICTM, Ljubliana, Slovenia. (September)

International Congress of Applied Ethnomusicology, Ljubliana, Slovenia. (September)

International Symposium of Voice, Stuttgart, Germany. (September)

International Meeting « Music as Memory », Oslo, Norway. (October)

The Global Forum on Civilization and Peace, Seoul, Korea. (November)

2007
Bilan du film ethnographique, Paris, France. (March)

Voice Festival / 9th session of the ILV/ CETC, Buenos Aires, Argentina. (March)

Symposium on music therapy, Sao Paulo, Brazil. (April)

Bergen International Music OI OI Festival, Bergen, Norway. (May-June)

Homage to Demetrio Stratos, Alberone di Cento, Italy. (June)

39th World conference of the ICTM, Vienna, Austria. (July)

PEVOC 7 International Congress on Voice, Groningen, The Netherlands. (August)

International Doromb Jew's Harp Festival, Hungary. (September)

2008

A Week of Sound Festival, Lyon, France. (January)

Unesco Congress of World Heritage, Canberra, Australia. (February)

Giving Voice, Aberystwith, New Wales. (March)

Bergen International Music OI OI Festival, Bergen, Norway. (May/June)

Homage to Demetrio Stratos, Alberone di Cento, Italy. (June)

"A Voix Haute" Festival, Bagnères de Bigorre, France. (August)

MELA music festival, Oslo, Norway. (August)

International Voice Festival, Dresden, Germany. (September)

2009

Voice Festival, Switzerland. (May)

Homage to Demetrio Stratos, Alberone di Cento, Italy. (June)

40th World conference of the ICTM, Durban, South Africa. (July)

International Congress of Voice Teachers, Paris, France. (July)

MELA Music Festival, Oslo, Norway. (August)

2010

Homage to Demetrio Stratos, Alberone di Cento, Italy. (June)

International of Sound, Saint John's, Canada (July)

ICTM 2 study groups meeting, Hanoi, Vietnam. (July)

Vietnamese Guiness Record Ceremony, Ho Chi Minh city, Vietnam. (December)

2011

International Symposium on Đờn ca tài tử Nam bộ, Ho Chi Minh City. (January)

International colloquial about 400 years of the birth of Phu Yen city, Phu Yên, Vietnam. (April)

World Jew's Harp Festival in Yakutsk, Yakutia. (June)

Homage to Demetrio Stratos, Alberone di Cento, Italy. (June)

International Festival of Mediterranean Music, Genova, Italy. (July)

World Conference ICTM in Saint John's, Canada. (July)

World Symposium of Choral Music, Puerto Madryn, Argentina. (August)

Spring Festival of South African Music, Fort Hare, South Africa. (September)

International Festival of Humour and Music, Stavanger, Norway. (September)

Peace Festival, Wroclaw, Poland. (October)

30th International Ethnographical Film Festival, Paris. (November)

International Conference of Arirang, Seoul, Korea. (December)

2012

Festival d'Auch, Auch, France. (April)

Festival Music Night, Munich, Germany. (April)

2013

Festival de la Voix, Colombes, France. (May)

42nd ICTM WORLD CONFERENCE, Shang Hai, China. (July)

Festival Les Nuits du Monde "Vietnam Style", Geneva, Switzerland. (November)

Exhibition VOICE – « Voices of the World ", City of Sciences, Paris, France (December 2013 – September. 2014)

Congress "Biomedical Signal Processing & Control (Elsevier) devoted to the workshop MAVEBA, Florence, Italy. (December)

World Marranzano Festival, Catania, Sicily, Italy. (December)

2014

Festival "Pauses Musicales", Toulouse, France. (February)

"Promenade Vietnam", City of Music, Paris, France (March)

International Conference "Safeguarding & Promotion of Folk Songs in the Contemporary Society", Vinh city, province of Nghệ An, Vietnam. (May)

Ancient Trance Festival – Jew's harp world festival, Taucha, Germany. (August)

10 Internationale Stuttgarter Stimmtage, Stuttgart, Germany. (October)

Opening ceremony of the World Vocal Clinic / Deutsche Stimmklinik, Hamburg, Germany. (October)

Festival « Il teatro vivo », Bergamo, Italy (November)

2015

Omaggio a Demetrio Stratos, Alberone, Italy. (June)

43rdICTM World Conference, Astana, Kazakhstan (July)

Festival of Hát Then Nùng Thái, Việt Bắc, Vietnam. (September)

Convegne, Concerti e master class dedicati al « canto sardo e canto armonico nel mondo », Sorso, Sardinia, Italy. (October)

2016

Festival of Chầu Văn (Vietnamese music of Possession), Nam Định, Vietnam. (January)

*Voice Encounters: Voice Pedagogy, Wroclaw, Poland. (April)

*International Meeting A GRAN VOCE, Vicenza, Italy. (May)

*Omaggio a Demetrio Stratos 2016, Alberone, Italy. (June)

*Ancient Trance Festival, Taucha, Germany. (August)

*12th international Voice Symposium « BRAIN & VOICE », Salzburg, Austria (August)

2017

*44th ICTM World Conference, Limerick, Ireland (July)

*Congress "Voci e Soni "Di Dentro e Di Fuori"", Padova, Italy (October)

*Congress La Voce Artistica 2017 XI edition, Ravenna, Italy (October)

Career

Ethnomusicologist: Musée National des Arts et Traditions Populaires, Paris,1968-1987

Ethnomusicologist: Musée de l'Homme, Paris, since 1968, retired in 2009

Professor: Centre of Studies for Oriental Music, Paris, 1970-1975.

Lecturer: Université de Paris X-Nanterre, 1987-1995.

Lecturers of many Universities and Museums in the World since 1969.

USA: University of Hawaii (1977), University of Maryland (1980), Columbia University, New York (1983), Museum of Modern Art, New York (1984), University of California, San Diego (UCSC, 1990), Cornell University, New York (1994), Saint Thomas University, Minnesota (1996), University of Wisconsin, Wisconsin (1998), George Mason University, Washington D.C. (2000)

Canada: University of Montreal, Montreal (1991), York University, Toronto (1994), University of Toronto (1994), Royal Ontario Museum, Toronto (1994)

Brazil: Conservatorium of Music, Rio de Janeiro (1983), University of Recife, Recife (1998), University of Rio de Janeiro (2006),

South Africa: Cape Town University, Cape Town (1984, 1997), Stellenbosch University (1984), University of Durban (2009), University of Fort Hare (2011)

Australia: Monash University, Melbourne (1986), University of Sydney, Sydney (1986), Western Australian University, Perth

(1986, 2008), Melbourne College of Advanced Education, Melbourne (1988)

Philippines: University of the Philippines, Manila (1988)

Japan: Tokyo University of Fine Arts, Tokyo (1981), Miyagi University of Music Education, Sendai (1999), University of Hiroshima, Hiroshima (1999), OsakaUniversity of Fine Arts, Osaka (2000)

Korea: Seoul National University, Seoul (1981)

Thailand: Mahasarakham University, Mahasarakham (1996), Chulalongkorn University, Bangkok (2012)

Taiwan : Université de Taiwan, Taipei (2000), Centre National des Arts, Taipei (2000)

China: National Conservatory of Music, Shanghai (2013)

Vietnam: Vietnamese Institute of Musicology, Hanoi (2002, 2017), Academy of Music, Hanoi (2017), National Conservatory of Music, Ho Chi Minh City (2007)

Liban : CLAC (centre de lecture et d'animation culturelle) de Sin El Fil, Mansoura, Kfar Debyan, Amioun, (2002)

Austria: University of Austria (2007)

Belgium: Institute of Musicology, Louvain (1976), Royal Museum of Central Africa (1976), Royal Museum of Musical Instruments, Brussels (1980, 2001), University of Anvers. (1984), Musee Royal de Mariemont, Mariement (2002)

Italy: Institute of Musicology, Bologna (1979), French Cultural Center, Napoli (1980),Academia Nacionale Santa Cecilia, Roma (1994), University of Roma (1994), Institute of Musicology and Linguistics, Venice (1995, 1996), University of Bologna, Bologna (2000), Institute of Musictherapry, Padova, Italy (2001, 2017), Fondazione Giorgio Cini, Venice (1979, 2001, 2002, 2003, 2004,2005,2006, 2007, 2008) , Institute IATGONG for traditional music, Genoa, (2003,2007,2013,2017)

The Netherlands: Jaap Kunst Center for Ethnomusicology, Amsterdam (1974), Gemeente Museum, The Haye (1980), Tropen Museum (1975, 1992, 1998), University of Leiden, Leiden (2000)

Germany: Volkerkunde Museum, Berlin (1985, 1990, 2000), La Charité Hospital, Berlin (1991), Musik Hochschole, Detmold (1994), Musik Hochschole, Stuttgart (1996, 2000,2014), University of Heidelberg, Heidelberg (1997), University of Aachen, Aachen (2003)

United Kingdom: Horniman Museum, London (1974), Durham University, Durham (1976, 1979, 1985), University of London, London (1991), City University, London (1992), SOAS (School of Oriental and African Studies), London (1998), Queen's University, Belfast (1985), Centre of Performance Research, Cardiff. (1995,1996), University of Reading, London (2005)

France: many universities in different towns from 1974 onwards: Universite de Paris IV-Sorbonne, Univeriste de Paris VIII-Saint Denis, Universite de Paris X-Nanterre, Paris; Universite de Nice; Universite deTours; University of Rennes ; Conservatoire National Régional de la musique, Strasbourg; Universite de Montpellier 3, Montpellier; Universite de Marseille; Universite Le Mirail, Toulouse, UniversitÃ© de Poitiers, Poitiers , Universite de la Reunion, Ile de la Reunion. (1999, 2000, 2001, 2002, 2003)

Switzerland: Volkerkunde Museum, Basel. (1969), Academy of Music, Basel (1993), Musée d'Ethnographie, Geneva. (2015)

Spain: Summer University, Madrid. (1990)

Yugoslavia: Academy of Music, Sarajevo. (1991, 2011)

Sweden: Lund University, Lund (1976), Stockholm University, Stockholm (1976), Musik Museet, Stockholm (1981), Royal Academy of Music, Stockholm. (1985)

Denmark: Musikhistorisk Museum, Copenhagen (1972), Danish Folk Archive Institute, Copenhagen (1972), Conservatory of music, Holstebro (1972), Nordisk Teaterlaboratorium, Holstebro (1998), Cantabile 2, Vordingborg. (2000)

Norway: Institute of Musicology, Trondheim (1976,1980, 1981), University of Oslo (1979), Music Academy Sibelius, Bergen (2004), Musik Folkehogskole, Oslo (2003)

Poland: 17th Summer Course for Young Composers, Polish Society for Contemporary Music, Radziejowice, Poland (1997), University of Wroclaw, Poland. (2011, 2016)

Russia: National Conservatory Tchaikovsky, Moscow (1993, 2013), Institute of Research for World Music Cultures, Moscow (1993), International Center of Khoomei, Kyzyl, Tuva. (1995).

Georgia: Conservatory of Music, Tbilissi. (2002)

Lithuania: Academy of Music, Vilnius. (1997)

Belarus: Academy of Music, Minsk. (1996)

Slovenia: University of Ljubljana. (2006, 2011)

Croatia: University of Zagreb. (2006)

Musician

15 LP records and 5 CDs as performer on Vietnamese Music (with different record companies: Le Chant du Monde, OCORA, Studio SM, Société Française de Productions Phonographiques, Playasound in France, Lyrichord, Music of the World in the USA, Albatros in Italy.

1. Cithare Vietnamienne (le Dan Tranh) par Tran Quang Hai. Le Chant du Monde LDX 74454, Paris, 1971, collection Special Instrumental.

2. Le Chant de la Rivière des Parfums. Productions et Editions Sonores PES 528 003, Paris, 1973.

3. Vietnam: Nouvelle Musique Traditionnelle. OCORA 558 012, Paris, 1976.

4. Musique du Vietnam: Tradition du Sud. Anthologie de la musique des Peuples AMP 72903, Paris, 1976.

5. Musique Traditionnelle du Vietnam. Aide à l'Enfance du Vietnam AEV 01, Paris, 1976.

6. Musica del Vietnam. Albatros Records VPA 8396, Milan, 1978.

7. Vietnam: Tran Quang Hai et Bach Yen. Playasound PS 33514, Paris, 1979, collection: Musiques de l'Asie traditionnelle, vol.10.

8. Cithare et Chants Populaires du Vietnam/ Tran Quang Hai et Bach Yen. Aide à l'Enfance du Vietnam AEV 02, Paris, 1979.

9. Music of Vietnam. Lyrichord LLST 7337, New York, 1980.

28

10. Vietnam/ Tran Quang Hai et Bach Yen. Studio SM 3311.97, Paris, 1983. Grand Prix du Disque de l'Académie Charles Cros 1983

11. Vietnamese Dan Tranh Music/ Tran Quang Hai. Lyrichord LLST 7375, New York, 1983.

12. Shaman/Tran Quang Hai et Misha Lobko. Didjeridou Records DJD O1, Paris, 1983.

13. MUSAICA: Chansons d'enfants des Migrants. DEVA RIC 1-2, Paris, 1984.

14. Landscape of the Highlands/ Tran Quang Hai. Music of the World MW 004, New York, 1984.

15. Le Monde Magique du Dan Tranh/ Tran Quang Hai. Viet Productions VN 1944, Paris, 1985.

16. CD: Rêves et Réalité - Tran Quang Hai et Bach Yen. Playasound PS 65020, Paris, 1988.

17. CD: Cithare vietnamienne/Tran Quang Hai. Playasound PS 65103, Paris, 1993.

18. CD: Landscape of the Highlands/String Music from Vietnam/Tran Quang Hai. Latitudes LAT 50612, North Carolina, USA, 1997.

19. CD: Phillip Peris/Didjeridu. Les Cinq Planètes CP 10296, Paris, 1997.

20. CD: Les Guimbardes du Monde / Tran Quang Hai. Playasound PS 66009, Paris, 1997.

21. CD: That's All Folk! Le Chant du Monde CML 5741015.16, 2CDs, Paris1997.

22. CD: International Jew's Harp Festival Molln Austria '98, CD-0513, 2CDs, Molln, 1999.

5 Commercialized cassettes on Pop music of Vietnam

1 Videocassette on Vietnamese Music (1984)

1 Videocassette "Music of Vietnam" produced by Ministry of Education in Perth. (Australia) (1989)

1 Videocassette on "Tran Quang Hai performance" produced by the Melbourne College of Advanced Education in Melbourne, Australia. (1989)

1 Videocassette on "Dan Tranh Music" produced by Volkerkunde Museum, Berlin, Germany. (1991)

Performer for film music in 25 commercialized films

Performer of more than 3,000 concerts in 70 countries around the world since 1966.

Performer of more than 1,000 school music concerts organized by JMF (Jeunesses Musicales de France), JMB (Jeunesses Musicales de Belgique), JMS (Jeunesses Musicales de Suisse), Rikskonsertene of Norway and Sweden.

Composer

300 pop songs in Vietnamese, French, English

100 musical compositions for different musical instruments: 16 stringed zither, monochord, spoons, Jew's harp, overtone singing.

3 compositions for electro-acoustical music (1975, 1988, 1989, see creative works)

Researcher

Author of a book Âm Nhac Việt Nam " (Music of Vietnam in Vietnamese), edited by Nhom Bac Dâu, 361pages, Paris, 1989.

Author of a book "Musiques du Monde" (in French), edited by J-M Fuzeau, 320 pages, 3 CD, Courlay, 1993. (with Michel Asselineau and Eugene Berel)

Author of a book "Musics of the World " (in English), edited by J-M Fuzeau, 320pages, 3 CD, Courlay, 1994. (with Michel Asselineau and Eugene Berel)

Author of a book "Musik aus aller Welt " (in German), edited by J-M Fuzeau, 320pages, 3 CD, Courlay, 1996. (with Michel Asselineau and Eugene Berel)

Author of a book "Musicas del Mundo" (in Spanish), edited by J-M Fuzeau, 320pages, 3 CD, Courlay, 1998. (with Michel Asselineau and Eugene Berel)

Author of a book "Musiques et Danses Traditionnelles d'Europe " (in French), edited by J -M Fuzeau, 380pages, 2 CD, Courlay, 1995.

Author of a book (in cooperation with Patrick Kersale), VOIX, DVD, edited by Lugdivine, Lyon, 2006.

Author or more than 250 articles on Vietnamese and Asian musics

31

Co-ordinator for New Grove's Dictionary of Musical Instruments on South East Asian Music (1st edition, 1984) 3 volumes

Author of articles in New Grove Dictionary of Music and Musicians (6ᵗʰ edition, 1980, 20 volumes), Algemeine Muziekencyclopedia (Holland, 1982, 12 volumes), Encyclopaedia Universalis. (France, 1984, 1986, 1988, 1990, 1991)

Co-author with Hugo Zemp for the film 16mm on the overtone singing style "Le Chant des Harmoniques" (The Song of Harmonics) produced by the National Center for Scientific Research-Audio Visual, Paris, 1989)

Contributor to the bilingual notes (188pages) accompanying the 3-CD set

"Voices of the World" edited by Le Chant du Monde, Paris, 1996.

Contributor to the bilingual notes (124 pages) accompanying the 2-CD set "Vietnam: Musics of the Montagnards " edited by Le Chant du Monde, Paris, 1997.

Researcher specializing in Vietnamese Music, South East Asian Music, Overtone Singing Style, Music Therapy, Music Pedagogy, Creation of NewTechniques for Vietnamese 16 stringed zither, Jew's Harps, Spoons.

Author of more than 500 articles in Vietnamese for 30 Vietnamese magazines in America, Europe, Asia and Australia.

Creative Works

Nhớ Miền Thượng Du (Nostalgia of the Highlands) for 16 stringed zither (1971)

Xuân Về (The Spring Is Coming Back) for 16 stringed zither (1971)

Tiếng Hát Sông Hương (The Song of the Perfumed River) for monochord (1972)

Ảo Thanh (The Magic Sound) for Spoons (1972)

Về Nguồn (Return to the Sources) with Nguyễn Văn Tường (1975)

Shaman for Voice, saxo, synthetizer (1982)

Hát Hai Giọng (Diphonic Song) (1982)

Ca Đối Ca (Song vs Song) for overtones (1982)

Tùy Hứng Muỗng (Improvisation of Spoons) for Spoons (1982)

Độc Tấu Đàn Môi Mông (Solo of Mong Jew's Harp) for Jew's Harp (1982)

Tiếng Hát Đàn Môi Tre (The Song of the Bamboo Jew's Harp) for Jew's Harp (1982)

Sinh Tiền Nhịp Tấu (Rhythm of Coin Clappers) for Coin Clappers (1982)

Tiết Tấu Miền Thượng (Rhythm of the Highlands) for 2 Jew's Harps (1982)

Núi Ngự Sông Hương (Royal Mount and Perfumed River) for monochord (1983)

Nam Bắc Một Nhà (North and South, the Same House) for 16 stringed zither (1986)

Chuyển Hệ (Modulation) (1986)

Trở Về Nguồn Cội (Return to the Origin) (electro-acoustical music) (1988)

Solo Thái for 16 stringed zither (1989)

Tambours 89 in cooperation with Yves Herwan Chotard (1989)

Envol for overtones (1989)

Chuyển Hệ Ba Miền (Metabole on three regions) for 16 stringed zither (1993)

Mộng Đến Vùng Việt Bắc (Dream of Viet Bac) for 16 stringed zither (1993)

Vịnh Hạ Long (Ha Long Bay) for 16 stringed zither (1993)

Sông Hương Núi Ngự (The Perfumed River and the Royal Mount) for 16 stringed zither (1993)

Tiếng Vang Đàn Trưng Tây Nguyên (Echo of the musical instrument Trung of the Highlands) for 16 stringed zither (1993)

Nhớ Miền Nam (Nostalgia of the South) for 16 stringed zither (1993)

Saigon-Cholon (Saigon-Cholon The Twin Cities) for 16 stringed zither (1993)

Vĩnh Long Thời Thơ Ấu (Vinh Long, My Childhood) for 16 stringed zither (1993)

Cửu Long Giang Thân Yêu (the Beloved Mekong River) for 16 stringed zither (1993)

Hồn Việt Nam (The Soul of Viet Nam) for 16 stringed zither (1993)

A Bali, on entend le genggong rab ncas (In Bali, one hears the jew's harp genggong) for Jew's Harp (1997)

Paysage des Hauts-Plateaux (Landscape of the Highlands) for Jew's Harp (1997)

Nostalgie au Pays Mong (Nostalgia of the Mong Land) for Jew's Harp (1997)

Souvenir à Alexeiev et Chichiguine (Souvenir of Alexeiev and Chichiguine) for Jew's Harp (1997)

Bachkir-Bachkirie (Bashkir-Bashkiria) for Jew's Harp (1997)

Orient-Occident (East-West) for Jew's Harp (1997)

Souvenir de Norvege (Souvenir from Norway) for Jew's Harp (1997)

Vietnam, mon Pays (Vietnam, my Country) for Jew's Harp (1997)

Tuva! Tuva! (Tuva! Tuva!) for Jew's Harp (1997)

La Mélodie des Harmoniques (The melody of Harmonics) for Jew's Harp (1997)

Ambiance des Hauts-Plateaux du Vietnam (Atmosphere of the Highlands of Vietnam) for Jew's Harp (1997)

Echo des montagnes (Echo of Mountains) for Jew's Harp (1997)

Taiga mysterieux (Mysterious Taiga) for Jew's Harp (1997)

Le Saut des Crapauds (The Jump of Toads) for Jew's Harp (1997)

Harmonie des Guimbardes (Harmonie of Jew's Harps) for Jew's Harp (1997)

L'Univers harmonique (The Harmonic Universe) for Jew's Harp (1997)

Consonances ! (Consonances !) for Jew's Harp (1997).

Vietnam, My Motherland for Jew's Harp (1998)

Welcome to Molln Jew's Harp Festival 1998 for Jew's Harp (1998)

Film music for the film Long Vân Khánh Hội (The Meeting of the Dragon and the Clouds) 1980

Film music for the film Le Chant des Harmoniques (The Song of Harmonics) 1989

Film music for the film La Rencontre du Dragon et du Coq (The Meeting of the Dragon and the Cock) 1997

Memberships in different Scientific Societies

Society for Ethnomusicology, USA, since 1969.

Society for Asian Music, USA, since 1978.

International Council for Traditional Music, USA, since 1976 (Liaison Officer since 1991)

International Musicological Society, Switzerland, since 1977.

International Association of Sound Archives, Australia, since 1978.

European Seminar in Ethnomusicology, Switzerland, since 1983.

Société Française d'Ethnomusicologie, France, since 1985 (founding member)

Société de Musicologie, France, since 1980.

Association Française d'Archives Sonores, France, since 1979.

Centre of Studies for Oriental Music, France, since 1962. (Professor from 1970 to 1975)

Vietnamese Penclub in Europe, France, since 1987.

Center of Vietnamese Studies, France, since 1987.

Association Française de Recherche sur l'Asie du Sud-Est, France, since 1983.

Société des Auteurs, Compositeurs et Editeurs de la Musique (SACEM), Paris, since 1983.

International Center of Khoomei, Tuva, Russia, since 1995.

Honorary Member of the Scientific Society of Vietnamese Professionals, Canada, since 1992.

Life Fellow, International Adviser, Deputy Governor of the American Biographical Institute and Research Association, USA, since 1987.

Life Fellow, International Adviser, Director Deputy General of the International Biographical Association, United Kingdom, since 1987.

Consultant of the Prize Diderot for the Encyclopaedia Universalis, France, since 1990.

Board Committee of the International Association of Jew's Harp, Austria, since 1998.

Founding member of the American Order of Excellency, USA, in 2002.

Honorary member of the Institute of Musicology, Hanoi, Vietnam, since 2004.

Board Member of the ICTM, Slovenia, since 2005.

Biographical Reference Books

1. Dictionary of International Biography, 15th edition, United Kingdom

2. Men of Achievements, 5th, 6th, 7th editions, United Kingdom.

3. International Who's Who in Community Service, 3rd edition, United Kingdom.

4. International Who's Who in Music, 8th, 9th, 10th, 11th, 12th, 13th, 14th, 15th, 16th, 17th, 18th editons, since 1982, U.K.

5. Who's Who in Europe, 2nd, 3rd editions, U.K.

6. Men and Women in Distinction, 1st, 2nd editions, U.K.

7. Ivnternational Register of Profiles, 4th, 5th editions, U.K.

8. International Who's Who of Intellectuals, 2nd, 3rd editions, U.K.

9. The First Five Hundreds, 1st edition, U.K.

10. Who's Who in the World, 5th, 6th, 7th, 8th, 9th, 10th, 11th, 12th, 13th, 14th, 15th,16th, 17th, 18th editions, since 1983, USA.

11. 5000 Personalities in the World, 1st edition, USA.

12. International Directory of Distinguished Leadership, 1st edition, USA.

13. International Book of Honor, 1st edition, USA.

14. International Register of Personalities, 1st edition, USA.

15. Nouveau Dictionnaire Européen, 5th,6th,7th,8th,9th editions,1985, Belgium.

16. Who's Who in International Art, 1st edition, 1989, Switzerland.

17. Who's Who in France, 29th, 30th, 31st, 32nd, 33th, 34th, 35th, 36th, 37th, etc... editions, since 1997, France.

18. Who's Who in Entertainment, 3rd edition, 1998-1999, U.K.

19. Who's Who in Popular Music, 2nd edition, 1998, U.K.

20. Vẻ Vang Dân Việt - The Pride of the Vietnamese, vol.1, 1st, 2nd editions, 1993, USA.

21. Fils et Filles du Vietnam, 1st edition, 1997, USA.

22. Tuyển Tập Nghệ Sĩ (Selection of Vietnamese Artists), vol. 1, 1st edition, 1995, Canada.

23. Guide du Show Business, from 20th to 40 th editions (since 1983), France.

24. Director Deputy General List of Honour, 1998, U.K.

25. The Europe 500 Leaders for the New Century, Barons Who's Who, USA. (2000)

26. QUID (since 2000), France

27. 500 Great Minds of the Early 21st Century, Bibliotheque World Wide, USA. (2002)

Prizes, Honours, Awards:

1983: Grand Prize of Academy Charles Cros, Paris for LP "Vietnam/Tran Quang Hai and Bach Yen (SM 3011.97)

1986: Médaille d'Or de la Musique (Gold Medal of Music) / Asian Cultural Academy, Paris.

1987: D.MUS (HON) / International University Foundation, USA.

1987: Life Fellow of the American Biograhical Institute and Research Association, USA.

1987: Deputy Governor (DG) of the American Biographical Institute, USA.

1987: Life Fellow of the International Biographical Centre (IBC), UK

1987: Director Deputy General (DDG) of the International Biographical Centre, UK.

1988: International Advisor of the American Biographical Institute, USA.

1988: International Order of Merit/ International Biographical Centre, UK.

1989: Ph. D (HON) / Albert Einstein International Academy Foundation, USA. 1990: Grand Prize of the International Festival of Anthropological and Visual Film for the film "The Song of Harmonics", Parnü, Estonia.

1990: Prize of the Best Ethnomusicological Film for the film "The Song of Harmonics" delivered by the Academy of Sciences, Parnü Estonia.

1990: Special Research Prize of the International Festival of Scientific Film for the film "The Song of Harmonics", Palaiseau, France.

1991: Grand Prize Northern Telecom of the 2nd International Festival of Scientific Film of Quebec for the film "The Song of Harmonics", Montreal, Canada.

1991: Van Laurens Award of the British Voice Association and the Ferens Institute for the best paper on overtone singing researc, London, UK.

1991: Honorary International Advisor of the International Biographical Centre, UK.

1991: Alfred Nobel Medal of the Albert Einstein Academy Foundation, USA.

1991: Man of the Year 1991/ American Biographical Institute, USA.

1991: International Man of the Year 1991/1992/ International Biographical Centre, UK.

1992: Honorary Member of the Vietnamese Scientific Society of the Professionals, Canada.

1994: Man of the Year / American Biographical Institute, USA.

1994 : Gold Record of Achievement par American Biographical Institute, Etats-Unis.

1995: Special Prize of the 2nd International Festival of Throat Voice, Kyzyl, Tuva.

1995: Honorary Scientific Member of the International Center of Khoomei, Kyzyl, Tuva.

1996: Medal of Cristal / National Center for Scientific Research, Paris, France.

1997: Prize of the Academy of Records Charles Cros for the CDs Voices of the World (collective work), Paris, France.

1997: Le Diapason d'Or of the Year for the CDs Voices of the World (collective work), Paris, France.

1997: Le CHOC of the Year for the CDs Voices of the World (collective work), Paris, France.

1998: The Medal of Citizen of Honor/ City Hall of Limeil Brevannes, France.

1998: The Platinum Record for Special Performance in Music and Overtone Singing, USA.

1998: Special Prize of Jew's Harp, 3rd World Jew's Harp Festival, Molln, Austria.

2002: Highest Distinction of France: Knight of the Legion of Honor (Chevalier de la Legion d'Honneur).

2009 Medal of Honor, category Great Gold (Médaille d'Honneur du Travail, catégorie Grand Or), France.

Other relevant informations

Tran Quang Hai is the first Vietnamese musician who performed at special events: Bicentennial of Australia in Melbourne (1988), Bicentennial of the French Revolution in Paris (1989), 700 Years of Switzerland in Lausanne (1991), 350 Years of Montreal in Montreal, Canada (1992), 500 Years of Christophe Columbus' Discovery of America in Paris (1992), 600 Years of Seoul in Seoul, Korea (1994), Jubilee of the King of Thailand in Mahasarakham, Thailand (1996), 1000 Years of Trondheim in Norway (1997).

He is the first Vietnamese musician who performed different works composed by contemporary composers such as NguyÃªn Van Tuong (died in 1996), Bernard Parmegiani, Nicolas Frize, Yves Herwan Chotard, and also film music composed by Vladimir Cosma, Philippe Sarde, Maurice Jarre, Gabriel Yared, Jean Claude Petit.

He practises 15 musical instruments belonging to Europe (violin, guitar, banjo, mandoline, flute), Vietnam (zither dan tranh, monochord dan doc huyen, 2 stringed fiddle dan co, coin clappers sinh tien, spoons muong), China (2 stringed fiddle nan hu), India (lutes tampura, vina) Iran (drum zarb), European and Asian Jew's Harps.

His research on overtones since 1969 has given him the title of the-greatest specialist of overtone singing with more than 8000 persons who have learnt this peculiar vocal style with him from 70 countries around the world. He got the Cristal Medal of the National Center for Scientific Research in 1996 for his research on overtones, and the recipient " Knight of the Legion of Honor " given by the French President Jacques Chirac in 2002 for his career as musician and musicologist since 1966 , the Medal of Work, Great Gold category in 2009 for his 41 years career at the National Center for Scientific Research, the Diploma of Vietnamese Guiness Book 2010 for the title "KING OF SPOONS" in 2010 in Ho Chi Minh City, Vietnam, and the Diploma of Vietnamese Guiness Book 2012 in Ho Chi Minh City for the title "The Musician who performed the Vietnamese Jew's harp in the biggest number of countries in the world", in 2012 in Vietnam.

Contact:

TRAN QUANG HAI 12 rue Gutenberg 94450 LIMEIL BREVANNES France Tel : (33-6) 50 25 73 67 (overseas) E-mail: tranquanghai@gmail.com

Websites: http://tranquanghai.com, http://tranquanghai.info

Blogs : http://tranquanghai1944.com , http://tranvankhe-tranquanghai.com

Vietnamese Music from a Cultural Perspective

Trần Quang Hải

National Center for Scientific Research, France.

Introduction

Geographically Vietnam occupies the eastern coast of the Indochinese peninsula, extending from China South to the Gulf of Siam, and is a part of Southeast Asia. Culturally, artistically and, above all, musically Vietnam is a part of the Sino-Japanese family grouping China, Japan, Korea, Mongolia and Vietnam. The music of the Far Eastern world shares many common characteristics: script (Chinese characters), musical terminology (the same theory for the determination of twelve basic tones and the names of musical instruments), musical instruments (most of them of Chinese origin),

45

musical genres (court music), village folk music, anhemitonic pentatonic scale for ritual music, theatre music and ceremonial music.

Ten centuries of Chinese rule (from 111 B.C. to A.D. 939) have profoundly influenced the life, culture and music of the Vietnamese people. Musical instruments, such as the 16-stringed zither, the 4-stringed pear-shaped lute, 3-stringed lute, 2-stringed fiddle, vertical and transverse flutes, the oboe, large and small drums, cymbal, stone chime, bell chime, undoubtedly originated from China. Names of musical instruments are written in Chinese characters but their pronunciation differs according to whether they are read by Chinese or Vietnamese (16-stringed zither ZHENG in Chinese, TRANH in Vietnamese, pear-shaped lute PIPA in Chinese, TỲ BÀ in Vietnamese, etc...).

During the Lê Dynasty (1428-1788) the first theory of Vietnamese music was copied from the Chinese (the theory of five degrees, of seven tones and twelve LYU or basic tones, and the eight categories of court music: music of the esplanade of heaven, temple music, music of the five sacrifices, music for helping the sun and the moon in the event of the eclipse, music for formal audiences, music for ordinary audiences, banquet music and palace music. Musical notation (hò, xự, xang, xê, cống, liu) was still written in Chinese until the eve of the World War I (1914-1918).

Owing to its geographical position, at the crossroads of different peoples and civilizations, Vietnam has also come into contact with the Champa Kingdom of Indian civilization. Indian influences can be found in the use of the improvised prelude RAO in the South, or DAO (read ZAO) in the North, preceding the performance of a set musical composition, in the use the TRỐNG CƠM, a long two-membrane drum covered with a rice paste in the centre of the drum head, similar to the MRIDANGAM of South India, and in the use

46

of onomatopoeia for drum playing (toong, tà-roong, táng, tà-ráng, cắc, tà-rắc, trắc, rụp, sậm, tịch, rù), as in the BOL and THEKA systems of Indian music.

Chinese and Indian influences have not, however, destroyed the creative culture instincts of the Vietnamese people. In fact, the national identity is reflected in the creation of three purely Vietnamese musical instruments:

The ĐÀN ĐÁY or ĐỚI CẦM or VÔ ĐỂ CẦM, the songstresses'3-stringed lute, which incorporates the peculiarities of the 2-stringed moon-shaped lute ĐÀN KÌM or ĐÀN NGUYỆT, of the 4-stringed pear-shaped lute ĐÀN TỲ BÀ, and of the 3- string lute ĐÀN TAM

The SINH TIỀN, or coin clappers, bearing all the characteristics of clappers, sistrum and scrapers,

The monochord ĐÀN ĐỘC HUYỀN or ĐÀN BẦU, differing from other Asian monochords (e.g. the Cambodian SADEV, the Indian GOPIYANTRA and EKTARA, the Chinese I HSIEN QIN, and the Japanese ICHIGENKIN), in the exclusive combination of the use of a unique string and the production of harmonics.

Vietnam is a multi-ethnic country with its main population of 85 million Vietnamese of Mongoloid race. There are also 20 million of aborigines grouping some 53 ethnic minorities. The composition of ethnic minorities is as followed : the Mường, Thổ, Chut (of Việt-Mường language), the Tày, Nùng, Thái, Cao Lan, Sán Chi, Lào, Puna (of Tày-Thái language), the Hmong, Dao, Patheng, Tông (of Hmong-Dao language), the Lolo, La Hu, Công, Phu La, Si La (of Tibeto-Burman language),the Bahnar, Khmer, Sedang, Mnong, Maa, Srê, Katu, Khmu, Hrê (of Môn-Khmer language), the Jarai, Êđê, Chàm, Churu, Rađê (of Austronesian language), the Co Lao,

La Chi, Pu Peo, La ha (of various languages of the Austroasiatic family), etc.

The history of Vietnamese music can be divided into four periods, from the foundation of the first Vietnamese Dinh Dynasty (968-980)

The first period (10th – 15th centuries), characterized by the conjugated influence of Chinese and Indian music,

The second period (15th – 18th centuries), characterized by the predominance of Chinese influence,

The third period (19th century to the eve of World War II), characterized by the originality and identity of Vietnamese traditional music, and by the introduction of superficial influence of Western music.

The fourth period (from 1945 onwards), characterized by the decline of traditional music and new attempts to restore it, and by the development of a new European style music.

The Vietnamese musical language is characterized by the use of musical scales such as:

- the ditonic scale C-G-C (e.g. the HÁT ĐÚM, as in the alternating voices song of the Hải Dương province in North Vietnam)

- the tritonic scale C-F-G-C (e.g. as in children's game-songs « TÙM NỤM TÙM NỊU »,

« OÁNH TÙ TÌ », folksongs « THUYỀN PHÊNH », « ĐÒ ĐƯA » of the Hải Dương province, « HÁT DẶM, » « VÍ ĐÒ ĐƯA » of the Nghệ Tĩnh province, « HÁT THAI» charade song of Central Vietnam, of the beginning of the classical piece «NAM XUÂN »

- the tetratonic scale C-F-G-Bb-C (e.g. « HÁT DÂNG QUẠT » of the Thanh Hóa province in North Vietnam, « HÒ DÔ HẬY, « LÝ HOA THƠM », « LÝ LẠCH » of the Quang Nam province in Central Vietnam, the lullaby « RU EM » and boatwoman's song "HÒ MÁI ĐẨY" of Central Vietnam,

- the pentatonic scale comprising five types:

C – D – E – G – A – C (folksongs)

C - D – F – G – A – C (Bắc modal system music)

C – Eb- F – G – Bb- C (Nam modal system music)

C – D – F – G – Bb- C (Ngũ Cung Đảo piece)

C C – E – F – G – A – (Vọng Cổ piece)

Vietnamese music is composed of many musical genres: court music, ceremonial music, religious music, village music, new Western style music and proto-Indochinese music.

COURT MUSIC

During the first years of the Lê Dynasty (1428-1788), Lương Đăng, a high Court dignitary, was asked to establish a new theory of Court music (Nhạc Cung Đình), which took its form from Chinese Ming music. Court music of Vietnam was highly formalized based on Confucian ideals and Chinese philosophy in general, showing a tendency in the royal court to consider Chinese culture more refined and sophisticated than the native music. Nonetheless, Vietnamese court music developed in a unique manner and integrated many aspects of Vietnamese folk music as well, making even traditions imported from China definitively Vietnamese. Eight categories were presented to King Lê Thái Tôn:

1. GIAO NHẠC: music of the « esplanade of Heaven », performed during the sacrifice for Heaven and Earth, and during the triennial ceremony celebrated by the Vietnamese emperors,

2. MIẾU NHẠC: Confucius temple music, performed at the Confucius temple and during the anniversary commemoration of the death of Vietnamese sovereigns,

3. NGŨ TỰ NHẠC: music of the Five Sacrifices,

4. CỨU NHỰT NGUYỆT GIAO TRÙNG NHẠC: music for helping the sun and the moon in the event of the eclipse,

5. ĐẠI TRIỀU NHẠC: music for formal audiences,

6. THƯỜNG TRIỀU NHẠC: music for ordinary audiences,

7. ĐẠI YẾN CỬU TẤU NHẠC: music for large banquets,

8. CUNG TRUNG CHI NHẠC: palace music

Apart from music performed for the Emperor, there were two large instrumental ensembles (ĐƯỜNG THƯỢNG CHI NHẠC – music of the upper hall; ĐƯỜNG HẠ CHI NHẠC – music of the lower hall). Court dances consisted of military dance (VÕ VŨ), civilian dance (VĂN VŨ), flower branches dance (HOA ĐĂNG VŨ), phoenix dance (PHỤNG VŨ), horse dance (MÃ VŨ), four fabulous animals dance (TỨ LINH VŨ), and the dance of the 8 barbarians presenting their gifts (BÁT MAN TẤN CỐNG VŨ).

CEREMONIAL AND RELIGIOUS MUSIC

Ceremonial music and religious music are heard less and less today. Funerals are held according to the Confucian, Buddhist, Caodaist or Christian rituals. In some parts of the country one can still witness the celebration of the worship of ancestors or local deities. The Buddhist or Caodaist prayers, the medium or medicine men or women incantations (CHẦU VĂN, HẦU VĂN, RỖI BÓNG) are still heard in numberless pagodas and temples in Vietnam. CHẦU VĂN is a Northern traditional folk art which combines trance singing and dancing, a religious form of art used for extolling the merits of beneficent deities or deified national heroes. Christian music is inspired from the Western Catholic liturgy, while new Buddhist music in Saigon (Ho Chi Minh City) is written by young composers who take their inspiration from Christian hymns.

MUSIC FOR ENTERTAINMENT

Music for entertainment purposes is performed by a small instrumental ensemble for a small audience:

In the North, the HÁT Ả ĐÀO (songstress' song) mostly vocal but accompanied by three musical instruments: a 3-stringed lute ĐÀN ĐÁY, wooden clappers PHÁCH, and a small drum TRỐNG CHẦU reserved for the listener-connoisseur. It has different names: CA TRÙ, HÁT NHÀ TRÒ, HÁT NHÀ TƠ, HÁT CÔ ĐẦU. CA TRÙ flourished in the 15th century in northern Vietnam when it was popular with the royal palace and a favorite hobby of aristocrats and scholars. Later it was performed in communal houses, inns and private homes. These performances were mostly for men. When men entered a ca trù inn they purchased bamboo tally cards. In Chinese, TRÙ means card. CA means song in Vietnamese. Hence CA TRÙ means tally card songs. The tallies were given to the singers in appreciation for the performance. After the performance each singer received payment in proportion to the number of cards received. CA TRÙ requires at least three performers. The singer is always a woman and plays the phách, an instrument made of wood or bamboo that is beaten with two wooden sticks. A musician accompanies the singer on the đàn đáy, a long-necked lute with three

51

silk strings and 10 frets. There is also a drummer who is a connoisseur. The drummer shows his approval of the singer or the songs depending on how he hits the drum. If he likes a song, he might hit the drum several times. If he is disappointed with the singer, he hits the drum twice. The long-necked lute player must follow the rhythm of the wooden clappers phách. The repertoire of the CA TRÙ has 15 styles namely: HÁT MƯỠU, HÁT NÓI, GỬI THƯ, ĐỌC THƯ, ĐỌC PHÚ, CHỪ KHI, HÁT RU, CUNG BẮC, TỲ BÀ, KỂ TRUYỆN, HÃM, NGÂM, VỌNG, SÁM CÔ ĐẦU, etc.....

In Central Vietnam, the CA HUẾ (Huế Music) of aristocratic origins was created when the Nguyễn kings settled in Thuận Hóa province at the beginning of the 18th century. The music of the North in contact with the Cham music which was influenced by Indian music gave birth to CA HUẾ. This music has a particular scale, characteristic to the Central part of Vietnam. It is often only instrumental (the orchestra called NGŨ TUYỆT – the five perfects - being composed of stringed instruments, including 16 stringed zither đàn tranh, 4 stringed pear-shaped lute đàn tỳ bà, 2 stringed fiddle đàn nhị, monochord đàn độc huyền and transverse flute sáo). After 2 centuries of existence, the repertoire is composed of 10 bài ngự (royal pieces) such as LƯU THỦY, CỔ BẢN, KIM TIỀN, TẨU MÃ, NGUYÊN TIÊU, XUÂN PHONG, PHẨM TUYẾT, LONG NGÂM, HỒ QUẢNG, LỘNG ĐIỆP in the Bắc mode and a certain numbers of songs in the Nam mode expressing Sadness like AI GIANG NAM , HÀNH VÂN, NAM XUÂN or HẠ GIANG NAM, NAM BÌNH, CHINH PHỤ, TƯƠNG TƯ KHÚC. The song TỨ ĐẠI CẢNH might be composed by King Tự Đức in the 19th century. As for the songs, the voice is always accompanied by the NGŨ TUYỆT ensemble.

In the South, it is the ĐỜN TÀI TỬ (the so-called « music of the amateurs») coming from the Hue and Quang traditions. This music is the origin of the music of the renovated theater HÁT CẢI LƯƠNG. Many pieces from the CA HUẾ repertoire were modified after the inspiration of South Vietnamese musicians and the specific scales of ĐỜN TÀI TỬ tradition. There are two distinct modal systems: Bắc (North) and Nam (South). All the pieces belonging to the Bắc system are rapid, joyful and the pieces of Nam system are sad, melancholic and tempo is slow. The principal short pieces of Bắc system are: LONG HỒ HỘI, XUÂN PHONG, LƯU THỦY, CAO SƠN, KHỔNG MINH TỌA LẦU, MẪU TẦM TỬ, BÌNH BÁN VẮN, KIM TIỀN HUẾ. Besides, there are 6 long pieces such as: TÂY THI, CỔ BẢN, LƯU THỦY TRƯỜNG, BÌNH BÁN CHÁN, XUÂN TÌNH. The Nam system has the following pieces NAM AI, NAM XUÂN, ĐẢO NGŨ CUNG, TỨ ĐẠI OÁN, VĂN THIÊN TƯỜNG, PHỤNG CẦU HOÀNG, TRƯỜNG TƯƠNG TƯ. Only the musical piece TỨ ĐẠI OÁN was the most popular and performed by musicians before the World War 2 (1939-1945). The piece TỨ ĐẠI OÁN combining with the piece HÀNH VÂN from the Ca Huế tradition inspired Mr. Cao Văn Lầu (his nickname was Sáu Lầu) to compose the piece DẠ CỔ HOÀI LANG (Hearing the drum in the night when thinking of his beloved) which was changed the name VỌNG CỔ (nostalgia of the past). This piece has since become the main piece of the renovated theater HÁT CẢI LƯƠNG There exist two other modal systems of the ĐỜN TÀI TỬ repertoire: Nhạc (from the term Nhạc Lễ - Ritual), and Quảng – Cantonese having the flavour of Chinese music. The piece NGŨ ĐỐI HẠ of Nhạc system is also performed in ceremonial music and at the traditional theater HÁT BỘI, while the piece XÀNG XÊ is used in the renovated theater HÁT CẢI LƯƠNG. Many pieces of Quảng system like NGŨ ĐIỂM, BÀI TẠ, KHỐC HOÀNG THIÊN, XANG XỪ LÍU, TÂY THI QUẢNG also belong the repertoire of the renovated theater HÁT CẢI LƯƠNG.

THEATER

Theater in Vietnam comprises the traditional theater of Chineseo rigin (HÁT TUỒNG, HÁT BỘI), folk theater (HÁT CHÈO in the North), and renovated theater (HÁT CẢI LƯƠNG). A new westernized theater (KỊCH NÓI) was born during the 30's. The water puppet theater (MÚA RỐI NƯỚC) is created by the Vietnamese people.

HÁT TUỒNG, also called HÁT BỘI in the south, came into being over eight hundred years ago, thanks to the transmission of the art of Chinese traditional theater by Lý Nguyên Cát during the Trần Dynasty (1225-1400). HÁT TUỒNG stage has a very concise symbolization. Only with some actors on the stage, the whole scene of the court with all the officials who are attending royal ceremonies could be seen, or two generals with some soldiers fighting also show a battle with hundreds of thousands of troops and horses fighting fiercely, and even a gourd of wine and four wooden cups also express a lowest banquet. It is a mistake to deal with Tuồng without mentioning the art of making up. It is because just looking at a made-up face, we may guess the personality and social class of that character; As for beards, a black, curly beard is for a fierce man, three-tuft beard for a gentleman; a dragon's beard for Kings and mandarins and for majesty; a mouse's whisker, a goat's beard and a fox's whisker for cunning and dishonest men. Beardless man must be students. The gestures of characters on the stage are stylized with symbolization, which attract the viewers passionately. To a western-style drama, when a general ride a horse, it must be a real one or a horse-like costume; but, to an actor of HÁT TUỒNG, only a white, brown red or black whip also means many kinds of horses: black, sorrel or white. The actor of Tuồng acts very concisely. Only with a whip, he is able to make the viewers passionate through delicate acting's with horses galloping or at full gallop, of which there are good-mannered or restive ones... With an oar, the actor of Tuồng is able to show the viewers the boat fast sailing, wavering due to waves, making the viewers feel as through they were on the boat.The accompanying drum in HÁT TUỒNG are very important, because they start the actor's sentiment; they bring the past time and space to the present; they unite the character's sentiment with the stage, and the actor with the audience. The art of HÁT TUỒNG in Vietnam includes those of painting, sculpture through the ways of making up, costumes and dance, pantomine, singing, saying through the actings of actors; as well as the combination of traditional musical instruments of Vietnam. The art of HÁT TUỒNG has raised the lofty view of desire to the true - the good - the beautiful (Chân - Thiện - Mỹ) as well as the viewpoints of life of the ancients: Benevolence - Civility - Righteousness - Knowledge - Loyalty (Nhân - Nghĩa - Lễ - Trí- Tín) through special characters who are benevolent and righteous.

HÁT CHÈO is a form of popular theatre in Vietnam that has its roots in ancient village festivals. It consists of folk songs with pantomime, intrumental music and dances, combined with instructive or interpretive sketches dealing with stories from legends, poetry, history or even daily life. Also brought into play are acrobatic scenes and magic. HÁT CHÈO tells tales of chiefs, heroes and lovely maidens and offers an eclectic mix of romance, tragedy and comedy. Traditionally HÁT CHÈO was composed orally by anonymous authors. Nowadays, HÁT CHÈO plays are composed along traditional lines: the characters in the plays sing time-tested popular melodies with words suited to modern circumstances. The costomes, makeup, gestures and language create typical characters familiar to every member of the audience. The props are simple. As a result, there is a close interchange between the performers and the spectators. A HÁT CHÈO play could be put on stage in a large theater, but it could also be performed successfully on one or two bed mats spread in the middle of a communal house with a cast of only three: a hero, a heroine and a clown. The sound of the HÁT CHÈO drum has a magical power and upon hearing it. Villagers cannot resist coming to see the play. The clown in a HÁT CHÈO play seems to be a supporting role, but actually he or she is very important to the performance. The clowns present a comic portrayal of social life, with ridiculous, satirical words and gestures, they reduce the audience to tears of laughter. The national CHÈO repertoire includes among others Trương Viên, Lưu Bình - Dương Lễ, and Quan Âm Thị Kính, which are considered treasures of the traditional stage. HÁT CẢI LƯƠNG (renovated theater) appeared in the southern part of Vietnam in the 1920s. The word "Cải lương" was coined after this sentence "**Cải** biến kỳ sự, sử ích tự thiên **lương**" (Changing old things and transforming them into better and newer ones). The first word and the last word of the sentence were combined to create the word CẢI

LƯƠNG around the year of 1920. This relatively modern form combines drama, modeled after French comedy, and singing. Scenes are elaborate and are changed frequently throughout the play. HÁT CẢI LƯƠNG is similar to the Western operettas and more easily depicts the inner feelings of the characters. Songs of the HÁT CẢI LƯƠNG are based on variations of a limited number, perhaps 20, of tunes with different tempos for particular emotions - this convention permits a composer to choose among 20 variations to express anger, and as many to portray joy. The principal supporting songs in HÁT CẢI LƯƠNG is the VỌNG CỔ (nostalgia of the past). CẢI LƯƠNG theater owes much of its success to the sweet voices of actors/singers (the most famous actors are Năm Nghĩa, Út Trà Ôn, and actresses are Út Bạch Lan, Thanh Nga, Bạch Tuyết), much appreciated by the audience. Upon hearing the first bars of the well-loved VỌNG CỔ, the audience reacts with gasps of recognition and applause. The HÁT CẢI LƯƠNG performance includes dances, songs, and music; the music originally drew its influences from southern folk music. Since then, the music of HÁT CẢI LƯƠNG has been enriched with hundreds of new tunes. An orchestra consists mainly of guitar with concave frets Lục Huyền cầm or Ghita phím lõm, and 2 stringed moon-shaped lute Đàn Kìm, 16 stringed zither Đàn Tranh; 2 stringed fiddle Đàn Cò and a percussion ensemble.

FOLK MUSIC

Folk music is composed by the people for the people without any artistic goals, illustrating the life of an individual from the cradle to the grave.

It is essentially vocal music (DÂN CA, literally DÂN: people; CA: songs).

Lullabies (HÁT RU in the North, RU CON in the Center, and HÁT ĐƯA EM in the South), children's game songs (THIÊN ĐÀNG ĐỊA NGỤC, tag games OÁNH TÙ TÌ – one two three, etc.), work songs associated with work in the field (irrigation HÒ ĐẬP NƯỚC, HÒ TÁT NƯỚC, rice grinding HÒ XÂY LÚA, lime crushing HÒ GIÃ VÔI. Boatman songs can be heard on the rivers (HÒ CHÈO GHE, HÒ CHÈO THUYỀN, HÒ MÁI NHÌ, HÒ MÁI ĐẨY, HÒ MÁI XÁP, HÒ KHOAN, HÒ SÔNG MÃ).

Love songs are countless in Vietnam. In the North, the birthplace of festival songs (TRỐNG QUAN, QUAN HỌ, CÒ LÃ, HÁT ĐÚM, HÁT PHƯỜNG VẢI, HÁT GIẶM, HÁT GHẸO, HAT XOAN). Songs are used for singing contests between girls and boys. In Central Vietnam, the HÒ or calls, are associated with many village activities and the LÝ, very numerous, include mostly love songs (LÝ THƯƠNG NHAU, LÝ HOÀI NAM, LÝ MONG CHỒNG, LÝ NĂM CANH, LÝ CHIA TAY, LÝ HÀNH VÂN, etc.). In the South, the most famous HÒ are the A LI HÒ LỜ, HÒ ĐỒNG THÁP, HÒ BA LÝ, HÒ LÔ TÔ, HÒ CẤY, The LÝ are: LÝ GIAO DUYÊN, LÝ VỌNG PHU, LÝ CHIM QUYÊN, LÝ CHUỒN CHUỒN, LÝ CÂY CHANH, LÝ BỎ BÌA, LÝ CON KHỈ ĐỘT, LÝ CON SÁO, LÝ NGỰA Ô, LÝ DĨA BÁNH BÒ, etc... HÁT GIẶM VÈ (stories told in flowery terms), HÁT VÈ, NÓI VÈ, HÁT XẨM (peddler's songs) are other types of Vietnamese folk songs. HÁT XẨM, or the song of the blind artists, has existed since the Tran dynasty (13th century). The beauty of the "XẨM" song is expressed in the rhythms and tones of the music. Its attractive and lively drum rhythms and numerous rules of song applications make it an interesting spectacle. The HÁT XẨM song tells of the fate or unhappiness of the poor. Besides theses common themes, there are funny songs with satirical implications about wrong doings, the condemnation of outdated customs, the crimes of rulers, and the deeds of heroes. These stories are well oved by many people. The instruments traditionally used for the HÁT XẨM are a 2 stringed fiddle đàn nhị, bamboo clappers phách, a monochord đàn bầu and two drums. People used to walk in a group of 2 to 5 and sing, mainly in residential areas such as a parking lot, a ferry-landing, or a market gate. Today, HÁT XẨM singers no longer exist, but their ancient art is still kept alive and respected thanks to the effort by a group of researchers and musicians led by Mr. Thao Giang. Mrs Hà Thị Cầu is the last Hát Xẩm singer in Việt Nam.

MODERN MUSIC

Modern music based on Western musical styles was introduced to Vietnam around the 1930s. On the eve of World War 2, the Youth movement gave origin to a new music corresponding to youth's aspirations for struggle (songs of struggle NHẠC CHIẾN ĐẤU), for love (love songs NHẠC TÌNH CẢM). During the last 75 years pop music has rapidly developed and now represents nearly 80% of the music heard in Vietnam. Songs associated with love, struggle, war, revolution, natural beauty etc. are a convincing means of expression for awakening or subduing the political conscience of the people,

The most famous composers in Vietnam are **Lưu Hữu Phước** (died in 1989), **Phạm Duy** (moved to the United States after the fall of Saigon in 1975 and now back to Vietnam since 2005, and died in Vietnam recently), **Trịnh Công Sơn** (died in 2001) **Lê Thương** (died in 1999), **Văn Cao** (died in 1995), **Nguyễn Văn Thương** (died in 2002).

Classical music in the Western idiom was late in developing in Vietnam: works for piano have been composed by **Mrs. Louise Nguyễn Văn Ty** and the late **Võ Đức Thu**. Symphonic works have been and are always written in Vietnam by **Đỗ Nhuận** (deceased) **Nguyễn Xuân Khoát** (deceased), **Nghiêm Phú Phi** (in the United States, and died in 2008). In France, some composers like **Nguyễn Văn Tường** (deceased in 1996), **Trương Tăng** (deceased in 1989), loved by many people. The instruments traditionally used for the HÁT XẨM are a 2 stringed fiddle đàn nhị, bamboo clappers phách, a monochord đàn bầu and two drums. People used to walk in a group of 2 to 5 and sing, mainly in residential areas such as a parking lot, a ferry-landing, or a market gate. Today, HÁT XẨM singers no longer exist, but their ancient art is still kept alive and respected thanks to the effort by a group of researchers and musicians led by **Mr. Thao Giang**. **Mrs Hà Thị Cầu** is the last Hát Xẩm singer in Việt Nam. and passed away recently. **Tôn Thất Tiết, Nguyễn Thiên Đạo** (died in 2015 in Paris) and **Trần Quang Hải** have written many compositions in electro-acoustical, contemporary or avant-gardist style. Some renowned young composers such as **Phan Quang Phục** (USA), **Vũ Nhật Tân** (Vietnam), **Hoàng Ngọc Tuấn** (Australia) have had their works performed in Western countries.

A great number of harmonized folksongs for part singing especially by **Lê Văn Khoa** (living in the United States) have attracted a certain category of the Vietnamese population. This westernized music, now in expansion, cannot however be judged at this time.

TRIBAL MUSIC

Tribal or Ethnic Minorities, living in the mountainous sections of the country, in an area equal to two thirds of the entire territory of Vietnam, and especially in the autonomous zone of Viet Bac, the Northwest mountains or Vietnamese Cordillera and the High

Plateaus of Central Vietnam, have a music which is completely different from that of Vietnamese of Mongolian origin. This music has a wealth of dances, songs and musical instruments (Jew's harps in metal and bamboo – RODING, TOUNG, GOC; mouth organ with divergent tubes – MBOAT, KOMBOAT, ROKEL; bamboophone – TRUNG, KLENG KLANG; monochord fiddle – KONI; gongs – CING; gong ensemble; hydraulic chime – TANG KOA; lithophone of the Mnong Gar from the village of Ndut Lieng Krak, etc.). This music has many common characteristics with the music of other tribal peoples in Southeast Asia.

Vietnamese Music in Exile since 1975 and Musical Life in Vietnam since Perestroika

The exile of some millions of Vietnamese refugees after the fall of Saigon in 1975 gave birth to a new type of music outside of Vietnam. Traditional music has been in regression because of the lack of interest among youngsters. Pop music, on the other hand, is flourishing, especially in the United States, where there is a big concentration of Vietnamese emigrants. Contemporary music in the Western idiom is in its early stages. In Vietnam, pop music has come back since around 1990, with perestroika. Traditional music has also gained in popularity due to the efforts made by the Institute of Musicology (Viện Âm Nhạc) in Hanoi, the capital of Vietnam, and thanks to a number of festivals organized in main cities.

Forty-three years have gone by since the fall of Saigon. **Forty-three** years during which many political, economical, and artistic events have changed the face of the history of humanity in general and that of Vietnamese history in particular. In terms of music, it has only been outside of Vietnam, notably among members of the exile community, that an exceptional development in quantity can be observed. Thousands of new music and video cassettes of pop music, as well as revivals of theater pieces, have been issued by twenty or so producers in America. These producers, who are centered in California (more precisely, in the area of Orange County nicknamed '*Little Saigon*') and in Europe (especially in Paris) have flooded the market with cassettes reserved for Vietnamese refugees.

In the framework of this article, the author will offer with some brief information on the musical activities in the Vietnamese community since April 30, 1975, the date of the fall of Saigon and the beginning of the major departure into exile of several hundreds of thousands of Vietnamese, as well as some comments on musical life in Vietnam since perestroika.

Four themes will be discussed:

1. The survival of traditional music (nhạc cổ truyền)

2. The development of new music (tân nhạc)

3. The beginning of a contemporary western-style music (nhạc cận đại tây phương)

4. Musical life in Vietnam since perestroika.

I. THE SURVIVAL OF TRADITIONAL MUSIC (NHẠC CỔ TRUYỀN)

Traditional music has long been treated as a poor parent in relation to westernized music.

Before April 1975, at the National Conservatory of music in Saigon, classes of traditional instruments and arts did not attract many students. Professors of traditional music had an inferiority complex in relation to professors of western music.

The Vietnamese refugees who now live abroad have been generally too busy setting up their new lives to have the time to appreciate the sound of the zither *Đàn tranh* or to attend performances of the revived theater form of *hát cải lương*. Children who arrived abroad when they were ten years of age are now 53 years old. They are really quite indifferent towards Vietnamese culture. They hardly speak their native language and prefer listening to Michael Jackson, Madonna, Prince, Céline Dion and others, because for them, it is the music of their present world.

Performances of modernized theater *hát cải lương*, concerts of traditional music are less and less numerous because of lack of spectators. Parents do not encourage children to attend Vietnamese concerts or theater performances, which are boring for youngsters who understand Vietnamese less and less, and tickets are expensive.

For the next few decades, Vietnamese **renovated** theater will probably have fallen into oblivion. Traditional music could probably survive longer but to a lower level, because young Vietnamese have turned toward western pop music or the new Vietnamese westernized music.

II. THE DEVELOPMENT OF NEW MUSIC (TÂN NHẠC)

The departure of many artists from Vietnam in May of 1975 marked the beginning of the development of exile music. This music, characterized by pop songs, can be divided into several themes:

1. Nostalgia for the country, nostalgia for Saigon (1975-1977) with songs evoking lost memories, such as '*Vĩnh Biệt Saigon*' (Farewell Saigon) by **Nam Lộc** (1976) and '*Saigon niềm nhớ không tên*' (Saigon, Nostalgia without Name) by **Nguyễn Đình Toàn** (1977).

2. Resistance and struggle for the reconquest of the country (1978-1981) in songs composed by **Phạm Duy** (*'Hát trên Đường tạm dung'* / Songs on the Road of Exile, 1978), songs of struggle by **Nguyệt Ánh** (*'Em nhớ màu cờ* / I Remember the Colors of the Flag, 1981); 'Dươi cờ phục quốc' / Under the Flag of the Reconquest of the Country, 1981), and songs by **Việt Dzũng** ('Lưu Vong Quốc '/ Melodies of the Exile, 1980; *'Kinh ty nạn'* / Prayers of Refugees, 1981), etc.

3. Description of prisoners' lives in Vietnam, found in a compilation of 20 songs by **Phạm Duy** based on poems written by **Nguyễn Chí Thiện** (*'Ngục Ca'* / Songs of Jail, 1981) and melodies by the poet-musician **Hà Thúc Sinh** (*'Tiếng Hát tủi nhục'* / The Song of Shame, 1982), etc.

4. Rebirth of prewar songs (1982-1985), with thousands of cassettes recording voices of male singers (**Elvis Phương, Duy Quang, Chế Linh**) and female singers (**Khánh Ly, Lệ Thu, Thanh Thúy, Thanh Tuyền, Hương Lan, Julie Quang**) well known to the Vietnamese; these revive memories of the golden age of Saigon.

5. Birth of the *Hưng Ca* movement (since 1985) gathered around ten young composers, including **Hà Thúc Sinh, Nguyễn Hữu Nghĩa, Nguyệt Ánh, Viêt Dzũng, Phan Ni Tấn**, and **Khúc Lan**. They have composed new songs on different themes: struggle, resistance, and love, and this movement works to collect and preserve some new songs.

6. Development of 'new wave' music and of Chinese serials music (since 1986), with about one hundred cassettes on these kinds of music ('top hit' western songs and music of Hong Kong and Taiwan movies with Vietnamese lyrics).

7. Diffusion of songs composed in Vietnam among Vietnamese communities overseas (since 1997). This new Vietnamese pop music has been developed in Vietnam, and many of its artists have become well known abroad. The overseas Vietnamese are interested in the newly composed songs and the young artists of Vietnam because they like to listen to another musical source and to discover new artistic faces. Vietnamese refugees are allowed to go back to Vietnam on vacation, where they discover new songs and new artists. This contact permits the export of music to foreign countries where the Vietnamese diaspora now lives.

III. BEGINNING OF WESTERN COMPOSERS CLASSICAL MUSIC (NHẠC CẬN ĐẠI TÂY PHƯƠNG)

In addition to the few Vietnamese composers of contemporary music living already for a long time in France such as **Nguyễn Văn Tường** (died in 1996), **Nguyễn Thiên Đạo** (died in 2015), **Tôn Thất Tiết** (composer of music for 3 films ' *Odeur de la papaye verte* ', '*Cyclo*', '*A la verticale de l'été*' directed by **Trần Anh Hùng**), **Trương Tăng** (died in 1989), **Trần Quang Hải**, and **Cung Tiến, Lê Văn Khoa** in the United States, some young Vietnamese composers have also emerged. In Australia, the guitarist **Hoàng Ngọc Tuấn**, gold medal winner of the 1978 music festival in Vietnam and author of more than 500 new songs, left Vietnam in 1982 by the sea and received a research grant to prepare his Ph.D. dissertation on Vietnamese folk songs. He wrote some modern arrangements for traditional songs in a new style. **Nguyễn Mạnh Cường** won a composition prize at the Asia Pacific Festival and Composers Conference in December, 1984, in New Zealand on the basis of his composition '*Phong Vũ*' (The Dance of Phoenix). Since 1985, he has continued to compose electronic music in Sydney (Australia). **Lê Tuấn Hùng** obtained his Ph.D. degree in Ethnomusicology at Monash University in Melbourne and has composed new music mixing Vietnamese musical instruments and

Western contemporary compositions. He has published 4 CD since 1992. **Phan Quang Phục** earned a doctorate of music at the University of Michigan and has taught composition at Indiana University (Illinois, USA). He is considered to be one of the six most talented young composers in the United States and won the Prize of Rome in 1998. **Võ Vân Ánh**, renowned musician of Vietnamese zither, monochord, has lived in the United States. She has combined East & West musical idioms for performances and creations and has obtained many awards.

Among interpreters of western classical music, the guitarist **Trịnh Bách** is the only one who has reached an international level of performance. Having arrived in New York in 1975 at the age of 13, he is now considered one of the best guitarists in the world. Several excellent young Vietnamese musicians have pursued their studies at conservatories of music in Sydney, Paris and the United States. In 2001, **Văn Hùng Cường**, a Vietnamese pianist, won the world piano competition organized by the American Music Scholarship Association in New York (USA). There are **Nguyên Lê**, a talented jazz guitarist, **Phạm Quân**, excellent violinist in France.

IV. MUSICAL LIFE IN VIETNAM SINCE PERESTROIKA

Since Perestroika policies began there, many foreign tourists have been visiting Vietnam, instigating a new dimension to the musical life of that country. Many hotels and restaurants for tourists hire musicians of traditional music to entertain their new customers. Spectacles of traditional music offer to tourists some aspects of the musical culture of the country. Instead of presenting the authentic music, though, musicians play westernized folk music to please European tastes. Because of the economical necessity, traditional artists have done this for money and have neglected aspects of art and tradition.

Many groups of artists like Tre Xanh, **Phù Đổng** have been sent abroad to participate in festivals or to present concerts to the exiled Vietnamese. Inside of the country, though, the emphasis is on pop music, as young singers turn toward the west. They dress like European pop singers on stage, imitate them and sing fashionable foreign songs (Western, Korean, Japanese, Taiwanese). Since 1995, many singers namely **Thanh Lam, Mỹ Linh, Hồng Nhung, Hồng Hạnh, Ánh Tuyết, Thanh Phương, Cẩm Vân, Lam Trường, Đan Trường, Quang Linh, Mỹ Tâm, Trần Thu Hà, Bằng Kiều** etc... have become famous inside and outside of the country. They can earn up to 20,000 US dollars per month with shows and recordings.

The rebirth of modernized theater (*Hát Cải Lương*) since 1990 in Ho Chi Minh City and the southern part of Vietnam has enabled young artists like **Ngọc Huyền** (moved to the United States in 2004), **Tài Linh** (moved to the United States in 2005), **Vũ Linh, Kim Tử Long, Ngọc Giàu, Bạch Tuyết, Lệ Thủy, Minh Phụng, Minh Vương** to earn more money and have a better life. A new kind of comic theater (*Tấu Hài*) appeared at the beginning of the 90's and has become popular with productions of video cassettes and DVD. Some actors like **Bảo Quốc, Minh Nhí, Thành Lộc, Lê Vũ Cầu, Hữu Châu, Hoài Linh** etc..; and actresses like **Hồng Nga, Hồng Vân, Ngọc Giàu** are well known in Vietnam and also among the Vietnamese abroad.

In spite of this disappointing aspect, some excellent festivals of traditional music take place, namely the Lullaby Festival, modernized Theater Festival, Theater Song contest, the Traditional Theater Festival, etc.

Composers for film music have been more and more after the unification of the country since 1976. Other composers like **Trọng Bằng, Đàm Linh, Hoàng Vân, Đặng Hữu Phúc, Trọng Đài, Dương Thụ** have contributed to film music in Vietnam.

Contemporary music with concertos, symphonies has been developed in Vietnam with some famous composers like **Đỗ Hồng Quân, Nguyễn Thị Nhung, Hoàng Dương, Hoàng Cường, Phúc Linh, Vũ Nhật Tân.**

Compositions for orchestra with traditional musical instruments (16 stringed zither, monochord, moon shaped lute, 2 stringed fiddle, bamboo transverse flute) and Western orchestra occupy an important place in musical creations in Vietnam nowadays.

In Hanoi over the past 43 years, the Institute of Musicology has carried out thousands of field work projects on the tribal music of 53 minorities. In addition to the collection stored in archives from 1956 to 1995, 34 field work projects have been carried out since 1996 throughout the country, from the mountainous regions in the north to the highlands in the central region and some provinces in the south. Stored in the Sound Archives of the Institute of Musicology are 8,850 pieces of instrumental music and nearly 18,000 folksongs performed by more or less 2,000 performers. Since 1995, with revisions in working methods, open and dynamic mechanisms based on the current situation have abolished the passive role of scientific research. The Institute of Musicology now has qualified collaborators in the entire country to carry out projects from the grassroots to the ministry level and up to the national level.

In January of 1999, this Institute of Musicology opened a showroom of 130 Vietnamese musical instruments from 54 ethnic groups belonging to four categories of classification: chordophones, idiophones, aerophones, and membranophones. Each instrument in the showroom is introduced in printed descriptions and audio and visual recordings. Of particular note, the showroom also displays many ancient musical instruments such as the lithophone, bronze drum, big drum with elephant skin of the Ede ethnic group, sets of gongs, etc. In addition to providing visual education, the displayed objects and musical instruments are also demonstrated in a lively way.

Thousands of technology products in the form of audio CD, video DVD, and videotapes featuring performances on folk music have been released. In addition, the Institute of Musicology has held symposiums and seminars on diverse and practical themes such as the Vietnamese lithophone, gongs of the central highlands of Vietnam, etc. In 1998, the Institute of Musicology held a scientific meeting on 'Reviewing a process of training, preserving and promoting Vietnamese traditional music'. More than 30 papers of a high scientific quality were presented. The research department of the Institute of Musicology is well equipped with modern apparatus that can help to restore and preserve traditional music and folk songs on compact discs for the longer and better conservation of sound documents. Thanks to these demonstrations, many scientific books on music and traditional songs have been published. This Institute of Musicology has many young researchers like **Hình Phước Long** (Cham music), **Dương Bích Hà** (traditional music from Central Vietnam), **Kiều Tấn** (traditional music from South Vietnam), **Võ Thanh Tùng** (Vietnamese musical instruments with a publication of a CD Rom and an important book on that subject), **Nồng Thị Nhinh** (folk music of the **Tày, Nùng**, Dao tribes from North Vietnam), **Kpa Ylang** (Bahnar music from the Highlands) **Romah Del** (Jarai music from the Highlands).

In Vietnam, the research on traditional music has been developing rapidly. Many senior reasearchers have contributed to enrich this field with hundreds of publications (books, CD, films**). Prof. Nguyễn Hữu Ba** (deceased) **Lê Thương** (deceased), **Lưu Hữu Phước** (deceased in 1989), **Đắc Nhẫn, Lê Huy, Huy Trần, Tú Ngọc** (deceased) **Đỗ Minh, Vũ Nhật Thăng, Đặng Hoành Loan, Thụy Loan, Tô Vũ** (deceased), **Tô Ngọc Thanh, Lư Nhất Vũ,** etc... are among the best known in Vietnam. Young researchers are many such as **Lê Văn Toàn, Nguyễn Bình Định, Nguyễn Thị Minh Châu, Bùi Trọng Hiền, Hồ Hồng Dzung, Phạm Minh Hương,** and **Nguyễn Thuỷ Tiên.**

A center of research on the preservation of court music was created in Huê in 1996 thanks to the help of Japan and has been under Prof. **Trần Văn Khê's** supervision.

For the last 23 years (since 1995), many artists of folk theaters and pop singers living in Vietnam have performed abroad at international music festivals or in America, Asia, Australia, and Europe where Vietnamese refugees have settled in. Since 1999, a great number of Vietnamese Oversea artists like **Hương Lan, Phượng Mai, Elvis Phương, Tuấn Ngọc, Khánh Hà, Hoài Linh, Dalena, Linda Trang Đài etc…** have been back to Vietnam many times to perform with other artists in Vietnam. This musical exchange has contributed to facilitate the relationship between Vietnamese artists outside/inside.

The influence that music has throughout the world is immeasurable. Music evokes many feelings, surfaces old memories, and creates new ones all while satisfying a sense of human emotion. With the ability to help identify a culture, as well as educate countries about other cultures, music also provides for a sense of knowledge. Music can be a tool for many things: relaxation, stimulation and communication. It is often transformed according to technological advancement, market demands, and political forces far from its home ground. As certain forms of music enjoy worldwide popularity, other forms of music mutate, sink into obscurity, and even cease to exist Within the reign of imported culture, cross cultivation and the creation of the so-called global village lies the need to expand horizons to engulf more than just what you see everyday. Globalization is becoming one of the most controversial topics in today's world.

Bibliography

Bulletin Thông báo khoa học (2003): 19 articles on teaching traditional music at school in Vietnam, n° 10 (September-December 2003), 156p. (English version), Viện Âm nhạc, Hanoi.

Bulletin Thông báo khoa học (2005): 13 articles on Ca Trù, special issue on Ca Trù singing of Viet people, n° 16 (September-December 2005), 176p, (Vietnamese version), Viện Âm Nhạc, Hanoi.

Bulletin Thông báo khoa học (2005): 9 articles on Ca Trù, special issue on Ca Trù singing of Viet people, n°15 (May-August 2005),160 p. (Vietnamese version), Viện Âm Nhạc, Hanoi.

Bulletin Thông báo khoa học (2006): 10 articles on Ca Trù, Gongs in Central Vietnam, tribal music in Ha Giang province, etc…, n° 17 (January – April 2006), 184p, Viện Âm nhạc, Hanoi.

Bulletin Thông báo khoa học (2006): 8 articles on Ca Tru in English, n° 18 (May-August 2006), 166p, Viện Âm nhạc, Hanoi

Condominas, Georges (1952): « Le lithophone préhistorique de Ndut Lieng Krak », 45 (2) : 359-392, Hanoi.

Đắc Nhẫn : 1987 : *Tìm hiểu âm nhạc cải lương,* (ed), 230p, Hô Chi Minh City.

Đắc Nhẫn (1987): *Tìm hiểu âm nhạc cải lương* , nhà xuất bản TP Hồ Chí Minh, 230p, Ho chi minh city.

Đặng Hoành Loan (editor) :2004 : *Hợp Tuyển tài liệu nghiên cứu lý luận phê bình âm nhạc Việt Nam thế kỷ XX,* 7 volumes, nearly 7,000 p, Viện Âm nhạc (ed), Hanoi.

Đặng Hoành Loan and others : 2006 : *Đặc khảo Ca Trù Việt Nam*, Viện Âm Nhạc (ed), 633p, Hanoi. Articles written by Nguyễn Xuân Diện, Trần thị Kim Anh, Vũ Nhật Thăng, Bùi Trọng Hiền, Nguyễn Đức Mậu, Trần Văn Khê, Đặng Hoành Loan, etc…

Đặng Nguyễn & others (1997): *Âm nhạc cổ truyền Quảng Trị*, Viện nghiên cứu âm nhạc, sở Văn Hóa Thông Tin , 352p, Quảng Trị.

Đặng Văn Lung, Hồng Thao, Trần Linh Quý (1978): *Quan Họ : nguồn gốc và quá trình phát triển*, Khoa Học xã hội (ed), 527p, Hanoi.

Đào Trọng Từ, Huy Trân, Tú Ngọc (1979): *Essais sur la musique vietnamienne*, Editions en langues étrangères, 287p, Hanoi.

Đào Trọng Từ, Huy Trân, Tú Ngọc (1979): *Essais sur la musique vietnamienne*, Editions en langues étrangères, 287p, Hanoi.

Đinh Lan, Sỹ Tiến (1971): *Hướng dẫn sử dụng một số nhạc cụ dân tộc*, Vụ văn hóa quần chúng và thư viện, 170p, Hanoi.

Đỗ Bằng Đoàn, Đỗ Trọng Huề (1962): *Việt Nam ca trù biên khảo*, 681p. Saigon.

Đỗ Minh: (1975): *Bước đầu tìm hiểu ca nhạc dân gian Việt Bắc*, Việt Bắc (ed), 163p, Việt Bắc.

Dương Bích Hà (1997): *Lý Huế,* nhà xuất bản Âm nhạc, Viện Âm nhạc, 256p, Hanoi.

Hinh Phước Long, A Thiên Hương, Lê Thị Kim Quý (1986): *Nghệ thuật cồng chiêng*, Sở văn hóa thông tin Gia Lai – Kontum, Viện Nghiên cứu âm nhạc Việt Nam (ed), 286p, Gia Lai – Kontum.

Hồ Trường An (1999): *Theo chân những tiếng hát*, nhà xuất bản Miền Đông, 385p, Virginia, USA.

Hồ Trường An (2000): *Chân dung những tiếng hát*, nhà xuất bản Tân Văn, 441p, Tokyo, Japan.

Hoàng Châu Kỳ (1973): *Sơ khảo lịch sử nghệ thuật tuồng*, nhà xuất bản Văn Hóa, 212p, Hanoi.

Hoàng Châu Kỳ (1973): *Sơ khảo lịch sử nghệ thuật tuồng*, Văn hóa (ed), 212p, Hanoi.

Hoàng Hiệp, Ca Lê Thuần, xuân Hồng, Lưu Hữu Phước (1986): *Âm nhạc ở thành phố Hồ Chí Minh*, TP Hồ Chí Minh (ed), 180p, Hô Chi Minh City.

Hoàng Kiều (2001): *Thanh điệu tiếng Việt và âm nhạc cổ truyền*, Viện Âm nhạc, 472p, Hanoi.

Hoàng Như Mai (1986): *Sân khấu cải lương*, nhà xuất bản Tổng Hợp Đồng Tháp, 198p, Đồng Tháp.

http://www.talawas.org/talaDB/showFile.php?res=6620&rb=0206

http://www.talawas.org/talaDB/showFile.php?res=6803&rb=0206

Kiều Tấn (1998-1999): *Music of the Talented / Nhạc tài tử Nam bộ*, 1st part, listing of sound documents archived at the Volkerkunde Museum in Berlin, manuscript, 262p., Berlin & Ho Chi Minh City.

Lê Giang, Lê Anh Trung (1991): *Những bài hát ru*, nhà xuất bản Văn Nghệ, 180p, Ho chi Minh City.

Lê Huy, Huy Trân (1984): *Nhạc khí dân tộc Việt Nam*, Văn Hóa (ed), 169p, Hanoi.

Lê Yên (1994): *Những vấn đề cơ bản trong âm nhạc tuồng*, nhà xuất bản Thế Giới, 181p, Hanoi.

Lư Nhất Vũ / Lê Giang (editors) 1995: *Dân ca Đồng Tháp*, nhà xuất bản Tổng Hợp Đồng tháp, 465p, Đồng Tháp.

Lư Nhất Vũ, Lê Giang (1981): *Dân ca Bến Tre*, ty Văn hóa thông tin Bến tre (ed), 346p, Bến Tre.

Lư Nhất Vũ, Lê Giang, Nguyễn Văn Hoa (1985): *Dân ca Kiên Giang*, Sở Văn Hoá Thông Tin (ed), 483p, Kiên Giang

Lư Nhất Vũ, Nguyễn Văn Hoa, Lê Giang (1985): *Dân Ca Kiên Giang*, sở Văn Hóa Thông Tin Kiên giang, 483p, Kiên Giang.

Many authors (1987): *Vietnamese Modern Theatre*, Vietnamese Studies no 17, 153p, Hanoi.

Many authors (1997): *Nghiên cứu văn nghê dân gian Việt Nam, vol.1*, nhà xuất bản Văn Hóa Dân tộc, 863p, Hanoi.

Nguyễn Chung Anh (1968): *Hát Ví Nghệ Tĩnh*, 147p, Hanoi.

Nguyễn Đình Lai (1956): Etude sur la musique sino-vietnamienne et les chants populaires du Vietnam, Bulletin de la Société des Etudes Indochinoises, 31 (1) 1-86, Saigon.

Nguyễn Đổng Chi, Ninh Viết Giao (1942): *Hát Giặm*, vol.1, 348p, Hanoi ; 1944 : *Hát Giặm*, vol.2, 340p, Hanoi.

Nguyễn Thị Nhung (1998): *Nhạc khí gõ trống để trong chèo truyền thống*, nhà xuất bản Âm nhạc, 190p, Hanoi.

Nguyễn Văn Huyên : 1934 : *Les chants alternés des garçons et des filles en Annam*, Paul Gueuthner (ed), 224p, Paris.

Nguyễn Văn Phú, Lưu Hữu Phước, Nguyễn Viêm, Tú Ngọc (1962): *Dân ca Quan Họ Bắc Ninh*, Văn Hóa (ed), Viện Văn Học, 340p, Hanoi.

Phạm Duy (1975): *Musics of Vietnam*, Dale H. Whiteside (ed), Southern Illinois University, Carbondale.

Phạm Phúc Minh (1994): *Tìm hiểu dân ca Việt Nam*, nhà xuất bản Âm nhạc, 328p, Hanoi.

Reyes Adelaida (1999): *Songs of the Caged, Songs of the Free / Music and the Vietnamese Refugee Experience*, Temple University Press, 218p, Philadelphia, USA.

Song Bân (1960): *Le Théâtre vietnamien*, 163p, Hanoi

Sỹ Tiến (1984): *Bước đầu tìm hiểu sân khấu cải lương*, nhà xuất bản TP Hồ Chí Minh, 160p, Ho Chi Minh City.

Sỹ Tiến (1984): *Bước đầu tìm hiểu sân khấu cải lương*, TP Hồ Chí Minh (ed), 159p, Ho chi Minh city.

Thái Văn Kiểm (1964): « Panorama de la musique classique vietnamienne des origines à nos jours », Bull.de la Société des Etudes Indochinoises, nouvelle série, 39 (1), Saigon.

Toan Ánh (1985): *Cầm Ca Việt Nam*, nhà xuất bản Xuân Thu, 270p (reprint), Los Alamitos, USA.

Trần Cường (1996): *Âm nhạc : tác giả và tác phẩm*, nhà xuất bản Âm nhạc, 348p, Hanoi.

Trần Hữu Lạc, Phạm Thùy Nhân, Sâm Thương : 1987 : *Dưới ánh đèn sân khấu*, Sở Văn Hóa Thông tin Tây Ninh, 192p, Tây Ninh.

Trần Kiều Lại Thủy (1997): *Âm nhạc cung đình triều Nguyễn*, nhà xuất bản Thuận Hóa, 268p, Huế.

Trần Quang Hải & Bạch Yến (2006): « Ca Trù on the acoustical point of view », Bulletin Thông báo khoa học n°18 : 71-97, Viện Âm nhạc, Hanoi .

Trần Quang Hải (1976): « Vietnamese Traditional Music », Oriental Music: 46-49, Durham University.

Trần Quang Hải (1985): *La musique du Vietnam*, Musique et Culture (ed), 8 : 20p, Strasbourg.

Trần Quang Hải (1987): « La musique et les réfugiés », Revue musicale (ed) nos 402-403-404 : 125-133, Paris.

Trần Quang Hải (1989): *Âm nhạc Việt Nam biên khảo* , Bắc Đẩu (ed),361p, Paris.

Trần Trung Quân (1999): *Hậu trường sân khấu cải lương trước năm 1975 và tại hải ngoại*, nhà xuất bản Nam Á, 364p, Paris

Trần Văn Khải (1986): *Nghệ thuật sân khấu Việt Nam* , nhà xuất bản Xuân Thu, 265p, reprint, USA

Trần Văn Khê (1959): « Place de la musique dans les classes populaires au Vietnam », Bull. de la Société des Etudes Indochinoises, 34 (4) : 361-377, Saigon.

Trần Văn Khê (1962): *La musique vietnamienne traditionnelle*, Annales du Musée Guimet, vol.66, Presses Universitaires de France (ed), 384p, Paris.

Trần Văn Khê (1967): *Vietnam (les traditions musicales),* Buchet /Chastel (ed), 224p, Paris.

Trần Văn Khê (1987): *Trân Van Khê et le Vietnam,* La Revue Musicale triple numéro 402-403-404, 146p, Paris, France .

Trần Văn Khê (2000) : *Văn hóa với âm nhạc dân tộc, tiểu luận,* nhà xuất bản Thanh Niên, 158p, Ho chi minh city.

Trường Kỳ (1995): *Tuyển tập nghệ sĩ , vol.1,* nhà xuất bản Trường Kỳ, 336 p, Montreal, Canada.

Trường Kỳ (1999): *Tuyển tập nghệ sĩ , vol.3,* nhà xuất bản Trường Kỳ, 268p, Montreal, Canada .

Trường Kỳ (2000): *Tuyển tập nghệ sĩ , vol.4,* nhà xuất bản Trường Kỳ, 368p, Montreal, Canada .

Trường Kỳ (2002): *Một thời nhạc trẻ,* nhà xuất bản Trường Kỳ, 384p, Montreal, Canada.

Trường Kỳ (2003): *Tuyển tập nghệ sĩ vol.6,* nhà xuất bản Trường Kỳ, 376p, Montreal, Canada.

Tú Ngọc (1994): *Dân ca người Việt,* nhà xuất bản Âm nhạc, 300p, Hanoi.

Tú Ngọc (1997): *Hát Xoan, dân ca lễ nghi – phong tục,* nhà xuất bản Âm nhạc, Viện Âm nhạc, 216p, Hanoi.

Tú Ngọc, Nguyễn Thị Nhung, Vũ Tự Lân, Nguyễn Ngọc Oánh, Thái Phiên : 2000 : *Âm nhạc mới Việt Nam : tiến trình và thành tựu,* Viện âm nhạc, 1000p , Hanoi.

Võ Thanh Tùng (2001): *Nhạc khí dân tộc Việt*, nhà xuất bản Âm nhạc, 435p, Hanoi

Vũ Tự Lân (1997): *Những ảnh hưởng của âm nhạc Châu Âu trong ca khúc Việt Nam giai đoạn 1930-1950*, nhà xuất bản Thế giới, 252p, Hanoi.

Vương Hồng Sển 1968 : *Hồi ký 50 năm mê hát* , nhà xuất bản Phạm Quang Khai, tủ sách Nam Chi, 254p, Saigon.

DISCOGRAPHY

1988   Vietnam: Rêves et Réalité, performed by Trần Quang Hải & Bạch Yến, CD.

      PLAYASOUND PS 65020, recordings (1979 & 1987), bilingual notes (French-English) (12p) by Trần Quang Hải, Paris.

1989   Hát Chèo / Théâtre populaire vietnamien, CD

      AUVIDIS D 8022, recordings and bilingual notes (French – English) by Trần Văn Khê, Unesco Collection, Paris.

1991   Music from Vietnam, CD

      CAPRICE CAP 21406, English notes (16p) , Stockholm, Sweden.

1993   Stilling Time / Người ngồi ra thời gian, CD

      INNOVA 112, recordings and English notes (12p) by Philip Blackburn, Minneapolis.

1993   Vietnam : chants des minorités des Hauts Plateaux du Nord Vietnam, CD

      PEOPLES, recordings and trilingual notes (French – English-German) (16p) by Patrick Kersalé, Paris.

1993   Cithare vietnamienne / Tran Quang Hai, performed by Trần Quang Hải, CD.

      PLAYASOUND PS 65103, recordings (1993), bilingual notes (French-English) (24p) by Trần Quang Hải, Paris.

1993 Vietnam: Tradition du Sud, performed by Nguyễn Vĩnh Bảo and Trần Văn Khê, CD.

OCORA C 560043, recordings (1972), bilingual notes (French-English) (32p) by Trần Văn Khê, Paris.

1994 Vietnam : Le Dàn Tranh : Musiques d'hier et d'aujourd'hui, performed by Hải Phượng and Trần Văn Khê, CD.

OCORA C 560055, recordings (1994), bilingual notes (French – English) by Trần Văn Khê, Paris.

1994 Vietnam / Poésies et chants, performed by Trần Văn Khê and Trần Thị Thủy Ngọc, CD.

OCORA C 560054, recordings (1993) and trilingual notes (French-English-German) (36p) by Trần Văn Khê, Paris

1994 Music from Vietnam 2: Huê, CD.

CAPRICE CAP 21463, recordings, English notes (16p), Stockholm, Sweden.

1995 Vietnam du Nord : chants de possession, CD.

Buda Records 92657-2, recordings and bilingual notes (French-English) (24p) by Patrick Kersalé, Paris.

1995 Vietnam : Ca Tru tradition du Nord, CD.

Maison des Cultures du Monde MCM W-260070, recordings (1995), bilingual notes (French-English) (24p), Paris.

1995 Vietnam : Musique de Huê, CD.

Maison des Cultures du Monde MCM W-26073, recordings (1995), bilingual notes (French-English) (24p) by Trần Văn Khê, Paris.

1996 L'art de la vièle vietnamienne, CD.

ARION ARN 60417, recordings and bilingual notes (French-English) (12p) by Patrick Kersalé, Paris.

1996 Fêtes traditionnelles vietnamiennes, performed by Trần Quang Hải & Bạch Yến, CD.

Studio SM D-2504, quadrilingual notes (French-English-German-Spanish) by Trần Quang Hải, Paris.

1996 Vietnam Music of the Trường Sơn Mountains, CD.

White Cliffs Media WCM 9990, recordings and English notes (12p) by Nguyễn Thuyết Phong and Terry Miller, USA.

1996 Tran Quang Hai / Landscape of the Highlands, performed by Tran Quang Hai , CD.

Latitudes LAT 50612, North Carolina, USA.

1997 Vietnam : Musiques des Montagnards, set of 2 CD.

Le Chant du Monde CNR 2741085/86, recordings (1958-1994), bilingual notes (French-English) (124p) by many authors, Paris.

1997 Tran Quang Hai / Guimbardes du Monde, performed by Tran Quang Hai, CD.

PLAYASOUND PS 66009, recordings (1997), bilingual notes (French- English) (12p) by Trân Quang Hai, Paris.

1998 Vietnam : Musique des Edê, CD.

Buda Records 92726-2, recordings and bilingual notes (French-English) by Patrick Kersalé, Paris .

2001 Dân Ca Miền Núi và Cao Nguyên (Folksongs of Mountainous Regions and Highlands), CD.

Viện Âm Nhạc, Hanoi, Vietnam.

2002 Âm Nhạc dân gian dân tộc Mông (Music of the Mông tribe), CD.

Viện Âm Nhạc, Hanoi, Vietnam.

2004 Musique du Vietnam, CD.

PROPHET 38, Philips 981 431-1, recordings (2003), bilingual notes (French –English) (20p) by Charles Duvelle, Paris.

2005 Ca Tru Vietnam / Vietnamese Ca Tru Singing, CD.

Viện Âm Nhạc (Vietnamese Institute for Musicology), Hanoi, Vietnam.

2006 Vietnam : Musiques vocales des plaines du Nord : Ca Trù – Hát Chèo – Quan Họ , CD.

VDE CD-1267, recordings (2005) and bilingual notes (English – French) (40p) by Yves Defrance, Geneva.

VCD & DVD

2001   Canh Hát Quan Họ VCD 2 (A session of Quan Họ Singing) , VCD.

Viện Âm Nhạc, Hanoi, Vietnam.

2001   Canh Hát Quan Họ VCD 1 (A session of Quan Họ Singing), VCD.

Viện Âm Nhạc, Hanoi, Vietnam.

2005   Âm Nhạc và Múa Cung Đình Huế (Music and Dance of Huế Court) , DVD.

Viện Âm Nhạc, Hanoi, Vietnam.

About the terminology used in overtone/undertone for the throat singing /overtone singing

Trần Quang Hải

National Center for Scientific Research, France.

"KHOOMEI" or "THROAT SINGING is the name used in Tuva and Mongolia to describe a large family of singing styles and techniques in which a single vocalist simultaneously produces two (or more) distinct tones. The lower one is the usual fundamental tone of the voice and sounds as a sustained drone or a Scottish bagpipe sound. The second corresponds to one of the harmonic partials and is like a resonating whistle in a high, or very high register. We transcribe in the simplest way the Tuvan term, for the lack of agreement between the different authors:

KHOMEI

KHÖÖMII

HO-MI

HÖ-MI

CHÖÖMEJ

CHÖÖMIJ

XÖÖMIJ

Throat Singing has almost entirely been an unknown form of art until rumours about Tuva and the peculiar Tuvan musical culture spread in the West, especially in North America, thanks to Richard Feynman, a distinguished American physicist, who was an ardent devotee of Tuvan matters (today, partly because of Feynman's influence, there exists a society called „Friends of Tuva "in California, which circulates news about Tuva in the West.

This singing tradition is mostly practised in the Central Asia regions including Bashkortostan or Bashkiria (near Ural Mountains), Altai and Tuva (two autonomous republics of the Russian Federation), Khakassia and Mongolia. But we can find examples worldwide in South Africa between Xhosa women, in the Tibetan Buddhist chanting, in Rajasthan, and also among the Dani tribes in Papu Guinea

The Tuvan people developed numerous different styles. The 5 different techniques are:

Sygyt (like a whistle with a weak fundamental)

Khoomei (general term for throat singing and a particular style)

Borbangnadyr (similar to Kargyraa with higher fundamental)

Ezengileer (rercognizable by the quick rhythmical shifts between diphonic harmonics)

Kargyraa (with very low fundamentals obtained by undertones)

In Mongolia, most throat singing styles take the name from the part of the body where they suppose to feel the vibratory resonance

XAMRYN XÖÖMI (nasal XÖÖMI)

BAGALZUURYN XÖÖMI (throat XÖÖMI)

TSEEDZNII XÖÖMI (chest XÖÖMI)

KEVLIIN XÖÖMI (ventral XÖÖMI)

XARKIRAA XÖÖMI (similar to Tuvan Kargyraa)

ISGEREX (rarely used style it sounds like a flute)

The Khakash people practise three types of Throat singing

KARGIRAR   like KARGYRAA (Tuva)

KUVEDER or **KILENGE**   like EZENGILEER (Tuva)

| **SIGIRTIP** | like SYGYT (Tuva) |

The peoples of the Altai Mountains use three terms

KARKIRAA	like KARGYRAA (Tuva)
KIOMIOI	like KHOOMEI (Tuva)
SIBISKI	like SYGYT (Tuva)

The Bashkiria musical tradition uses the throat singing UZLAU similar to Tuvan EZENGILEER) to accompany epic song.

The **Tibetan GYUTO** monks have also a tradition of diphonic chant, related to the religious beliefs of the vibratory reality of the universe. They sing in a very low register in a way that resembles the Tuvan KARGYRAA method. The aim of this tradition is mystical and consists in isolating the 10th harmonic partial of the vocal sound.

IN THE WESTERN WORLD

There are in the literature many terms to indicate the presence of different perceptible sounds in a single voice. If you have a look at the motor of reaearch (www.google.com), you will be astonished by the number of websites linked to throat singing KHOOMEI. I am going to establish a listing of unmbers of sites linked to each term according to GOOGLE motor research (28 December 2003, date of consultation of GOOGLE).

KHOOMEI	*1,710 sites*
KARGYRAA	*883 sites*
SYGYT	*673 sites*

EZENGILEER	*141 sites*
BORBANGNADYR	*129 sites*
THROAT SINGING	*8,980 sites*
OVERTONE SINGING	*2,500 sites*
DIPHONIC SINGING	*65 sites*
BIPHONIC SINGING	*121 sites*
OVERTONING	*615 sites*
HARMONIC SINGING	*901 sites*
FORMANTIC SINGING	
HARMONIC CHANT	
MULTIPHONIC SINGING	*158 sites*
BITONALITY	
DIPLOPHONIA	*190 sites*
VOCAL FRY	
CANTO DIPLOFONICO	*27 sites*
CANTO DIFONICO	*138 sites*
OBERTONSEGANG	*256 sites*

According to the pioneer work in the domain of the vocal sounds made by the Extended Vocal Techniques Ensemble (EVTE) of San

Diego University and bearing in mind that there is little agreement regarding classifications, the best distinctive criterion for the diphonia seems to be the characterization of the sound sources that produce the perception of the diphonic or multiphonic sound.

Following that principle, we can distinguish between BITONALITY and DIPHONIA

BITONALITY: in this case, there are two distinct sound sources that produce two sounds. The pitches of the two sounds could be or not in harmonic relationship. This category includes DIPLOPHONIA, BITONALITY, and VOCAL FRY.

DIPHONIA: the reinforcement of one (or more) harmonic partials produces the splitting of the voice in two (or more) sounds. This category includes KHOMEI, THROAT SINGING, OVERTONE SINGING, DIPHONIC SINGING, BIPHONIC SINGING, OVERTONING, HARMONIIC SINGING, HARMONIC CHANT.

BITONALITY

Diplophonia:

The vibration of the vocal folds is asymmetrical. It happens that after a normal oscillatory period, the vibration amplitude that follows is reduced. There is not the splitting of the voice in two sounds, but the pitch goes down one octave lower and the timbre assumes a typical roughness. For example, assuming as fundamental pitch a C3 130.8 Hz, the resulting pitch will be C2 65.4 Hz. If the amplitude reduction happens after two regular vibrations, the actual periodicity triplicates and then the pitch lowers one octave and a 5th. The diplophonic voice is a frequent pathology of the larynx (as in unilateral vocal cord paralysis), but can be also obtained willingly for artistic effects (Demetrio Stratos was an expert of this technique).

Bitonality

The two sound sources are due to the vibration of two different parts of the glottis cleft. This technique requires a strong laryngeal tension. In this case, there is not necessarily a harmonic relationship between the fundamentals of the two sounds. In the Tuvan KARGYRAA style, the second sound is due to the vibration of the supraglottal structures (false folds, aryepiglottic folds that connects the arytenoids and the epiglottis, and the epiglottis root). In this case generally (but not always) there is a 2:1 frequency ratio between the supraglottal closure and vocal folds closure. As in the case of Diplophonia, the pitch goes down on octave lower (or more).

Vocal fry

The second sound is due in this case to the periodic repetition of a glottal pulsation of different frequency. It sounds like the opening of a creaky door (another common designation is "creaky voice"). The pulse rate of vocal fry can be controlled to produce a range from very slow single clicks to a stream of clicks so rapid to be perceived as a discrete pitch. Therefore, vocal fry is a special case of bitonality: the perception of a second sound depends on a pulses train rate and not on the spectral composition of a single sound.

DIPHONIA

Diphonic and **Biphonic** refer to any singing that sounds like two (or more) simultaneous pitches, regarless of technique. Use of these terms is largely limited to academic sources. In the scientific literature the preferred term to indicated Throat Singing is **Diphonic Singing**.

Multiphonic Singing indicates a complex cluster of non-harmonically related pitches that sounds like the vocal fry or the creaky voice. The cluster may be produced expiring as normal, or also inhaling the airflow.

Throat Singing is any technique that includes the manipulation of the throat to produce a melody with the harmonics. Generally, this involves applying tension to the region surrounding the vocal folds and the manipulation of the various cavities of the throat, including the ventricular bands, the arytenoids, and the pharynx.

Chant generally refers to religious singing in different traditions (Gregorian, Buddhist, Hindu chant, etc...). As regards the diphonia, it is noteworthy to mention the low singing practised by Tibetan Buddhist monks of the Gyutö sect. As explained before, they reinforce the 10th harmonic partial of the vocal sound for mystical and symbolic purposes. This kind of real diphonia must be distinguished from resonantial effects (enhancement of some uncontrolled overtones) that we can hear in Japanese Shomyo Chant and also in Gregorian Chant.

Harmonic Singing is the term introduced by David Hykes to refer to any technique that reinforces a single harmonic or harmonic cluster. The sound may or may not split into two or mor notes. It is used as a synonym of Overtone Singing, Overtoning, Harmonic Chant and also Throat Singing.

Overtone Singing can be considered to be harmonic singing with an intentional emphasis on the harmonic melody of overtones. This is the name used by Western artists that utilizes vowels, mouth shaping and upper throat manipulations to produce melodies and textures. It is used as a synonym of Harmonic Singing, Overtoning, Harmonic Chant and also Throat Singing.

OVERTONE SINGING IN THE WEST

In the West, the Overtone Singing technique has unexpectedly become very popular, starting into musical contests and turning very soon to mystical, spiritual and also therapeutic applications. The first to make use of a diphonic vocal technique in music was Karlheinz Stockhausen in STIMMUNG. He was followed by numerous artists and amongst them : the EVTE (Extended Vocal Techniques Ensemble) group at the San Diego University in 1972, Laneri and his Prima Materia group in 1973, Tran Quang Hai in 1975, Demetrio Stratos in 1977, Meredith Monk in 1980, David Hykes and his Harmonic Choir in 1983 , Joan La Barbara in 1985, Michael Vetter in 1985, Christian Bollmann in 1985, Noah Pikes in 1985, Michael Reimann in 1986, Tamia in 1987, Bodjo Pinek in 1987, Josephine Truman in 1987, Quatuor Nomad in 1989, Iegor Reznikoff in 1989, Valentin Clastrier in 1990, Rollin Rachele in 1990, Thomas Clements in 1990, Sarah Hopkins in 1990, Les Voix Diphoniques in 1997, Mark Van Tongeren in 2000, etc... The most famous proponent of this type of singing is David Hykes. Hykes experimented with numerous innovations including changing the fundamental (moveable drone) and keeping fixed the diphonic formant, introducing text, glissando effects, etc... in numerous works produced with the Harmonic Choir of New York.

CONCLUSION

All these sounds contain overtones or tones that resonate in fixed relationships above a fundamental frequency. These overtones create tone color, and help us to differentiate the sounds of different music instruments or one voice and another

Different cultures have unique manifestations of musical traditions, but what it is quite interesting, is that some of them share at least one aspect in common: the production of overtones in their respective vocal music styles.

The diversity of terminology designating this vocal phenomenon shows us the interest of people in discovering overtones /undertones. The most used term is THROAT SINGING (8980 websites linked according to GOOGLE motor of research) more than OVERTONE SINGING (2500 linked websites). This attitude is understandable because the term "Throat Singing" is the correct translation of the Tuvan and Mongolian terms KHOOMEI which means "pharynx", or "throat".

Cithare vietnamienne, guimbarde, cuillères au service de la musique électro-acoustique

Trần Quang Hải

National Center for Scientific Research, France.

Dans le cadre de la manifestation consacrée aux 50 ans de musique électro-acoustique, en hommage à Pierre Schaeffer, le père de la musique concrète, j'évoque ici mon travail avec le regretté Nguyên Van Tuong, compositeur et ancien collaborateur de Monsieur Pierre Schaeffer, concernant l'oeuvre Vê Nguôn (Retour aux Sources) où ont été utilisés les instruments traditionnels avec le soutien des éléments électroniques.Je mentionnerai également le prolongement de mes recherches expérimentales avec d'autres compositeurs français comme Yves Herwan Chotard et Nicolas Frize et Michel

Moglie, inventeur d'orgue à feu.

Vê Nguôn (" Retour aux Sources") en quatre mouvements ou quatre pensées, pour bande magnétique quatre pistes (quadruple stéréophonie) et soliste en direct : cithare vietnamienne à 16 cordes, guimbardes, cuillères, cloches-bols iraniennes et voix diphonique.

1. LE POURQUOI ET LE COMMENT

Vê Nguôn est construit avec des matériaux sonores issus d'une part de la nature, d'autre part des traditions musicales. Mais ces matériaux, qui contribuent à l'élaboration de cette architecture musicale, varient par l'utilisation même qui en est faite. Présentés à l'état brut, ils sont alors utilisés dans leur état originel. Sinon, passés au crible des systèmes électroacoustiques et électroniques, ils deviennent alors travaillés, laminés, broyés, modelés, sculptés... par ces "machines étranges".

Les bruits naturels tels que vent, tonnerre, chants d'oiseaux, de grillons, battements de coeur, voix humaines, etc. confèrent à "la musique de la nature" ses lettres de noblesse.

Quant à la tradition musicale, elle fait appel aux sons des instruments musicaux traditionnels, principalement ceux du Viêt-nam tels que cithare à 16 cordes, vièle à 2 cordes, cliquettes, bloc de bois *song lang,* cuillères ; ils font partie du catalogue sonore des traditions de l'Extrême Orient.

Les sons d'instruments occidentaux (cordes, ondes Martenot, percussions), ajoutent eux aussi leur pierre à cet édifice grandiose; mais ils ne cimentent pas la matière sonore de base. Utilisés comme répliques aux ambiances sonores issues de la nature ou des musiques traditionnelles, ils viennent renforcer les contrastes et enrichir les couleurs sonores spécifiques d'une tradition musicale fruit de la pensée ou de l'imagination.

Nulle hiérarchie de valeurs ne vient ici interférer entre ces sons et ces bruits: c'est à l'homme-auditeur-observateur de les capter, de les accepter, et d'opérer en lui l'alchimie secrète qui fera naître d'eux la "musique" en tant que telle.

Nulle volonté, non plus, de localisation géographique et ethnique des traditions musicales en fonction des critères propres à certaines, et que l'auteur utilise ici. Il s'agit plutôt d'offrir à l'auditeur, à travers un travail de reconstitution d'ambiance sonore, l'approche sensible d'une Asie musicale imaginaire. Cette "mise au diapason" avec les traditions du passé s'opère grâce à l'intervention des moyens technologiques du présent. Simples, complexes, artisanales ou super élaborées, peu importe, - pourvu que les "étranges machines " puissent satisfaire la curiosité de l'homme envers la matière sonore qu'il considère comme "musicale".

A travers cette oeuvre, l'auteur approfondit sa recherche sur la spatialisation du son, qu'il considère comme "technique d'orchestration en relief". Il emploie les moyens électroacoustiques et électroniques :

1) comme un **pont** susceptible de créer un trait d'union entre une perfectibilité technique encore instable mais souvent sollicitée par des "pensées", et l'assise bien ordonnée des traditions des penseurs.

2) comme un **mode d'expression** indépendant à la fois de la tradition orale, et des artifices conventionnels d'une écriture musicale dont les routines risquent d'entraver la transmission intégrale d'une pensée.

3) comme une **voie de synthèse** encore possible entre un présent bousculé anxieux, et un passé serein, et méditatif, mais ô combien

respectable !

<u>Pourquoi le titre "Vê Nguôn"</u> (retour aux sources) ?

Dans son article "Retour aux Sources" (in cahiers d'études de la Radio-Télévision numéro 27/28, 1960) Pierre Schaeffer, réfléchissant sur l'évolution de la recherche musicale, écrivait : "*Pas d'expédition en Amazonie, au Sikkim, au Kilimandjaro, sans magnétophone. Pas d'exploration magnétique, pas de phonogène ni de musique électronique à Paris, à Milan ou à New York sans zoulous, sans sorciers, sans lamas* ".

Constatation ? Défis ? Ou..., tout simplement, semailles d' une graine de sagesse issue de la terre riche d'une certaine philosophie !?

Mais, en des terres trop souvent stériles à force d'intellectualisation outrancière, quel fruit ce premier germe a-t-il pu engendrer ?

Quinze ans après cette déclaration pleine de "ferveur et de croyance" - et faite d'encre et de papier - de Pierre Schaeffer, les zoulous ont bien débarqué à Paris, et les magnétophones, toujours incrédules, se laissent docilement ou "indocilement" manipuler au Groupe de Recherches Musicales de l'ORTF à Paris.

Profitant de la présence effective des uns et des autres, nous tentons donc ici une aventure, citant une dernière fois Pierre Schaeffer "*en nous promenant sans grâce et la conscience peu tranquille, dans de vieux monuments des civilisations disparues, pour essayer de déchiffrer le "Présent" dans les traces énigmatiques du "Passé*".

2. FICHE ANALYTIQUE

Vê Nguôn comprend quatre phases ou "manières de penser" ; ces phases ne sont pas des fins en elles-mêmes, mais des directions

96

compositionnelles permettant d'agencer, d'amalgamer les différents matériaux entre eux. Le soliste s'intègre au cheminement de l'oeuvre par des improvisation libres et spontanées, à partir des directives de l'auteur.

Première pensée : EXPOSITION.

C'est une présentation progressive, dans le temps et dans l'espace, des matières et des manières qui seront utilisées dans le déroulement des phases suivantes. L'auditeur est invité à pénétrer dans le monde sonore proposé, à s'y accoutumer, à s'en imprégner, afin d'être prêt à accueillir les périodes ultérieures.

1/ Matières : pures ou métamorphosées, les sonorités issues des instruments orientaux contrastent avec celles de l'Occident, ou fusionnent avec la musique de la nature.

2/ Manières : mouvement et vie animent les sons sous l'effet de la spatialisation. Le dialogue musical s'instaure dans le temps et dans l'espace, ceux-ci étant pris comme paramètres techniques de l'orchestration en relief. La coexistence des ambiances sonores différentes s'impose alors, plus dans l'interaction que dans l'alternance des différents éléments.

Deuxième pensée : ALLÉGORIE.

La bande magnétique donne le "Hò", note de base modale (sol), qui se déploie à travers différentes manières et permet au soliste d'accorder sa cithare selon le mode BAC (sol, la, do, ré, mi).

Les arabesques des chants d'oiseaux électroniques illustrent l'élément nature, tandis qu'une masse sonore floue symbolise, avec une intensité grandissante, le martèlement obstiné des battements de coeur. Cette pulsation lancinante s'enfle, puis disparaît peu à peu,

97

faisant place aux harmoniques de la cithare, prolongées en itératif par un écho artificiel qui tournoie dans l'espace, puis se transforme en un élément contrapuntique.

Ces harmoniques servent de "canevas modal et temporel" au jeu du soliste qui improvise en dialogue, en contrepoint avec la bande.

Troisième mouvement : TOURMENTE.

Tableau sonore abstrait, cette phase réfléchit l'état d'âme de l'homme ébranlé par une inquiétude profonde devant la vie, harcelé par les problèmes métaphysiques de sa condition.

Homophonie : une voix seule et unique, avec de nombreuses variations dans l'émission vocale, module, toujours à la même hauteur de base; mais cette hauteur, non stable, fluctue (en micro-intervalles selon le terme européen) à la manière orientale où la gamme n'est pas tempérée.

Personnage principal de cette phase, la voix s'amplifie dans des développements de plus en plus denses et fournis; elle se trouve brodée, enveloppée, assaillie, par les signaux sonores provenant de la musique de la nature et des sons instrumentaux orientaux et européens, montant graduellement jusqu'aux limites d'un sommet sonore, comme monte l'oppression si douloureuse à ceux qui la ressentent et la supportent.

Quatrième pensée: EUPHORIE

Cette sensation de bien être, de plénitude, a souvent été perçue à travers le dialogue des musiciens classiques hindous, dont la rythmique extrêmement évoluée est sans doute la plus complexe et savante du monde.

C'est à partir de cette idée d'un jeu de "lutte musicale" empreint de la sensibilité et de la finesse tant recherchées des maîtres de l'Inde et d'autres contrées, que l'auteur propose ici une autre forme de dialogue. En effet, entre le soliste et la bande magnétique, pullulent questions, réponses, choeurs rythmiques, phrases et paraphrases, temps et contretemps. L'un cherche à déséquilibrer l'autre musicalement à "faire perdre pied à l'antagoniste", selon le procédé si populaire dans les arts martiaux et musicaux de l'Extrême Orient.

Le soliste se sert de sa voix, en longues tenues ou en onomatopées, des cuillères, etc... pour donner la réplique aux figures imprimées sur la bande; il doit à d'autres moments assumer dignement et efficacement son rôle de virtuose - soutenu par la base rythmique de la bande. Enfin, soliste et bande se rejoignent dans un choeur rythmique de plus en plus précis et pressant, vers la fulgurance finale où les deux interlocuteurs cherchent, avec des moyens différents, à exprimer une même pensée pour parvenir à une même fin.

3. SPATIALISATION

L'auditeur sera placé au milieu d'un "mur de son" que l'auteur a conçu au moyen de sept points fixes de diffusion, à savoir les hauts parleurs, reliés entre eux par les trajectoires du son qui passe de l'un à l'autre.

La distribution spatiale dépend de plusieurs facteurs:

1) La bande quatre pistes a été réalisée avec quatre bandes stéréophoniques sur lesquelles la matière sonore est toujours en mouvement, ce qui donne un effet de quadruple stéréophonie, ou "octaphonie".

2) Le soliste qui joue en direct dispose de plusieurs micros; chacun d'eux étant relié à un haut-parleur placé dans un emplacement donné de la salle, le soliste a la responsabilité de localiser le son de ses

instruments dans l'espace, et même de le déplacer, en passant d'un micro à l'autre.

L'emplacement des hauts-parleurs sera déterminé, pour chaque exécution, en fonction de la salle, plusieurs schémas préparés par l'auteur étant proposés.

Vê Nguôn, oeuvre de synthèse, en quatre mouvements ou quatre pensées, pour bande magnétique quatre pistes et soliste en direct: cithare vietnamienne, guimbardes, cuillères, cloches-bols iraniennes, et voix diphonique , fut écrite en hommage à Pierre Schaeffer. Créée en 1975, en sa présence puisque l'oeuvre lui était dédiée, elle faisait également appel à l'art visuel à travers un montage audiovisuel en fondu enchaîné de 600 diapositives prises à partir d'un microscope.

Trân Quang Hai, musicien soliste Vietnamien, dans un contexte de recherche nouvelle, à la fois classique et contemporaine, tente d'établir un dialogue mélodique, rythmique et temporel avec la bande magnétique imprimant un "canevas musical" dans le temps et dans l'espace. Cette conception originale d'une trame spatio-temporelle, il la doit à son compatriote compositeur Nguyên Van Tuong.

Ce dernier lui a permis, dès 1965, de rencontrer Pierre Schaeffer avec lequel il travaillait à la réalisation de films au G.R.M. Entraîné dans le sillage de la musique électroacoustique, Nguyên Van Tuong était considéré comme le père de la musique concrète au Viêt-nam. Décédé en 1998, délaissé par ses amis de l'I.N.A. G.R.M. qu'il avait quittés dix ans plus tôt à cause de sa maladie, il est pourtant l'auteur d'oeuvres presque totalement inconnues à ce jour. Trente ans plus tôt, il eut l'idée avec Trân Quang Hai de combiner des éléments de musique traditionnelle avec les innovations de la musique concrète, ... ce qui fit d'eux des précurseurs dans le domaine de la musique électroacoustique. L'apport de Pierre Schaeffer se mesure à travers l'influence qu'a exercé sur Trân Quang Hai " le Traité des Objets Musicaux ", véritable Bible pour qui s'engage dans l'expérimentation de sons a priori "impossibles".

Trân Quang Haï poly-instrumentiste virtuose, joue ici de la cithare vietnamienne, des guimbardes, des cuillères, et produit des effets vocaux.

Les cuillères présentent la particularité de se transformer en un instrument qui n'a rien à envier au synthétiseur, tant elles recèlent de richesses aussi bien mélodiques que rythmiques. Instrument de musique entré depuis peu dans le dictionnaire, appelé "Moon" en vietnamien, cet instrument prouve comme disait Pierre Schaeffer que *"l'on peut transformer un objet quotidien - en l'occurrence culinaire - en instrument de musique "*

La guimbarde, utilisant toutes les ressources résonantielles de la cavité buccale, est loin d'être l'instrument ordinaire que l'on croit. Exploitée à l'extrême limite de son potentiel, elle donne des sons identiques aux sons électroniques, la langue se déplaçant pour moduler les fréquences, le souffle donnant le rythme. La présence de huit guimbardes différentes, de textures différentes et de hauteurs différentes permet donc une combinaison époustouflante de timbres. Si Trân Quang Haï a même été jusqu'à se risquer à l'utiliser pour bruiter des dessins animés (imitation de robot), ou encore à prouver qu'elle peut donner naissance à une parole synthétique, il lui confère ici un rôle noble d'instrument à part entière.

Quant à la voix, elle s'inspire de la technique du chant diphonique que l'on rencontre entre autres chez les Mongols, les Touvains, les Bachkirs et les Tibétains. Jouant sur la présence simultanée du bourdon et des harmoniques sélectionnés grâce à une technique rigoureuse de contrôle de la mobilité des cavités de résonance, elle magnifie les possibilités spectrales de la voix qui devient ici "instrument de l'étrange".

Il utilise ces intruments comme "armes pacifiques" durant cette longue aventure sereine ou tumultueuse, parfois étrange mais rassurante et persuasive, à travers des forêts sonores de l'Occident et des jungles musicales de l'Orient pour nous démontrer qu'il pourrait rester encore une "coexistence possible entre les langages musicaux des peuples du monde", bien que ceux-ci se cherchent continuellement dans la communication mais ne se comprennent pas toujours.

- Une tentative aventurière ?

- Certainement ! .... et au fond de leurs coeurs sincères et décidés, Nguyên Van Tuong et Trân Quang Haï cherchent à s'unir dans un même élan, pour aller de l'avant, solidaires et crédules, vers cette inconnue "le Mieux est l'ennemi du Bien" en courant le risque de gâter le BIEN pour obtenir le MIEUX.

Mais plus que d'aventure, c'est bien d'union au sens noble du terme qu'il s'agit. L'alliance entre les éléments électroacoustiques et la musique traditionnelle continue dans d'autres oeuvres ultérieures.

La rencontre avec Misha Lobko, musicien de free jazz, a donné naissance à la création de Shaman" (1982), composition improvisée entre la clarinette basse, la guimbarde, le synthétiseur et la voix humaine.

En 1989, Trân Quang Haï s'est joint à Yves Herwan Chotard pour l'oeuvre "Tambours 89" marquant le bicentenaire de la Révolution Française (1789-1989) avec bande magnétique et 300 percussionnistes venant de 30 pays. Cette création mondiale a eu lieu deux fois au Parc de la Villette vers la fin du mois de mai 1989, en la présence de 70 000 spectateurs. Cette fois encore, le mariage de la technologie moderne (séquenceurs, échantillonneurs de l'ordinateur) et la musique vivante des traditions diverses demeure l'élément principal de cet événement musical.

En 1991, un autre compositeur français Nicolas Frize, en collaboration avec Trân Quang Haï a mis en oeuvre une pièce intitulée "Composition Française", coexistence linguistique et musicale où des langues étrangères (le polonais, l'arabe, le chinois, le japonais) et la langue française fleurissaient côte à côte sur le sol français. L'ensemble, soutenu par des éléments électroacoustiques sur bande magnétique, a été donné au Festival de Saint Denis, lors du concert inaugural du mois de Juin qui s'est déroulé à la basilique même.

En 1999, la rencontre avec Michel Moglia, inventeur de l'Orgue à Feu, instrument terrifiant et bouleversant, a permis à Trân Quang Haï de se replonger dans le monde électronique par la production insolite du jeu des guimbardes et de nouvelles techniques expérimentales du chant diphonique.

Le feu vient donc couronner là trente ans d'une carrière qui s'est jouée de tous les éléments du monde sonore, propulsant à travers l'élément air, et à partir d'instruments faits de bois et de métal, tout ce que la terre avait pu produire d'"'étrangement musical", confié à ce musicien dont le prénom "Haï" signifie ... "Océan" ...!

Music of The Montagnards of Vietnam

Trần Quang Hải

National Center for Scientific Research, France.

INTRODUCTION

Whoever looks for the first time at a coloured ethnolinguistic map of this region- such as the one published in 1949 by the École française d'Extrême-Orient-may have the impression of being in front of a tachiste canvas, or a fairly complicated mosaic. Such an impression would be justified, since Southeast Asia is the most

105

complex region in the world from either the linguistic or ethnographic point of view.

This complexity of human groupings is a reflection of the habitats. If we step back and glance at a physical map of outheast Asia as a whole, we see it has a surprising relief, cut by five great rivers with sources in the Himalayan foothills which, as they distance themselves, look like the five spread fingers of a hand placed flat. Long mountain chains fan out,

following in general the directions west-east and north-south of the major water-flows, with each reaching the sea via vast deltas, interrupting the winding, jagged Southeast Asian coasts. The climate of the region is that of the humid tropics, perhaps better characterised when recalling that this is part of monsoon Asia.

We spoke above of the complexity of human groupings, evident on all maps.

All possible forms of technological level and political systems are there side by side, from bands of nomadic hunter-gatherers in the deep forest to states of vast size with highly hierachical political structures. In between, there is a whole range of political forms: from acephalic villages to chiefdoms, from principalities to confederations. A considerable varietyof agricultural techniques for the cultivation of rice is deployed, ranging from different kinds of shifting slash-and-burn methods, to different types of flooded rice-paddies, by rains or by irrigation.

As for religions, one may say that, in general, animism reigns in the mountainous regions, with the sacrifice of buffalos as culminating rite.

Islam is implanted on the coast of central Vietnam, among the Cham, where a rump form of Brahmanism also survives. Finally, if Catholicism has almost failed in areas of Hinayist Buddhism (the "Base Career"), it has succeededin implanting itself among the Mahayanists (the "Great Career") and on the Highlands.

It is above all on the linguistic side that the greatest complexity is manifest. South-east Asia is in fact the territory for five families of languages. Of course, in each of these families, the speakers of different

languages do not understand one another any more than do the French, Russians and Germans (who are notwithstanding all part of the one Indo-European language family). Let us stress the fact that belonging to a particular language family is no indication at all of a given technological level nor of any particular political or religious system. Indeed, there is a large variety of technological levels and of politico-religious systems.

We may now look at each of these language families. If we cite first the Austro-Asiatic linguistic family (or the Mon-Khmer) this is because it seems autochthonous to Southeast Asia in its largest sense. Apart from that, this is the family that has the most varied range of social organisation: from forest-dwelling nomads, like the Ruc, to those speakers residing in powerful states, like the Viet.

Between these two extremes, we may distinguish a great variety of social spaces wherein Austro-Asiatic languages are spoken. In the north the most numerous are the Khmu and the Muong (see CD-II). The Muong language belongs

to the same sub-group as the Viet language of which it constitutes in some ways an archaic form. In the centre are the Montagnards of the highlands-a term preferable to "Moï" as used by explorers and colonial administrations,

which is highly pejorative and was borrowed from the Viet language. We thus suggested a more neutral term, Proto-Indochinese, to characterise in a general way those populations, wherever in the country they may live. The great mass of Austro-Asiatics of the Centre may be subdivided into two groups, separated by the Austronesians. North of the latter, one may find the Katu, the Sedang, the Bahnar (see CD-I), the Reungao, the Jeh· South of the Austronesians is the Mnong-Ma ensemble, represented on CD-I by the Sre, the Ma and the Lac.

The Austronesian family is present here thanks to recordings on CD-I collected among the Proto-Indochinese Jörai and Rhade (or Edê). As regards the Cham, the descendants of the former maritime kingdom of the Champa, they are, according to George Coedès, "Hinduised Rhade".

The name of the Thai-Kadai family was made-up in 1942 by the linguist P.K.

Benedict, following the evidence of Auguste Bonifacy in 1904 of a direct linguistic relationship between residual groups living on either side of the Sino-Vietnamese border. A.G. Haudricourt associated the Thai and Chuang languages. This linguistic family includes (on CD-II) the Tay, the Nung, the Lü and the Black Thai.

The Miao-Yao family brings together languages which are among the most complex that be in the world. The Hmong (see CD-II) belong to the first group (Miao), and the Mien who belong to the second (Yao), live along the mountain tops and owe their wide renown to the beauty of their costumes and jewellery.

The Tibeto-Burmese family includes small groups living in the high mountains traversed by the frontier separating Laos and Vietnam from China.

Here we may cite, among others the Hani (see CD-II), the Lolo (or the Yi), and the Phula.

We have emphasised the linguistic complexity of Vietnam. Now, the mosaic of the ethnolingustic map is only partially revelatory, above all in the northern regions. As early as the beginning of the XXth century, Edouard Lunet de la Jonquière emphasised the overlapping and terracing of different groups. At the valley bottoms, on the banks of watercourses, the Thai are to be found, and at the beginning of the slopes, hamlets of Austro-Asiatics. Above the latter, and sometimes above the proper Kadai, one finds settlements of Yao and Tibeto-Burman speakers. Finally, on the crests, among clearings for cultivated poppies and maize, are the latest arrivals, the Miao. Although this schema is not quite complete everywhere, most of the time we find two or three different populations on levels according to altitude.

We find a comparable diversity and complexity in music, as shown by an extraordinary variety of musical instruments. These range from a simple blade of grass to elaborate orchestras of gongs and drums (among other instruments), not to mention a multitude of diverse sound-makers whose prime material is bamboo. We should not overlook stone (such as sonorous scarecrows), and above all the lithophones of central Vietnam, of which the oldest type (without going back to the Hoabinhien period) illustrates a southern feature of the Dongsonien (a bronze-age civilisation of ca.

2300-2000 BP of Northern Vietnam whose most characteristic surviving object is the bronze drum). This lithophone has intrigued musicologists because of its unusual scale, as also has the specific voice-placements of certain present-day Montagnard minorities. Now, this musical richness, belonging to the Vietnamese cultural heritage, is in danger of disappearing: it has been made fragile through thoughtless actions by agents of development, insensitive to the diversity of modes and genres-which they ought, for all that, to be able to appreciate in the music and poetry of the Viet (or Kinh), the majority people. The preservation of diversity and musical richness is not only important in its own terms, but would also help to recall the sources of the originality of Vietnamese music.

ETHNOGRAPHIC NOTES

As with its neighbours, Laos and China, Vietnam shelters (on a rather limited territory) one of the largest varieties of ethnic groups to be found anywhere. There are fifty-three minorities besides the ethnic majority of the Kinh (or Viet) which make up the pluricultural Vietnamese nation. These minorities represent 15% of the total population, some 12 million people, and include all the five major linguistic groups to be found throughout Southeast Asia and southern China. This mosaic of cultures reflects the past migrations which constitute today's Vietnamese population.

On the central highlands, the Austro-Asiatic minorities-who are the genuinely autochthonous people of this Asian region-have particularly suffered from the war, and their way of life has changed. Family and social relations have been transformed, the longhouses abandoned in favour of nuclear residences, rites are tending to be folklorised, traditional costumes are no longer worn· In the north live populations more nomadic than in the centre, coming from the south of China (some of them very recently). In such mountainous regions, difficult of access, these minorities have been better protected from external influences: each strongly asserts its identity, in particular through the use of its own language and the daily wearing of costumes specific to each sub-group.

PEOPLES OF CENTRAL VIETNAM

The Jörai

With more than 240,000 individuals, the Jörai are the most numerous of the montagnard peoples of the highlands of Central Vietnam. The majority of them live in the province of Gia Lai, while smaller numbers are found in the provinces of Kon Tum and the north of Dac Lac. Speaking an Austronesian language, they are related to the Cham and other Proto-Malay cultures of the Indonesian archipelago

They grow rice, for the most part by slash and burn cultivation, but also in wet paddies without irrigation systems. They are good herdsmen and skilled hunters who have developed a great variety of fishing and trapping techniques.

Group cohesion depends on a social organisation based on the maternal clan. A clan is primarily defined by its name, transmitted by the mother to her children, and those bearing the same clan name cannot intermarry. After marriage, a husband will settle with his wife in the longhouse to which she belongs. This large building, erected on piles, shelters several households, those of an elder woman, her daughters, and sometimes even her grand-daughters.

A village is made up of parallel longhouses, all oriented on a north-south axis. The grain-stores are built on the periphery. Each village has a community house at its centre, the place for the communal activities of themen, above all the young unmarried men. The cemetery, close to the village, is an extremely important place for the Jörai, who have particularly developed funerary rites. On the very elaborate tombs there are figurative sculptures-human beings and animals-keeping company with the deceased.

The Jörai recognise the political and spiritual authority of three Pôtau, best known under the name of Sadet: The Lords of Fire, Water and Air, whose prestige extends to neighbouring ethnic groups, as far as Cambodia. One of the richest elements of Jörai culture, but the most difficult to understand, is its oral literature-long poetic songs dealing with customs, tales of love, epic and mythic recitations-which Jacques Dournes has collected for over twenty years, and untiringly made known during his life.

The Bahnar

The Bahnar are part of the Austro-Asiatic linguistic family, numbering about 136,000 in the provinces of Kon Tum and western Binh Dinh. They are divided in several regional sub-groups such as the Reungao or the Alacong.

As with all populations of the region, the Bahnar grow rice by shifting cultivation, with vegetables, cotton, and all the edible and useful plants they need. They are skilled herdsmen, and rear buffalo, beef-cattle and poultry for their own diet, but also for commercial exchange.

Everyone lives in houses raised on piles, which are rather smaller nowadays than the traditional longhouses where all couples of an extended family used to gather. Every village has a community house, a remarkable edifice topped by a thatched roof, where men meet to deal with village affairs or to organise various rites. The village community is led by a chief and a council of elders.

The Bahnar have developed a particularly egalitarian society. They follow a cognatic system of kinship and residence. Children share inheritance equally. As equals, girls may select their husbands, and young couples may choose to go and live with one or other of their parents, as opportunity arises.

The Edê (or Rhade)

The Edê (Rhade is a name attributed to them by the French colonial administration) number about 195,000, spread in the provinces of Dac Lac, the south of Gia Lai, and the west of Khanh Hoa and of Phu Yen. As with the Cham and the Jörai, with whom they share a great number of cultural traits, the Edê speak an Austronesian language. The village is dense with both houses and grain-stores in the same orientation, an ensemble which evokes the scales on a tortoise's shell. The longhouses are always built on piles and in the past sometimes extended a hundred metres. Today they are smaller, the most usual being from 30 to 40 metres according to the number of persons they shelter. A house is divided in two parts: one is communal, where visitors are received and where the men gather, and the other consists of compartments, each for a couple, closed off with a bamboo partition, each with its own kitchen.

As with the Jörai, the Edê follow a system of matrilineal descent: mothers transmit their family names to their children, and only women have inheritance rights. A husband settles with his wife in her longhouse, where the extended matrilineal family lives under the authority of the eldest woman, who leads the community and rules on conflicts.

The Edê possess a very old and rich oral tradition, which only a few men in any village will know how to present in its poetic and rhymed forms, but of which everyone knows the subject-matter. The Srê and the Lac Vietnamese researchers have included the Lac and the Srê with the Cil under the name of the Coho, to show that their language in fact resembles that of the Ma and is akin to the Mon-Khmer family. The three groups thus called Coho total over 100,000 people living in the province of Lam Dong, south of Dalat. The most numerous, the Srê, live on the Di Linh plateau. With the Lac, they are the most ancient sedentary rice-cultivators, living in longhouses on piles sheltering several couples, under the authority of an elder. The Lac and the Srê follow a matrilineal and matrilocal system. After marriage, the young man settles with the family of his wife, and their children will take the name of the maternal family. Each nuclear family has its own fields and paddy storehouse.

The Srê and the Lac both believe in a large number of genies, yang, dwelling in nature or certain prestigious objects: the sun, moon and water-courses, or jars of rice-wine. One of these yangs is chosen by each family as its genie-protector. The sacrifice of buffaloes remains an essential social and religious act.

The Ma

Speaking Austro-Asiatic Coho, like the Srê and the Lac, the Ma number about 26,000, in the province of Lam Dong. They live in dispersed villages, in longhouses on piles, with only one lineage in each. Some of these longhouses reached nearly 100 metres of length. The greater part of the Ma practise shifting cultivation, using very rudimentary implements.

Their craft activities are strictly familial and utilitarian. The Ma are very adept weavers, as the finesse of their different baskets continue to demonstrate. The women make remarkable textiles with woven figurative motifs. The family of the Ma is patrilineal, the extended family giving way more and more to the small nuclear family. Inheritance goes to the eldest son.

Most of their rites are connected to the agricultural cycle. As with other groups in the Mon-Khmer language family, the Ma believe in yang genies, dwelling in nature or in everyday life or prestigious artefacts.

Peoples of the north of Vietnam

The Hani

There are about 12,500 Hani spread between the provinces of Lai Chau and Lao Cai. They belong to the Tibeto-Burmese ethno-linguistic group, which in Vietnam is only represented by some small, rather little-known groups: the Lolo, the Phula, the Xapho, the Sila, the Lahu and the Hani. Coming from the Chinese province of Yunnan, as from the 15th century, but above all since the 18th century, they are established in the mountains of the northernmost part of Vietnam, preferring altitudes above 1500 metres.

Most of their houses are built either on the ground, as among the people practising shifting cultivation, or on piles, as among the cultivators of wet rice. Of all groups living in the mountains of northern Vietnam, the Hani are highly experienced in the construction of rice-paddy terraces, dug from the mountainsides, fed with water by canal networks.

The Hani are patrilineal, the father and the eldest son having authority over the whole family. They regularly honour their ancestors on the family altar found in each house. Some offerings are also made to the spirits of nature, such as those of rice or of wild game, to ensure abundant harvests or good hunting.

The Hani sing long poems recounting myths, heroes of the past, tales and legends. One of the marriage songs of the Hani of Lai Chau is known to have 400 verses.

The Yao

The Yao are called Dao (but pronounced as Zao) by the Viets, and known as Man in French texts of the colonial epoch. There are two million Yao in China, half a million in Vietnam, and several thousand in Laos. There are a dozen Yao groups in Vietnam

115

speaking one of two different languages: Mien and Moun. Thus, the Yao Do (the Red Yao), the Yao Tiên (the Yao with sapekes), the Yao Quan Chet (the Yao with tight trousers), or the Yao Lo Gang, speak the Mien language, while the Yao Lan Tien (the indigo-blue Yao) or the Yao Quan Trang (the Yao with white trousers) speak the Moun language.

The Yao arrived in Vietnam as from the 18th century and settled at many different altitudes, from the plains up to the mountain heights, but generally lower down than the Hmong. According to their zone of habitation, their house styles differ. The most frequent is a house built on the ground, but one also finds among the Yao living in the valleys, in the proximity of the Tay or the Nung, some large houses on piles of wood or of bamboo. A third style of house also encountered is constructed on mountainsides, half on piles and half on the ground. The forms of agriculture practiced, from irrigated rice-paddies to slash and burn cultivation, is also diverse. The social unit is the patrilineal family.

Monogamy and patrilocality are de rigeur.

The Yao have been strongly influenced by Chinese culture, adopting writing and Taoist rites. Shamanic trance is widely practiced as a mode of direct action towards the invisible.

The Hmong

The popular name for the Hmong is the Meo. There are about ten million Hmong today, of whom nine million are in China, nearly 600,000 in Vietnam, with the remainder spread between Laos, Thailand and Burma (Myanmar). The Hmong arrived in Vietnam rather late, the greatest wave of migration coming in 1868 after the crushing of the Tai Ping in China. They settled near the Chinese and

Laotian frontiers, in the Vietnamese provinces of Thanh Hoa and Nge An.

We find several groups of Hmong in Vietnam: The White Hmong, the Flowered Hmong, the Green Hmong, the Black Hmong and the Hmong "with striped sleeves". These groups speak different dialects of the same language and can only be differentiated through details of their dress. Women's dress, in very varied styles, everywhere includes an ample skirt, generally wrapped with hemp, decorated with batik, embroidered and appliquéd. The Hmong rarely settle below 1000 metres, practising shifting cultivation on steeply sloped fields. After one or two rotations of the crop cycles, when the soil is near exhaustion, the cultivated territory is abandoned and the village community disperses. When the relief permits, the Hmong settle today around irrigated terrace rice-paddies. Kinship and residence are patrilineal, the head of the family controlling the finances of the household.

The Nung

The Nung number today more than 700,000, settled in the same regions as the Tay (the former Tho), living along the Chinese frontier in the provinces of Lang Son, Cao Bang, Ha Giang and Lao Cai, and also as far as Bac Thai and Tuyen Quang. They are divided into sub-groups, named after their places of origin in China (Nung Inh, Nung An, Nung Phan Sinh, Nung Loi·). Belonging to the Thai-Kadai linguistic group, the Nung language is very close to that of the Tay, both of them having adopted a form of writing based on Chinese ideograms.

The Nung left Guangxi in south China as from the 12th and 13th centuries, reaching the territories of the Tay, who conceded them mediocre, barely fertile land. This they improved with considerable effort, and now cultivate irrigated rice-paddies with success in the valley bottoms, as well as terraced paddies on the mountainsides. Other products are grown with slash and burn cultivation above the paddies. In the villages, the basic unit is the patriarchal family, a woman once married becoming totally dependent on her husband and parents-in-law.

The Nung are Buddhists and Confucianists. Shamans continue to play an important rôle in village society, and are the last ones who can read the traditional ideograms.

The Pa-y (or Pa Di)

Classified as part of Tay ethnic group by the Vietnamese authorities, the Pa-y (which is Pa Di in Vietnamese, pronounced "Pazi") live in only a few villages in the north of the province of Lao Cai.

The women's costume consists of a long tunic decorated with a large band of silver buttons across the breast, and a long skirt covered by an apron.

Their headdress is very characteristic, a kind of rigid helmet of indigo cotton, which is decorated with a silver jewel at the rear, with a ribbon of silver nails over the forehead.

The Pa-y remain poor, and as agriculturalists they grow maize and mountain rice for the most part by shifting cultivation. They live in cob-wall houses, with floors of beaten earth. Living in close relations with their neighbours the Nung, the Pa-y have adopted a number of their traditions, in particular the rites attached to birth and death.

The Lü

There are only about 3,700 Lü, spread among several villages of the province of Lai Chau, in the districts of Phong Tho and Sin Ho. They speak a Thai language, and are much more numerous in the north of Laos, but mainly in the Sip Song Panna of the south of Yunnan.

Their villages group together over fifty houses which, as with other Thai, are built on piles, well-aerated and spacious. Basic nourishment is of sticky rice cultivated in irrigated paddies. Other plants may be grown by slash and burn cultivation. Women's costume is particularly elaborate, with its small short vest, whose waisted form is emphasised by decorations of pieces of silver. The upper part of the skirt is brocaded with traditional motifs, a weaving technique in which the Lü women are among the best. A long turban is enrolled around a chignon, worn always on the left.

The Lü family is patrilineal. As among other Thai groups, a young husband comes to live with his wife's family for two or three years, before settling in his own house. Young people are relatively free to choose their marriage partners, although the agreement of the parents is always necessary, together with that of the astrologer, who plays an important rôle in social and religious life.

The Lü are the only Thai minority to have adopted Hinayana Buddhism which is, as in Laos and Thailand, strongly impregnated with animistic beliefs.

The Thai

From the south of China, their original habitat, the Thai have spread over a vast territory, extending from the east of India to Vietnam, passing through Burma (Myanmar), Thailand and Laos. The beginning of their migrations is very ancient, seeming to have started about 2000 years ago.

Some of them created states, as in Laos and Thailand; others have remained minorities, among whom the Thai of Vietnam, numbering over a million today, spread in the provinces of Lai Chau, Son La, Hoa Binh and Nghe An, in the northwest of the country.

Two principal sub-groups, the White Thai and the Black Thai, may be differentiated by the colour of the women's vests. The short, close-fitting vests are today in different colours, but have kept to their traditional buttoning of chased silver butterflies. All women wear a long black skirt fastened around the hips.

Constructed of wood and bamboo and perched upon high piles, the houses of both the White and Black Thai are surprisingly spacious. The most beautiful of them are often over ten metres long and shelter, around a central stove, a family of a dozen persons (usually three generations). The houses of the Black Thai have magnificent, rounded thatched roofs, said to be in the form of "the carapace of a tortoise".

We find a social organisation based on a feudal system among all the Thai, which remained rigorous among the Thai in the west of Vietnam up until the beginning of the 20th century. The society, strongly hierarchised, included the aristocratic class of lords and their kin, the one of the highest-placed notables; the remainder of the society was constituted of freemen-peasants and of servants, emancipated former slaves coming most often from neighbouring minorities, in particular the Khmu.

Feudal social organisation has now disappeared, but traditional beliefs in spirits, phi, and the strongly hierarchised genies of the soil, impregnate the religious life of all Thai. With a script adapted from the Sanskrit alphabet, as in Laos and Thailand, their cultural and spiritual heritage has great richness.

The Khmu

With 43,000 individuals in the provinces on the frontier with Laos, from Nghe An to Lai Chau, the Khmu constitute the most important Mon-Khmer linguistic group in the north of Vietnam. Coming from Laos (where they are still very numerous), their immigration into Vietnam seems to go back to the 17th or 18th centuries. Settled in Thai principalities, the Khmu constituted, until the beginning of the 20th century, a class of peasants enslaved to local lords. Strongly influenced by the Thai, the Khmu have adopted a number of their cultural traits, such as the Thai's feminine costume, which more and more replaces their own traditional garments.

Generally settled above the Thai, the Khmu practise slash and burn cultivation on often steeply sloping fields which quickly lose fertility.

Hunting and food gathering are therefore a far from negligible addition to the diet. The Khmu, for the most part, still lead a nomadic life, and are rather poor.

The family name of a Khmu most often designates a plant, an animal, or an object considered as the ancestor of the lineage, which is recalled in the origin myth that each lineage possesses. The Khmu thus retain an important heritage of myths, cosmological accounts and popular tales, marking an ethnic identity that is still strong today.

The Muong

The Muong number more than 900,000, mostly settled in the province of Hoa Binh and in part of Thanh Hoa. Originally, the Viet and the Muong formed a single, unique population, and did not separate until about 2000-1700 years ago. The Muong remained in the valleys and foothills of the mountainous zones, and did not fall under the influence of Chinese culture as did the Viet, but to that of the Thai, their most immediate neighbours.

As with the Thai, the traditional social system of the Muong was organized in chiefdoms, some of which could expand to a hundred villages. Each of these chiefdoms was ruled by a single lordly family, sharing power under the authority of the eldest, the head of the family. Thai Family and administration form the one and only structure.

A Muong family lives in a large house built on piles, with large openings. The women wear a long black skirt of which the belt, woven in coloured motifs, is drawn high upon the breast. They cultivate irrigated rice-paddies in descending terraces on hillsides. To irrigate, large bucket-waterwheels drawing water from the rivers are in current use. Other cereals and vegetables are also grown in shifting cultivations above the paddies. Fish have an important rôle in the diet, and the means and techniques of fishing are very varied, and known to everyone.

Up until today, during funerary rites, séances by medium and sacrifices to the spirits, historical, legendary and cosmological accounts of the Muong are sung or chanted.

NOTES ON THE MUSIC

Musical Instruments

Only a few instruments will be described below. Other instruments were used in times past, such as bronze drums and lithophones. Some instruments are still played today: tubes of struck or pounded bamboo, lutes with two or three strings (called tinh tâu among the Thai), the tube-zither with two strings (the bro' of the Jörai), etc. Apart from those made of metal, instruments are ordinarily made by their players and should be destroyed or buried with them when they die.

IDIOPHONES

Gongs

To designate gongs, one and the same term cing is employed by several Montagnard populations from two linguistic families of the highlands of the centre (Jörai, Edê, Bahnar, Köho, Sedang, Mnong Gar). The gongs are made from an alloy of copper and other metals. Either imported or purchased, the most recent have been made in Vietnam, the older ones which came from Laos or Cambodia being now very valuable (as much as 30 buffaloes for the largest gong). Tales and epic songs often mention gongs, which have always been exchange goods among the Montagnards of the highlands of central Vietnam.

There are two sorts of gongs: the flat gong struck on the interior with a mallet of green wood or by the bare hand, and the bossed gong struck with a cloth-covered mallet.

Among the Jörai, "every gong has its edge pierced by two holes where a cord is passed through for portability, as a shoulder-strap (light gongs]), or for suspended carriage from a beam over two men's shoulders (heavier gongs), or for hanging permanently in the house (very heavy gongs). Except in special cases, gong-players stand in line or March in file. The place for each gong in the series is ordained by a rule as inviolable as the placing of notes on a musical staff; if a man changes place to take another gong that he knows better, it is he who changes place and not the gong. Each instrumentalist sounds just one note, at the time required by the melody. The air is often sung through before it is performed [this being also the case among the Lac. The right hand of the player

123

strikes the gong, and the left (when it is a light gong) is placed, or not, on the other side to deaden vibrations and resonance" (Dournes 1965, p. 218).

Several gongs of different sizes are habitually grouped in instrumental ensembles, sometimes including a drum. Thus, it is among the montagnards of north Vietnam (Thai, Tay, Muong, Kho Mu) that two bossed gongs and a large drum beat the rhythms of the dances. In the central Vietnam, small ensembles of three bossed gongs with a large drum are the most widespread, but we also find some ensembles comprising a bigger number of instruments: among the Jörai, Bahnar, Sedang, Ro Ngao, Edê, Ma, Koho, Lac, Horê. Among the Ma, women can play gongs as well as men.

Cymbals

Among the Jörai, the körac-körang "are cymbals of copper [about 15 cm in diameter], bossed and hammered, that one rubs one against the other, with alternating rotational movement. These instruments, bought elsewhere (Cambodia or Laos) at the same time as the gongs, serve only for accompaniment, when desired, to the cinq arap gong-playing " (Dournes 1965, p.214).

Xylophones

Among the Jörai, the trüng xylophone consists of eleven bamboo tubes of 94 to 36 cm in length, bevelled at one end and attached by a cord, so that alternate tubes have their bevels on one side, and the others on the opposite. One end of the cord will be tied to a house-post or to a tree-trunk, and the other end tied around the ankle of the player, so as to suspend the instrument like a hammock. The tubes are struck with two wooden mallets, or with four if it is a duet. Each tube has its name according to its pitch, being ania (94 cm), ci (80 cm), krah (74 cm), kêu (72 cm), hloai (64 cm), ania hloi or böt (54 cm, octave of ci (53 cm), octave of krah (52 cm), octave of kêu (42 cm), octave of hloai (37 cm) and ania ddat, double octave of the longest tube (36 cm).

Neighbouring peoples know the same type of instrument under different names: dding dol (Köho), kleng klong, deng or to glong gloi (Bahnar), kleng klang (Sedang). When two musicians play in duet, one plays the principal melody and the other an accompanying part.

The xylophone is played for simple pleasure in the village or at the rice-paddy. It is also played to chase away animals which might damage the harvest. Today it also accompanies songs and dances, or is played with other instruments such as the leaves kèn la, the one-string fiddle köni, or various flutes.

Bamboo buzzing-forks

The dao of the Khmu is made from a tube of bamboo between 100 and 120 cms in length. One of the ends is shaped into two facing tongues 30 cm in length, at the base of which, and on each side, a slit of about 20 cm is kept slightly apart by a string (or wire) crossing the diameter of the tube. When one of the tongues is struck against the palm or the forearm, the instrument starts vibrating and the two slits cause a buzzing sound.

The other end is left open, some 15 or 20 cms past a pierced node of the bamboo. Two small holes are placed so that they can be closed or opened by a thumb and one of the fingers, to modify the timbre.

Several of these instruments, of different sizes, may be struck simultaneously while accompanying a song. Playing the dao is the preserve of Khmu women of the regions of Tây Bac and the mountains in the west of the province of Nghê An. The Black Thai of Son La have learned to play it and call it hüm may.

Jews-harps

The montagnards of Vietnam have two main types of jews-harp whose forms differ according to the material used, whether bamboo or brass.

The bamboo jews-harp-called gôc (Ma, Lac), röding (Jörai), tuong (Köho), then (Bahnar), hûn toong (Thai), cô ech (Edê)-is made from a sliver of bamboo into which a tongue is cut. The musician holds the instrument between his lips with the left hand and plucks the extremity of the tongue with the right thumb. By modifying the volume of the mouth's cavity, the player selects overtones to make a melody. A small ball of wax fixed to the middle of the vibrating tongue can be adjusted in position to change the pitch of the fundamental.

The djam jews-harp of the Hmong is made from a piece of hammered brass, into which a slim tongue is cut. The instrument is held in front of the mouth, and its tongue is set in vibration by plucking with the thumb. This instrument is much prized among the Hmong youth, and used for courtship.

Often a girl will give one to a boy in the hope that he will come after nightfall to her bedroom and murmur some amorous messages.

MEMBRANOPHONES

Drums

Drums with double skins (one at each end) have a body made from hollowed wood. The skins are of buffalo or oxen, held in place with small wooden pegs.

"The Jörai have two kinds of drum: the big one (a metre or more in diameter) is placed horizontally in the house, upon two wooden supports, as if cradled, and the small portable drum used for processional rites (with shoulder-straps, or carried on a beam by two porters). There are two ways to play the drum: tông when it is struck with a piece of green wood (stripped of its bark); pah when it is struck with the open hand. The drum, which marks the metre, is a primary element of Jörai music, being much more rhythmic than melodic. The first of the drummers has the rôle of a conductor of the other instrumentalists, by giving the cues to start and to stop, by deciding on the rhythm and the loudness" (Dournes 1965, p. 222).

Among the Montagnards of central Vietnam the generic term for the drum is högor (Jörai), or högör (Bahnar), sönggör (Köho). The big drum-högor m'nang or högor prong (Jörai), ho gor tak or p'nung (Bahnar)-is used by the Jörai to send messages or to play with the gongs in the course of rites for the spirits or for tutelary genies in the house of the head of the clan. It is often struck by the village chief during various rites. The presence of drums of medium size-po nuong yun (Bahnar) and ho gor cing arap (Jörai)-is indispensible for gong ensembles. Because of this, the drum is held in high regard among the Muong, Bahnar, Jörai and E-dê. The northern minorities (Hmong, Tay, Nung, Thai, Muong, Dao) use a large number of differently sized drums, each with its own name.

CHORDOPHONES

Tube-zithers

The gông tube-zither of the Jörai is made from a single internode of bamboo, the node walls left intact at each end, of 70 to 90 cms in length and from 5 to 8 cms in diameter, furnished with a calabash resonator.

127

Thirteen metal strings, usually recycled bicycle brake-cables, are stretched in a semi-circle across the bamboo tube, lifted by ring-like bridges and tightened by pegs.

"One holds the instrument in front, the pegs upwards. The left hand has six strings; the right has seven-three are for the melody and three for accompaniment, plus the high-pitched thirteenth. The strings are named by their notes: three böt, one ding and two kêu on the left; on the right, three krah, one ci, two ania and a small high-pitched ania. The notes have the same names as on the copper gongs and one can play the same melodies on them. The gông is in favour with young men who have a good ear; they play it for pleasure in the evenings, by themselves or at a friend's place; itattracts girls just as the dding-dek [bundle-panpipes] attracts boys" (Dournes 1965, p. 227).

The tube-zither also exists with idioglottal strings, of skin prised up from the body of the bamboo tube. It was found among the Bahnar, Jörai, Sedang, Rongao, Gie Triêng, Lac and the Ma in the two provinces of Kontumand Gia Lai.

The one-string fiddle köni and the zither ddong.

Among the Jörai, "one finds that one is here in the presence of an original and complex ensemble, that I have never found elsewhere among the Proto-Indochinese, while other instruments here and there have their equivalents.

"The ddong is very simple: it is a two-string zither with a calabash resonator, like a bro' [not presented on these CDs] with neither frets nor sound-holes, being lighter and shorter (50 rather than 80 or 90 cms). It is plucked, like other zithers. Its particularity is that it is not an instrument in itself, but is only part of an ensemble; it is only played with the köni, in the same hand, holding a stick serving as a bow.

"Köni. Its essential element is a vibrating string, whose vibrations are produced by two sources: a bow moving back and forth on the string; a piece of thread fastened to the bowed string, of which the far end is held in the mouth of the instrumentalist; vocal modulations, on the one hand, and stopping the string above the frets; on the other, modify the effect of the vibrations of the single [bowed] string.

"The body of the instrument is a section of bamboo about 50 cm long, terminated at one end with a piece of wood shaped as a 'coiled fern-tip' and decorated with a pompom. The metal string is fixed at its foot, tightened by a peg and tunable with a bridge; it passes over four frets of wax. The bow is a single stick of bamboo, rubbed with the wax of bees living in tree-hollows. At the position of the peg, a string of china-grass, its length precisely that of the bamboo tube, is fastened to the metal string and fixed at its free end to a rounded plastic tongue which is placed in the instrumentalist's mouth, behind the incisors.

"The instrumentalist is seated; he rubs the bow with wax, turns the peg to obtain the tuning desired; he places the köni almost vertically and holds it with the left hand, between the thumb (towards him) and the four fingers, placed on the frets (away from him), the foot of the instrument held between two toes. He puts the [plastic] tongue behind his teeth, tilting his head back enough to stretch the thread. His right hand holds the bow, a simple stick, like a spoon, making it pass back and forth on the [metal] string, while his left-hand fingers touch its frets, and he hums between clenched teeth, only his lips moving. All song melodies may thus be played, especially (success assured) in imitation of funeral laments. The köni is easy enough to make, but its interpreters are rare; it is played in the house or in the fields, by a man, for musical pleasure. Its sound is strange, distant, plaintive, nuanced, elusive and disquieting.

129

"The köni is an instrument complete in itself, usually played solo. However, as often happens, musicians know how to play the köni simultaneously with the ddong, invented to accompany it. The bow is therefore held in the right hand, placed against the ddong, between its foot and calabash; thumb and index-finger keep the bow and the ddong together, middle and ring fingers plucking its two strings, and the combination sets off, the bow continuing to cross the [metal] string. One artist thus plays a zither and a fiddle at once, while also transmitting his song by means of a piece of thread connected to the bowed string and its resonating tube" (Dournes 1965, p. 227-230).

Two-string fiddles

The two-string fiddle-cò ke for the Muong and io for the Black Thai- is made of a slender tube of bamboo inserted in a resonator made of a larger tube of bamboo, the latter open on one side and covered on the other by a piece of frog- or snake-skin. The two strings, tuned at the fourth or the fifth, are made of banana fibre or of horse-hair. The bow-string is of horse-hair, and is not resined.

AEROPHONES

Flutes

The ding klia is a vertical bamboo flute, 50 to 60 cm long, with four holes in the case of the Lac. It is played for diversion, in front of the house or in the fields. This kind of flute is found more or less everywhere in

Vietnam, under different names: rleet (Mnong), klia (Bahnar), pi thiu (Thai), ôông ôi (Muong), tiêu (Kinh or Viêt). It is an instrument for men only. Pribislav Pitoëff observes that the kalien duct flute of the Black Hmong is ade of a reed-tube of 60 cm pierced with four playing-holes. One end is chamfered about 3 cm, and the opening for expiration for the air is cut 1cm farther. Inside the beak, the tube's orifice is stuffed with a piece of screwed-up cloth: when more or less inserted, this plug alters the volume of air in oscillation, thus permitting the tuning of the instrument.

Bundle-panpipes

The dding dek of the Jörai "are panpipes of thirteen unequal bamboo tubes, from 35 to 125 cm in length, bevelled at one end and bound together. Each tube bears the name of its pitch: böt or but-bung, ci, ding, ania, kêu, krah and six tubes of the upper octave, plus a high-pitched thirteenth tube. The breath is directed from some distance towards the tubes, which the left hand holds from underneath, while the right thumb acts as a valve for the longest (deepest) tube, pe' böt. The dding dek is tuned by trimming the bevels. Though it is rather tiring to play these panpipes, it is the preferred instrument of Jörai girls, making use of it to attract boys. All tunes sung by these young girls can also be played on the panpipes; it is generally for courtship, where feminine imagination is inexhaustible. The dding dek is played once evening falls, on the steps of the house, in a seated position, facilitating the breathing required" (Dournes 1965, p.231).

Among the Bahnar, the same kind of instrument is called the dding jöng. Besides being present among these two groups of Vietnam Montagnard peoples, bundle-panpipes are known particularly in Melanesia, where they extend from New Guinea in the west to Vanuatu in the east, passing by the Solomon Islands. The Jörai piece presented here is the first to be published from South-East Asia.

Ensemble of whistles

The dding töjuh ("tube-seven" in Jörai) is an ensemble of seven to nine bamboo whistles, unequal in size (10 to 20 cm long, 1.6 to 2.3 cm in diameter), in use among the Jörai and the Edê (or Rhade).

131

Among the Lac, the ensemble consists of only five whistles. Each tube is closed at the bottom end by a node, the players each blowing a whistle as if blowing into a keyhole. The playing of the whistles is reminiscent of the music of the gongs.

The leaf

The use of leaves as musical instruments is widespread among the Hmong and the Dao of Northern Vietnam, and among several populations of the province of Gia Lai in the central highlands. The Hmong employ banana leaves, or any other kind of leaf provided it is flexible, smooth, and has an oval shape.

The player, by blowing on the leaf, pressed to his upper lip or between his lips, makes it vibrate. This instrument is intended to attract young girls during courtship.

Clarinets

The dding bbot of the Jörai is a five-holed bamboo clarinet. The mouthpiece has a beating reed, and the far end is bevelled. Known among the Jörai and the Edê, this instrument is played by both men and women for diversion. The instrument called pilang bhang of the Khmu is probably a clarinet of this type.

Free-reed instruments

Pribislav Piroëff has observed an instrument with a free reed called pi among the Lü, consisting of a tube of 40 to 50 cm, with seven playing-holes (six on the front and one at the back). Near the mouthpiece, closed and rounded, a rectangular opening is made on which a thin brass plate is fixed, into which a free reed is cut. The instrumentalist places all of this in his mouth, obliquely. Players use circular breathing, drawing air through their nostrils and not interrupting the air-flow after expiration through the mouth. Among the Lü, the pi accompanies different kinds of songs. The pipap of the Black Thai is a free-reed aerophone similar to the pi of the Lü. Instruments of the same type are called buot tak ta among the Edê, ponung bôc among the Lac, and töliö among the Bahnar.

The dding klut of the Jörai is a free-reed instrument made from a tube pierced with three holes for fingering, and an aperture having an added reed. A whole calabash, whose neck serves as embouchure, is fixed over the window with wax.

The töki of the Jörai "is a transverse horn, also known as as tödiap or dding-röwang, 'tube gone-to-war'. This is a buffalo or a wild-cattle horn, or an elephant's tusk (a more ancient version and, of course, more appreciated). The horn is opened at each extremity and in the middle of the concave curvature; at this latter point it has a reed, covered by a parallelepiped embouchure of wood, fixed in place with wax. The mouth blows, the right thumb operates as a valve, and the flat left-hand claps and closes or opens the larger opening. It is a very ancient instrument, made for war, exclusively. Formerly the tödiap was carved into an elephant's tusk; in default of ivory it was made from horn, and thus was it named töki, or horn. On leaving for war, it was worn as a necklace; on returning from war, if victorious and if prisoners were being brought, it was played before re-entering the village; on hearing the sound of the elephant tusk, the men remaining in the village played the warrior-rhythm juar on the drums. Today, as with sabre and shield, it is just an object for parade, but still used (held only by the hands) during rites of confirmation of manhood of the youths." (Dournes 1965, p. 232).

The instrument has the same name, tödiap, among the Bahnar, while it is called koyol among the Lac.

Mouth-organs

The mouth-organ is widespread among the Montagnards of Vietnam, except among the Jörai of Chöreo, where it is rare. It is generally made of six tubes of different length, fixed in two series into a calabash serving as air-reservoir, hence the name given to it by the Jörai: the dding nam, or "six tubes". Each tube has a free bamboo reed at its base, and has a hole on the side which must be blocked by a finger to obtain a sound.

Small-sized instruments are called by the name rökel among the Srê and the Lac; larger instruments are called kombuot among the Lac and komboat among the Ma. The mouth-organ is used to play the melodies of songs, old or modern.

Changes

The "evolution" of music since the 1960s lets us see transformations in the usage of musical instruments. The young generation prefers the guitar to the 13-string zither, the gông, plastic pipes to the dding clarinet, the western harmonica to the traditional mouth-organ, the dding nam or the komboat.

The Vietnamese, of the Viet or Kinh majority, have modernised some of the Montagnards' instruments, such as the flute of the Hmong (sao mèo), used especially by the musician Luong Kim Vinh. The cooangtac, a running-water carillon, has had several bamboo tubes of different sizes added to it. The mouth-organ of the Thai, the khèn bè, is today adapted to play major and minor chords. The play upon bamboo tubes-klong put (Sedang), dding but (Jörai) or pah pung (Bahnar), which one makes resonate by clapping the two hands in front of the opening-went from a dozen tubes in 1965 to twenty-one in 1968. The Vietnamese have adopted and transformed the one-string fiddle, the köni. The trüng xylophone (called dàn trüng in Vietnamese) has been modified by the musician Nay Pha of the Song and Dance Ensemble of the Highlands, of the

Ministry of Culture (which has become known as the Troupe Artistique Dam Sam). Since 1960, Nay Pha has considerably enlarged the number of tubes (up to forty-five tubes, in three tiered ranks), following the chromatic scale, and has played it at numerous international festivals.

VOCAL EXPRESSIONS

Colours and timbres, range and register, inflexions of the voice, intonations between the spoken and the sung, procedures of ornamentation of the melodies and/or of sound-emission· One could ask to what degree such vocal expressions are not the characteristics of certain Montagnard peoples or sub-groups, or whether of genres (such as the epic songs) beyond ethnic and linguistic boundaries, or yet again of individual singers, male or female. In our present state of knowledge, we can't answer these questions.

The following paragraphs ae simply meant to attract attention to the variety of vocal expressions.

Ornamentation

The work-song of the Yao Lan Tien and the epic song of the Bahnar contain passages of long-held notes characterised by tremulation (oscillation between two notes) of a melodic range from about a minor second for the first, and from a major second to a minor third for the second; this tremulation is perceived, by its speed-seven oscillations per second-as a tremolo (rapid repetition on the one and same note). In the case of the first song, such passages are followed by ornaments made by a slower and wider oscillation, from a minor to a major third. Some similar ornaments, oscillating up to a fifth, are also found in a song of the Nung Loi, characterised as well by an ornament of sound-production, which is strongly "hatched".

Repeated impulses (around 3 per second) on the commencements (attacks) of vowels periodically appear in the epic songs of the Ma, where the voice may be said to be "guttural". Some songs make frequent use of melisma (melodic ornaments on one syllable): for example, the courtship song of the Khmu], the monodic, alternating song of the Lac, and the polyphonic, alternating song of the Nung Loi in which the melismas are primarily by the principal voice.

Vocal inflexions and changes of register

The singers make free use of glissando, ascending and descending. These vocal inflexions appear at different places in the melodic lines of a song of the Red Yao, but systematically, at the ends of musical phrases, they are descending. Some descending glissandos are to be heard in the middle of melodic phrases, from the secondary voice in a courtship song of the Nung An, and at the end of the musical phrases, alternating with a long-held note, in a work-song of the Yao Lan Tien. By contrast, an ascending glissando, again in alternance with a long-held note, marks the end of some musical phrases in another work-song of these same Yao Lan Tien.

A song of the Nung Loi consists of two musical phrases in which the first ends with a long-held unison note for the men, and a descending glissando for the women; contrary to this, at the end of the second phrase, there is an ascending glissando in head-voice, which also signals the alternance of men/women respectively with women/men. Some phrase-endings in head-voice are also to be heard in a song of the Nung Giang, in alternance with descending glissandos, but what is specific here is a change of register on the same pitch, among both men and women; we will return to this song in the section on vocal polyphony. Some changes of register-chest voice/head-voice-are not only made at the endings but also in the middle of musical segments, e.g. in the voice of a Hani woman] or in Nung Giang and Pa-y songs.

Between the spoken and the sung

Some songs of different peoples of the central highlands-but not those of Northern Vietnam-have passages in recto tono, in which several words are pronounced one after the other on the same pitch. In the epic song of the Jörai each of the four principal degrees, succeeding one another in a descending melodic contour, is sounded in turn as recto tono. Some passages in recto tono are also to be heard in a song of the Ma, in an alternating song of the Bahnar, and in an epic song of the same Bahnar which is also singular for sections in spoken-sung, i.e. by a recitation without fixed pitches.

Finally, let us mention the song of the Jörai köni fiddle-player: this voice is characterised by large ascending and descending glissandos (together with the sounds of the fiddle), and above all by a very particular articulation, due to the fact that the singer-musician pronounces the words while holding behind the incisors a small plastic disc tied by a thread to the string of the fiddle. The unique colour of this voice is different from what one knows of voices sung or spoken, from all intermediary forms found either in Vietnam or elsewhere in the world.

POLYPHONY

The Montagnards of Vietnam use different kinds of polyphony: the drone (long-held notes, on one pitch, underneath one or several melodic lines); polyphony by ostinato (short repeated melodico-rhythmic formulæ upon which are superimposed one or several other voices); diaphony (two or more voices separated by certain intervals, progressing in a homorhythmic manner, i.e. in the same rhythm); counterpoint (superimposition of voices which are melodically and rhythmically differentiated). At the edge of polyphony and monody, one should add heterophony (enlargment of a single melodic line by a second performer) and the use of echo

137

(brief temporal delays). While the forms of vocal heterophony and instrumental ostinato-polyphony (above all on the mouth-organ and in gong-playing) of the highlands of the centre were relatively well-known, the vocal polyphonies of the Montagnards of the extreme north of Vietnam have remained for a long time unknown in the West.

Instrumental polyphonies

The instrumental polyphonies of the Montagnards may be the result of simultaneous playing on two instruments with melodic possibilities (such as fiddle and zither), or may be from several instruments playing together, each with its own single note (as with ensembles of gongs or whistles), or may also be the simultaneous sounding of two or three notes on a soloist's instrument when its construction permits (zither, mouth-organ, bundle-panpipes).

At the edge of polyphony, the playing of the io fiddle and the pipap free-reed instrument among the Black Thai, is heterophonic. The melody, built on an anhemitonic pentatonic scale (five notes without a semitone), ranges over an octave, with two principal long-held notes: the tonic C (at the beginning at the upper octave), and the fifth G. The piece is also characterised by downward glissandos from E to the lower tonic.

At certain points of the piece, the Jörai flautist directs the breath simultaneously into two neighbouring tubes of the bundle-panpipes, thus obtaining intervals of the fifth and the sixth played in a homorhythmic manner. By applying the regular tapping of a finger to the lower opening of the tube for E, she sounds once in each of the two musical phrases a superimposition of three notes, B-E-G. But the unison is more frequent and, as is the general rule in the polyphony of the Montagnards, it characterises the ends of musical phrases and of the piece. The hemitonic pentatonic scale (of five

138

notes with two semitones) is characteristic of Jörai music. It is well-known among Vietnam musicians today, who use it in some of their new compositions to lend local colour evoking the central highlands in general (without specific reference to the Jörai).

The rule of the final unison for a polyphonic piece is broken by the ensemble of five whistles of the Lac where the piece ends on the chord C#-E-G# with the G# a little sharp). The whole of the piece is built on an alternation of this chord with an interval of a minor sixth, A#-F#. The uniformity of this alternation is broken by rhythmical playing.

Most of the other instrumental musical pieces presented on these two discs are characterised by ostinato-polyphony, which is above all widespread among the Montagnards of central Vietnam. This consists of the repeated playing of a short formula, in the bass, while the melodic formula, longer, is simultaneously played higher.

Thus, in a piece for an ensemble of gongs of the Ma the ostinato in the bass, made of three notes, is played four times under the duration of the melodic formula, which itself is made of three notes. The beginning of the melodic formula varies slightly, the first note being interchangeable between A or F. In a piece for mouth-organ, again of the Ma, constructed on the same principle, the variations of the melodic formula are more numerous: one can count 15 variants out of a total of 39 passages of the melodic formula. A piece for ensemble of gongs among the Lac comprises two melodic formulæ of a duration equal to four passages of the ostinato formula; the second melodic formula can be shortened by half.

To indicate the next piece to play to the members of the gong ensemble, one of the players (generally the leader) sings sometimes the melodic formula or formulæ by itself or in alternance with the bass ostinato formula.

In the playing of a gong ensemble among the Edê and in a Jörai xylophone piece, the bass ostinato is made from two notes, while the melody is on three notes. In the piece for mouth-organ of the Lac, the two notes of the ostinato are combined with four melodic notes.

The bass ostinato may be replaced by a single sound, an intermittent drone or bourdon. This is the case for the mouth-organ of the Lac where the melody is built on five notes. In the second Jörai xylophone piece, the melody, with a wider range (an octave plus a fourth), descends lower than the intermittent drone. In the Jörai zither piece, the intermittent drone consists of two notes played simultaneously at the interval of a fifth.

The principle of polyphony by ostinato is also present in the piece for the sac bùa orchestra of the Muong, composed of two oông khao transverse flutes, a co ke two-string fiddle, four bua bossed gongs, and a plôông drum. The three high gongs vary an ostinato formula; a stroke on the lowest gong intervenes regularly on each fourth beat of the cycle (ie, every eighth pulsation). The two flutes and the fiddle play melodic phrases at the unison, with slight variations, exceeding in length the cycle of the gongs. The drum often intervenes with three unequally spaced strokes, of which the first sometimes coincides with the stroke of the bass gong.

The Jörai musician who plays the one-string fiddle accompanies himself on the gông zither of which he plucks either the two strings (G-C) simultaneously or only the string for the C, making thus a drone on the tonic and the lower fourth. The fiddle rarely plays the same C, but rather on the notes E, F and G. As for the voice transmitted the fiddle's string by a piece of thread, it rises and covers a ninth. In certain passages there is a superimposition of three components-fiddle, zither, voice-in others, the musician does not sing. As we have already pointed out, the hemitonic pentatonic scale (of five notes with two semitones) is characteristic of Jörai music.

Songs with instrumental accompaniment

The accompaniment on the gông zither of a Jörai man is characterised by ostinato formulæ.

The flute which accompanies the alternating song of the Black Hmong plays essentially two notes a fourth apart, linked by passing notes; the singers commence and finish the musical phrases at the unison, respectively at the lower octave of the flute, distancing from it by weaving above and below.

The flute is playing here the rôle of the second voice of the songs for two voices, which often is notable for long-held notes. In the songs accompanied by free-reed instruments of the Lü, some purely instrumental passages alternate with sung passages. The two instruments of different sizes play at the octave, with the exception of a note added by the smaller instrument. In accompanied passages, instrumental and vocal melodies partially diverge, while keeping the same rhythm, which seems to be determined by the syllabic division of the text. The performers come together at the unison or at the octave at the ends of phrases.

Vocal polyphony

The Montagnards of central Vietnam rarely sing together, but at the same time, if it happens as in the case of the song of three Srê women, it is at the unison and not in polyphony. In their alternating songs, a solo singer (male or female) alternates with a second performer. In the north, to the contrary, in particular among the sub-groups of the Nung (Nung Loi,

Nung An, Nung Phan Sinh, Nung Giang), the alternating songs, known as sli, are performed by two women in alternation with two men. Each Nung group possesses a characteristic sli air; si oi (Nung

Loi), hà lêu (Nung An) soong lan, nhi hào (Nung Phan Sing), ta sli (Nung Giang). Their two-voice polyphony emphasises the harmonic interval of the second, at the same time as using minor and major thirds, the fourth and the fifth. Generally, at the ends of musical phrases, the two voices come back to the unison.

The alternating song of the Nung An is intoned by two men. The first voice sings four notes in the range of a fifth (G#, B, C#, D#) while the second voice is limited to two notes (G#, B) enters on the tonic G#-and makes the lower fourth in relation to the C#-sung at that moment by the first voice, then the fifth in relation to the D#. The two voices periodically return to the unison. The interval of a major second is often produced when the first voice sings on the third degree (do) and the second voice on the second degree (ti). The women sing a minor third higher than the men according to the same procedure. Besides the interval of the second, the Nung An, in their songs in two voices, favour the interval of the fifth. The behavior of the second voice, limiting itself to two degrees evokes an intermittent drone on two pitches; the impression of a drone is reinforced by the fact that the tonic (so+ for the men and ti for the women) is sounded on the longest-held notes.

The women's / men's alternating song of the Nung Giang is organised in the following manner: a first musical phrase ends on the unison, with-as we have already emphasised-an abrupt change of register, from chest-voice to head-voice, while staying on the same pitch. The second musical phrase does not end at the unison, but at the interval of the second, with a simultaneous fall of the voices. The third and last musical phrase of a strophe ends anew at the unison and in head-voice. The end of the alternating parts of the women (but not of the men) is marked by a passage of one of the voices at a lower fourth, then by a crossing-over of the voices, at the major second, before ending at the unison and in head-voice.

In the courtship song of the Nung Inh, the women sing at the unison, with some heterophonic variants. Two men respond periodically, but simultaneously and not successively as in the majority of alternating songs. They also sing at the unison, following a similar melodic contour, but rhythmically shifted and transposed to a fourth lower in relation to the women. The voices of the women and of the men thus develop in an independent manner.

The Yao sub-groups seem to prefer heterophony with slight temporal delays; when these delays become more marked and more systematic, one could speak of the practice of echo.

The alternating song of the Hani combines several of these procedures. Certain passages are sung alternatively by one of the girls and by the young man, the girl sometimes completing the unfinshed musical phrase of the boy; in other passages they sing simultaneously, the young man at the lower octave, with variants. When the second girl intervenes, she sings at the same time as the first, but with a different melody, making a veritable counterpoint. Further on, the first feminine voice joins the second, with variations and temporal delays, like a sort of varied canon. During some brief moments, the three voices sing together.

The music of the Tribal peoples in Vietnam represents some characteristics which cannot be found in Vietnamese music of the Kinh people. It should be developped in the future. And it is the duty of Vietnamese musicologists living in Vietnam to pursue their research in the years to come.

Recherches Introspectives et Expérimentales sur le chant diphonique

Trần Quang Hải

National Center for Scientific Research, France.

La présence d'harmoniques et de leurs effets dans les prières lamaïques tibétaines est connue depuis une quarantaine d'années. L'existence du chant diphonique chez les Bachkirs et les Mongols a été signalée dix ans plus tard. Vers le début des années 1980, fut « découverte » la richesse du chant de gorge des Touvains. Le développement des effets harmoniques dans la musique méditative en Europe depuis les dix dernières années a poussé la recherche vocale dans le domaine de la résonance harmonique, notamment en Europe et en Amérique. Des travaux de recherches sur la *quintina* (la cinquième voix virtuelle obtenue par la fusion de quatre voix dans le chant polyphonique sarde) ont été menés par Bernard Lortat-Jacob.

Avant d'entrer dans les détails de ce sujet, il me semble nécessaire d'avoir un aperçu sur le phénomène du chant **diphonique.**

Description du chant diphonique

Le chant diphonique est un style vocal « découvert », pour ma part, en 1969 grâce à un document sonore rapporté de Mongolie par Roberte Hamayon, lors du dépôt de ses bandes magnétiques au département d'ethnomusicologie du Musée de l'Homme. Il repose sur une voix nommée « guimbarde », qui se caractérise par l'émission conjointe de deux sons, l'un dit « son fondamental » ou « bourdon », tenu à la même hauteur tout le temps d'une expiration, pendant que l'autre, dit « son harmonique » (qui est l'un des harmoniques naturels du son fondamental), varie au gré du chanteur. Ainsi, une personne parvient à chanter à deux voix simultanément. Ce son harmonique a un timbre proche de celui de la flûte (voix flûtée) ou de celui de la guimbarde (voix guimbarde).

Historique du phénomène vocal

Par le passé, le chant diphonique a été mentionné à plusieurs reprises. M. Rollin, professeur au Conservatoire de Paris, au XIXè siècle, affirme qu'à la cour de Charles le Téméraire, un baladin chantait à deux voix simultanées, la deuxième étant à la quinte de la première. Manuel Garcia, dans son *Mémoire sur la voix humaine* présenté à l'Académie des sciences, à Paris, le 16 novembre 1840, a signalé le phénomène de double voix chez les paysans russes. Plusieurs voyageurs ont mentionné dans le récit de leurs pérégrinations qu'au Tibet se pratiquait le dédoublement de la voix pendant certaines récitations de mantras. Mais cette déclaration ne fut pas prise au sérieux. En 1934, des chercheurs russes enregistrèrent des disques 78 tours de chant diphonique chez les Touvains, lesquels disques ont été étudiés par Aksenov. Ce dernier, par la suite, a publié en 1964 en URSS, un article – traduit en allemand en 1967 et en anglais en 1973 –, considéré comme le premier de valeur scientifique sur le chant diphonique.

Depuis les quarante dernières années, de nombreux chercheurs, acousticiens, ethnomusicologues ont essayé d'élucider à leur tour les mystères du chant diphonique[1]. Des appellations diverses furent proposées par des chercheurs français au cours des trente dernières années: « chant diphonique » (Émile Leipp, 1 971 ; Gilles Léothaud, 1 971 ; Trân Quang Hai, 1974), « voix guimbarde » (Roberte Hamayon et Mireille Helffer, 1973), « chant diphonique solo » (Claudie Marcel-Dubois, 1978), « chant diplophonique » (Trân Quang Hai, 1993), « chant biformantique » (Trân Quang Hai, 1994). Plutôt que parler de « chant diplophonique » (« *diplo* », « deux » en grec[2]), ou de « chant biformantique » (chant à deux formants), j'utiliserai dans cet article, pour ne pas créer de confusion, l'expression « chant diphonique ». Certains chanteurs adoptent le terme de « chant harmonique » qui me semble impropre, car tout chant, quel que soit le type de voix, est produit par une série d'harmoniques.

On peut citer parmi eux : Lajos Vargyas (Hongrie, 1967), Émile Leipp (France, 1 971), Gilles Léothaud (France, 171), Roberte Hamayon et Mireille Helffer (France, 1973), Suzanne Borel-Maisonny (France, 1974), Trân Quang Hai (France, 1974), Richard Walcott (États-Unis, 1974), Sumi Gunji (Japon, 1980), Roberto Laneri (1983), Lauri Harvilahti (Finlande, 1983), Alain Desjacques (France, 1984), Ted Levin (États-Unis, 1988), Carole Pegg (Royaume Uni, 1988), Graziano Tisato (Italie, 1988), Hugo Zemp (France, 1989), Mark Van Tongeren (Pays-Bas, 1993), Johanni Curtis (2006).

1. Le terme « diplophonie », emprunté à la terminologie médicale, désigne l'existence simultanée de deux sons de hauteur différente dans le larynx.

Ces harmoniques sont renforcés différemment et sont sélectionnés suivant la volonté du chanteur pour créer une mélodie harmonique ou plus exactement « formantique ».

Des chanteurs ou compositeurs[3] ont introduit l'effet du chant diphonique dans la musique contemporaine (« musique du monde » ou « *world music* », « musique nouvelle » « *new music* »), que ce soit en musique électro-acoustique, en musique improvisée, en musique d'inspiration byzantine, grégorienne, en musique méditative, en musique *new age*, en jazz, en rap...

Comme Trân Quang Hai (France, 1975), Dimitri Stratos (Grèce, 1977), Roberto Laneri (Italie, 1978), David Hykes et son Harmonic Choir (États-Unis, 1983), Joan La Barbara (États-Unis, 1985), Meredith Monk (États-Unis, 1980), Michael Vetter (Allemagne, 1985), Christian Bollmann (Allemagne, 1985), Michael Reimann (Allemagne, 1986), Noah Pikes (Angleterre, 1985), Tamia (France, 1987), Quatuor Nomad (France1989), Valentin Clastrier (France, 1990), Bodjo Pinek (Yougoslavie, 1987), Josephine Truman (Australie, 1987), Iegor Reznikoff (France, 1989), Rollin Rachelle (Pays-Bas, 1990), Thomas Clements (France, 1990), Sarah Hopkins (Australie, 1990), Mauro Bagella (Italie, 1995), Lê Tuân Hùng (Australie, 1996).

Des musicothérapeutes, tels Jill Purce (Angleterre) ou Dominique Bertrand (France), ont utilisé la technique du chant diphonique comme moyen thérapeutique. J'ai personnellement, depuis 1998, combiné le chant diphonique avec la gymnastique holistique en utilisant vibrations harmoniques et mouvements corporels : pratique favorisant la concentration.

Divers styles de chant diphonique

La technique du chant diphonique a été rencontrée autour du mont Altaï, en Haute-Asie, chez les Mongols, Touvains, Khakash, Bachkirs, Altaïens, mais aussi de façon inégale, parmi les Rajasthani de l'Inde, les Xhosas d'Afrique du Sud, les moines tibétains des monastères Gyütö et Gyüme, et depuis peu chez les Dani en Irian Jaya (partie indonésienne de la Nouvelle-Guinée).

Chez les Touvains, il existe cinq techniques principales avec bourdon, du plus grave au plus aigu, selon les styles *kargyraa*, *borbannadyr*, *ezengileer*, *sygyt* et *khoomei*. En ce qui concerne le style *kargyraa*, le fondamental a un timbre spécial (cor de chasse) avec une fréquence variant entre 55 Hz (*la* 0) et 65 Hz (*do* 1). Les harmoniques se dispersent entre H6, H7, H8, H9, H10 et H12. Chaque harmonique correspond à une voyelle déterminée. Le fondamental dans le style *borbannadyr* (autour de 110 Hz) reste fixe, et un timbre plus doux que celui du *kargyraa*. Le chanteur peut produire deux formants harmoniques au-dessus du fondamental. La parenté technique entre *kargyraa* et *borbannadyr* permet au chanteur d'alterner les deux styles dans la même pièce musicale. Le style *sygyt* possède un fondamental plus aigu (entre 165 Hz [*mi* 2] et 220 Hz [*la* 2]) qui varie avec les chanteurs. La mélodie harmonique utilise les harmoniques H9, H10 et H12 (maximum jusqu'à 2640 Hz). Le style *ezengileer* est une variante de *sygyt*, caractérisé par un rythme dynamique particulier, provenant de l'appui périodique des pieds du cavalier sur les étriers. Le style *khoomei* est la base du chant diphonique touvain.

Les types de chant diphonique touvins sont fondés sur les mêmes principes d'émission sonore que ceux de la guimbarde. La mélodie est créée par les harmoniques d'un fondamental, engendrés par le résonateur d'Helmholtz que constitue la cavité buccale dont on modifie les dimensions. Pour la guimbarde, c'est la lame vibrante

149

qui attaque le résonateur. Pour le chant diphonique, ce sont les cordes vocales qui seront ajustées sur des hauteurs différentes, ce qui crée plusieurs fondamentaux, donc plusieurs séries d'harmoniques. Depuis 1985, le chant diphonique touvain a trouvé son second souffle grâce aux intérêts des chercheurs chanteurs occidentaux. D'autres techniques secondaires ou moins connues ont été « retrouvées », à savoir *sygyt* moyen, *kargiraa* de steppe ou *kargyraa* de montagne, *stil oidupa* (ce style inspiré du style *kargyraa*, et appelé d'après le nom du créateur, est considéré comme le premier style urbain).

Chez les Mongols, il existe six techniques différentes de chant diphonique : *xamryn xöömi* (*xöömi* nasal), *bagalzuuryn xöömi* (*xöömi* pharyngé), *tseedznii xöömi* (*xöömi* thoracique), *kevliin xöömi* (*xöömi* abdominal), *xarkiraa xöömi* (*xöömi* narratif avec un fondamental très grave) et *isgerex* (voix de flûte dentale, d'usage rare). D. Sundui, le meilleur chanteur diphonique mongol, possède une technique de vibrato et une puissance harmonique exceptionnelle.

Les Khakash utilisent le style *xaj* et les Gorno-Altaïens possèdent un style *kaj* semblable pour accompagner les chants épiques. Avant la domination soviétique, les Khakash possédaient des styles de chant diphonique très proches de ceux pratiqués par les Touvains, à savoir *sygyrtyp* (comme *sygyt* touvain), *kuveder* ou *kylenge* (comme *ezengileer* touvin), et *kargirar* (comme *kargyraa* touvain). Chez les Gorno-Altaïens, on découvre les styles *kiomioi*, *karkira* et *sibiski* (correspondant respectivement à l'*ezengileer,* au kargyraa et au *sygyt* touvain). Les Bachkirs possèdent le style *uzlau*, proche du style *ezengileer* touvain.

Chez les moines tibétains des monastères Gyütö et Gyüme, le chant des *tantras* (écritures bouddhiques) et des *mantras* (formules sacrées), les *mudras* (gestes des mains), et des techniques permettant de se représenter mentalement des divinités ou des symboles se pratiquent régulièrement. Leur tradition remonte à un groupe de maîtres indiens – le plus connu étant le *yogin* Padmasambhava – qui visitèrent le Tibet au VIIIè siècle et, plus récemment, au fondateur de l'un des quatre courants du bouddhisme tibétain, Tzong Khapa. C'est Tzong Khapa (1357-1419) qui aurait introduit le chant diphonique et le style de méditation pratiqués dans les monastères Gyüto. Il tenait ce type de chant, dit-on, de sa divinité protectrice, Maha Bhairava qui, bien qu'étant une incarnation du Seigneur de la compassion (Avalokiteshvara) possédait un esprit terrifiant. Le visage central de Maha Bhairava est celui d'un buffle en colère. Ses trente quatre bras portent les trente-quatre symboles des qualités nécessaires à la libération. Aujourd'hui encore, les maîtres de cette école aiment comparer leur chant au beuglement d'un taureau.

Il existe plusieurs manières de réciter les prières : la récitation dans un registre grave avec vitesse modérée ou rapide sur des textes sacrés, les chants avec trois styles (*Ta* chanté avec des mots clairement prononcés sur une échelle pentatonique ; *Gur* avec un tempo lent utilisé dans les cérémonies principales et au cours des processions ; *Yang* avec une voix extrêmement grave sur des voyelles produisant l'effet harmonique pour communiquer avec les dieux). Les moines tibétains du monastère Gyüto produisent un bourdon extrêmement grave et un harmonique H10 correspondant à la tierce majeure au-dessus de la troisième octave du bourdon, tandis que les moines du monastère Gyüme génèrent un bourdon grave et un harmonique 12 équivalant la quinte au-dessus de la troisième octave du bourdon. On dit que le chant des moines Gyütö correspond à l'élément « feu » et que celui des moines Gyüme exprime l'élément « eau ». Ces moines obtiennent cet effet harmonique en chantant la voyelle « O » avec la bouche allongée et les lèvres arrondies.

Au Rajasthan, en Inde, un chanteur enregistré en 1967 par le regretté John Levy, est arrivé à utiliser la technique du chant diphonique proche du style *sygyt* touvain pour imiter la guimbarde et la flûte double *satara*. Cet enregistrement unique représente la seule trace qui nous soit connue de l'existence du phénomène du chant diphonique en ce pays.

En Afrique du Sud, les Xhosas, plus particulièrement les femmes, pratiquent le chant diphonique. Cette technique, *umngqokolo ngomqangi*, est une imitation de l'arc musical *umrhube*. *Ngomqangi* désigne le coléoptère. La chanteuse explique que cette technique à double voix simultanée est inspirée du bruit du coléoptère placé devant la bouche utilisée comme bourdon : la cavité buccale module sur ce modèle les harmoniques produits. Dave Dargie a découvert ce chant diphonique chez les Xhosas en 1983.

À Formose (Taiwan), les Bunun, une des minorités ethniques taïwanaises, chantent les voyelles avec une voix très tendue et font sortir quelques harmoniques dans un chant à l'occasion de la récolte du millet (*Pasi but but*). Est-ce bien un style de chant diphonique semblable à celui pratiqué par les Mongols et les Touvins ? Faute de documents sonores et écrits, nous ne pouvons poursuivre nos recherches.

En 2002, j'ai « découvert » l'existence d'un type de chant diphonique chez les Dani, en Irian Jaya. Dans certains types de chants où l'émission des voyelles est très résonantielle, cela permet aux chanteurs de créer un deuxième formant non intentionnel (chant bouddhique japonais *shômyô*, certains chants bulgares, chants polyphoniques d'Europe de l'Est), ou intentionnel (phénomène *quintina* des chants sacrés sardes, étudié par Bernard Lortat-Jacob).

Il faut donc faire la distinction entre chant diphonique (créant une mélodie d'harmoniques) et chant à résonance harmonique (accompagné ponctuellement par des effets harmoniques).

Aspect acoustique et spectral

Perception de la hauteur des sons

J'essaierai, dans un premier temps, de décrire la notion de perception de hauteur à la lumière de l'acoustique et de la psycho-acoustique. Dans un second temps, je présenterai l'espace de liberté du chant diphonique. Enfin, il serait profitable de formuler quelques hypothèses sur les mécanismes de formation de ce chant, sur la réalisation du chant diphonique (diplophonique, biformantique…).

Préalablement, il est nécessaire de comprendre le sens de la terminologie spécifique appliqué au chant diphonique, et qui utilise des termes tels que « hauteurs des sons » ou « tonalité ». Cette notion présente beaucoup d'ambigüités, et ne répond pas au principe simple de la mesure des fréquences émises. La hauteur des sons tient plus de la psycho-acoustique que de la physique. Mes propos s'appuient d'une part sur les découvertes récentes de certains chercheurs, d'autre part sur mes propres observations et expérimentations effectuées à partir du sonagraphe. Le sonagraphe permet en effet d'obtenir l'image du son à étudier. Sur un seul papier, figure en abscisse l'information « temps », en ordonnée l'information « fréquence », et au moyen de l'épaisseur du trait tracé, l'information « intensité ». Les manuels d'acoustique classiques enseignent que la hauteur des sons harmoniques, donc les sons comportant un fondamental de fréquence F et une suite d'harmoniques (F1, F2, F3… multiples de F) est donnée par la fréquence du premier son fondamental. Ceci n'est pas tout à fait exact, car il est possible de supprimer électroniquement ce fondamental sans pour cela changer la hauteur subjective du son perçu. Si cette théorie était exacte, une chaîne électro-acoustique ne reproduisant pas l'extrême grave changerait la hauteur des sons. Il n'en est rien car le timbre change mais pas la hauteur. Certains chercheurs proposent une autre théorie plus cohérente : la hauteur des sons est donnée par l'écartement des raies harmoniques ou la différence de fréquence entre deux raies harmoniques. Que devient la hauteur des sons dans ce cas pour les spectres sonores dit « à partiels » (les partiels sont les harmoniques qui ne sont pas des multiples entiers du fondamental) ? Dans ce cas, l'individu perçoit une moyenne de l'écartement des raies dans la zone qui l'intéresse. Ceci, en effet, concorde avec les différences de perception avérées d'un individu à l'autre.

On désigne par l'expression « spectre à formant » le renforcement en intensité d'un groupe d'harmoniques constituant un formant, c'est à dire une zone de fréquences où l'énergie est grande. En rapport avec l'existence de ce formant, une deuxième notion de la perception de hauteur se fait jour. On s'est en effet aperçu que la position du formant dans le spectre sonore donnait la perception d'une nouvelle hauteur. Dans ce cas, il ne s'agit plus de l'écartement des raies harmoniques dans la zone formantique mais de la position du formant dans le spectre. Cette théorie doit être nuancée, car elle est soumise à conditions.

À titre d'expérience, si l'on chante trois *do* (*do* 1, *do* 2, *do* 3) à une octave d'intervalle entre deux *do* en projetant la voix comme en direction d'un grand auditoire. On constate à la lecture du sonagramme que le maximum d'énergie se trouvait dans la zone sensible de l'oreille humaine (2 à 3 KHz). Il s'agit bien d'un formant situé entre 2 et 4 KHz. Si on enregistre trois *do* dans la même tonalité, mais cette fois en posant la voix vers un auditoire restreint, et on observe la disparition de ce formant.

Dans ce cas, la disparition du formant ne change pas la hauteur des sons. La perception de la hauteur par la position du formant n'est possible que si celui-ci est très aigu, à savoir que l'énergie du formant n'est répartie que sur deux ou trois harmoniques. Donc, si la densité d'énergie du formant est grande, et que le formant est étroit, celui-ci donnera une information de hauteur en plus de la tonalité globale du morceau chanté. Par ce biais, on parvient à la technique du chant diphonique. Cette notion de formant prenant le pas sur les raies harmoniques fut par la suite confirmée grâce aux recherches expérimentales sur la formation du chant diphonique.

Comparaison entre technique vocale diphonique et technique vocale classique

Dans le chant diphonique, le formant (son aigu) se déplaçant dans le spectre pour donner une certaine mélodie, la hauteur donnée par cette seconde voix génère parfois une certaine ambigüité. Une accoutumance, ou une éducation, est souhaitable pour l'oreille occidentale. Par contre, la mise en évidence du bourdon, son grave et consistant, est relativement facile grâce aux sonagrammes. Il se voit très nettement. Auditivement, il est très net. Après la mise en évidence du son fondamental, la comparaison des deux spectres est la suivante : l'un d'un chant diphonique, l'autre d'un chant dit « classique », les deux étant produits par le même chanteur. Le chant classique se caractérise par un doublement de l'écartement des raies harmoniques lorsque le chant passe à l'octave. Le chant diphonique présente un écartement égal des raies (ceci est prévisible puisque le bourdon demeure constant) pendant le passage d'une octave où l'on voit le déplacement du formant. En effet, on peut mesurer avec facilité la distance entre les raies pour chaque son émis : dans ce cas, la perception de la mélodie du chant diphonique se fait par le biais du déplacement du formant dans le spectre sonore.

Il convient d'insister sur le fait que ceci n'est vraiment possible que si le formant se concentre dans l'aigu, et c'est précisément le cas du chant diphonique. L'énergie sonore est principalement divisée entre le bourdon et la deuxième voix constituée de deux harmoniques – trois tout au plus. Il a parfois été dit qu'une troisième voix pouvait être produite. J'ai effectivement constaté, grâce aux sonagramme (sur les techniques touvines) que ceci existait, mais il m'est impossible d'affirmer que cette troisième voix est contrôlée. À mon avis, cette voix supplémentaire résulte plus de la personnalité de l'exécutant que d'une technique particulière. À cette occasion, on peut déjà établir un parallèle entre chant diphonique et guimbarde. La guimbarde produit, comme le chant diphonique, plusieurs « voix » différentes: le bourdon, le chant et le contre-chant. On pourrait considérer cette troisième voix comme un contrechant: celui-ci peut être produit délibérément, mais sans doute pas contrôlé.

Espace de liberté du chant diphonique

Du point de vue de l'espace de liberté, le chant diphonique équivaut au chant normal sauf pour ce qui concerne l'*ambitus*. Le temps d'exécution dépend évidemment de la cage thoracique du chanteur, donc de la respiration, mais également de l'intensité sonore, car l'intensité est en rapport avec le débit d'air. Le champ de liberté concernant l'intensité est par contre relativement restreint et le niveau des harmoniques est lié au niveau du bourdon. Le chanteur a intérêt à garder un bourdon d'intensité suffisante afin de faire émerger un maximum d'harmoniques. J'ai constaté précédemment que les harmoniques étaient d'autant plus claires que le formant était étroit et intense. On peut donc en déduire des liens entre les phénomènes d'intensité, de temps et de clarté. Le champ de liberté concernant le timbre se passe de commentaire, le son résultant étant dans la majorité des cas formé d'un bourdon et d'un ou deux harmoniques.

La question la plus intéressante concerne l'*ambitus*. Il est généralement admis que pour une tonalité judicieuse (en fonction de l'exécutant et de la pièce musicale à interpréter), un chanteur peut moduler ou choisir entre les harmoniques 3 et 13. Ceci est vrai mais mérite quelque précision. L'*ambitus* est fonction de la tonalité. Si la tonalité est en *do* 2, la réalisation se fait sur quatorze harmoniques du sixième au vingtième, ce qui représente une octave et une sixte. Si la tonalité est élevée, par exemple *do* 3, le choix se fait entre les harmoniques 3 et 10 soit huit harmoniques, représentant également une octave et une sixte. Les remarques suivantes s'imposent. D'une part, l'*ambitus* du chant diphonique est plus restreint que celui du chant normal. D'autre part, en théorie, le chanteur choisit la tonalité qu'il souhaite entre *do* 2 et *do* 3. En pratique, il réalise instinctivement un compromis entre la clarté de la deuxième voix et l'*ambitus* de son chant – le choix de la tonalité étant également fonction de la pièce musicale à exécuter. En effet, si la tonalité est élevée, par exemple *do* 3, le choix des harmoniques se trouve restreint, mais la deuxième voix est alors très claire. Dans le cas d'une tonalité en *do* 2, la deuxième voix est plus confuse, alors que l'*ambitus* atteint son maximum. La clarté des sons peut s'expliquer par le fait que dans le premier cas le chanteur ne peut sélectionner qu'un harmonique, alors que dans le deuxième il peut en sélectionner presque deux. Pour la question de l'*ambitus,* je sais que la mise en action des résonateurs buccaux est indépendante de la tonalité des sons émis par les cordes vocales. Autrement dit, le chanteur sélectionne toujours les harmoniques dans la même zone du spectre, que ceux-ci soient écartés ou resserrés.

De tout ceci, il résulte que le chanteur choisit la tonalité instinctivement pour déployer à la fois l'*ambitus* maximum et le maximum de clarté. Dans mon cas personnel, le meilleur compromis se trouve entre *do* 2 et *la* 2. Je peux ainsi produire avec les harmoniques à partir d'un son fondamental entre *do* 2 et *la* 2, une mélodie couvrant jusqu'à deux octaves.

Mécanismes de production du chant

Diphonique

Il est toujours très difficile de connaître de l'extérieur ce qui se passe à l'intérieur d'une machine. Tel est le cas de l'appareil phonatoire. Ce qui va en être dit ici est donc grossier et schématique, et ne doit pas être pris à la lettre. En traitant le système phonatoire par analogie, on peut se faire une idée des mécanismes, mais sûrement pas en fournir une explication complète. Un résonateur est une cavité munie d'un col pouvant vibrer dans un certain registre de fréquences. Le système excitateur – le pharynx et les cordes vocales, en l'occurrence – émet un spectre harmonique, à savoir les fréquences $F1$, $F1$, $F3$, $F4$... de résonateurs qui choisissent certaines fréquences et amplifient celles-ci. Le choix de ces fréquences dépend évidemment de l'habileté du chanteur. Il en va ainsi lorsqu'un chanteur porte la voix pour une grande salle. Instinctivement, il adopte ses résonateurs pour émettre le maximum d'énergie dans la zone sensible de l'oreille. Il est à noter que les fréquences amplifiées sont fonction du volume de la cavité, de la section de l'ouverture et de la longueur du col constituant l'ouverture.

Grâce à ce principe, je perçois déjà l'influence de la grandeur de la cavité buccale, de l'ouverture de la bouche, de la position des lèvres sur le chant. Mais ceci ne me donne pas un chant diphonique. En effet, il me faut deux voix. La première provient simplement du fait que celui-ci est intense à l'émission et que, de toute manière, il ne subit pas le filtrage des résonateurs. Son intensité, supérieure à celle des harmoniques, lui permet de maintenir grâce à un rayonnement buccal et nasal. J'ai constaté qu'en fermant la cavité nasale, le bourdon diminuait en intensité. Ceci s'explique de deux manières : d'une part une source de rayonnement est bouchée (il s'agit du nez), et d'autre part le débit d'air se trouve réduit, et avec lui l'intensité sonore des cordes vocales.

L'intérêt d'avoir plusieurs cavités est primordial. J'ai pu mettre en évidence que seul le couplage de plusieurs cavités permet d'obtenir le formant aigu indispensable au chant diphonique. Pour cette étude, j'ai en premier lieu procédé aux vérifications du principe des résonateurs, à savoir l'influence des paramètres fondamentaux. J'ai ainsi constaté que la tonalité du son monte en ouvrant plus grand la bouche. Pour mettre en évidence la formation d'un formant aigu, j'ai tenté de produire deux sortes de chants diphoniques : l'un avec la langue au repos, c'est à dire la bouche devenant une grande et unique cavité, et l'autre avec la pointe de la langue remontant et touchant la voûte palatine, divisant ainsi la bouche en deux cavités. La constatation faite grâce à la théorie des résonateurs couplés est la suivante : dans le premier cas, les sons ne sont pas clairs. Certes, on entend très bien le bourdon mais la deuxième voix est difficile à entendre. Il n'y a pas une différenciation distincte entre les deux voix. De plus, la mélodie s'impose difficilement à l'écoute. Selon les sonagrammes analysés, avec une cavité buccale unique l'énergie du formant se disperse sur trois ou quatre harmoniques, et donc la sensation de la deuxième voix devient beaucoup plus faible. Par contre, quand la langue divise la bouche en deux cavités, le formant aigu et intense réapparaît. Autrement dit, les sons harmoniques émis par les cordes vocales subissent, avec une seule cavité, une amplification et un filtrage grossiers, ce qui a pour conséquence de faire disparaître l'effet diphonique. Le chant diphonique nécessite donc un réseau de résonateurs très sélectifs filtrant uniquement les harmoniques désirés par le chanteur. Dans le cas d'un couplage serré entre les deux cavités, celles-ci donnent une résonance unique très aiguë. Lorsque le couplage devient lâche, le formant a une intensité moins grande, et l'énergie sonore est étalée dans le spectre. Lorsque ces cavités se réduisent à une seule, la courbe pointue devient encore plus ronde et on aboutit au premier exemple évoqué, consistant en un chant diphonique très flou (langue en position de « repos »).

On peut donc en conclure que la bouche avec la position de la langue joue un rôle prépondérant. On peut grossièrement l'assimiler à un filtre pointu qui se déplacerait dans le spectre uniquement pour choisir les harmoniques intéressants.

Réalisation du chant diphonique

Après la découverte de cette technique, et après quelques années de tâtonnement, je suis parvenu à maîtriser la pratique, et ai constaté qu'on peut produire les deux sons simultanés grâce à trois méthodes distinctes.

Première méthode avec une cavité buccale

La langue peut être à plat, en position de « repos », ou bien la base de la langue être légèrement remontée sans jamais toucher la partie molle du palais. Seules la bouche et les lèvres bougent. Par cette variation de la cavité buccale en prononçant les deux voyelles « ü » et « i » liées sans interruption (comme si l'on disait « oui » en français), on perçoit une faible mélodie des harmoniques qui ne dépasse guère l'harmonique 8.

Deuxième méthode avec deux cavités buccales

1.   Chanter avec la voix de gorge ;
2.   prononcer la lettre « l ». Dès que la pointe de la langue touche le centre de la voûte palatine, maintenir cette position ;
3.   prononcer ensuite la voyelle « ü », toujours la pointe de la langue collée fermement contre le point de fixation entre le palais dur et le palais mou ; 4. contracter les muscles du cou et ceux de

l'abdomen pendant le chant comme pour soulever un objet très lourd ;

5.   donner un timbre très nasalisé en l'amplifiant à travers les fosses nasales ;

6.   prononcer ensuite les deux voyelles « i » et « ü » (ou bien « o » et « a ») liées mais alternées, plusieurs fois de suite ;

7.   ainsi sont obtenus le bourdon et les harmoniques, en pente ascendante comme en pente descendante, selon le désir du chanteur.

Pour moduler la mélodie des harmoniques, il est possible de varier la position des lèvres ou celle de la langue. La forte concentration musculaire augmente la clarté harmonique.

Troisième méthode

Celle-ci consiste à utiliser la base de la langue remontée et mordue par les molaires supérieures pendant que le son de gorge est produit sur les deux voyelles « i » et « ü » liées et répétées plusieurs fois pour créer une série d'harmoniques descendants et ascendants. Cette série d'harmoniques se trouve dans la zone entre 2 KHz et 3,5 KHz. Cette troisième méthode ne permet pas le contrôle de la mélodie formantique, mais il ne s'agit ici que d'une démonstration expérimentale sur les possibilités de timbre harmonique.

Le chant diphonique : nouvelle thérapeutique

Le chant diphonique, en dehors de son expression traditionnelle (en Mongolie, au pays Touva, au Tibet), et de l'usage expérimental qu'en ont fait de nombreux chanteurs contemporains, tant en Europe qu'en Amérique, représente également un nouvel outil pour des applications thérapeutiques (Trân Quang Hai[4], Jill Purce, Dominique Bertrand, Bernard Dubreuil).

Jill Purce (Royaume Uni) propose un travail fondé sur la respiration et le chant diphonique auprès des personnes qui bégaient, ou éprouvent des sensations de blocage dans la gorge, ou sont effrayées par leur propre voix, ou encore souffrent d'inhibition, de troubles respiratoires, d'anxiété, de fatigue. Les principaux effets du chant diphonique concernent avant tout la concentration et l'équilibre psychologique. Pour des raisons techniques, le chant réclame de la part du patient une grande attention.

Le chanteur talentueux peut coordonner la structure musicale avec les forces énergétiques, la puissance vibratoire de l'œuvre. Quand l'harmonie émerge puis s'épanouit, le nettoyage de l'inconscient peut commencer. Pour les uns, le chant diphonique « vous envoie au septième ciel ». Pour les autres, il vous plonge au cœur du mystère musical, où les ondes sonores pénètrent le secret de la naissance de l'univers. Les chamans du Tibet, de Sibérie et d'Amérique du Nord font résonner les harmoniques de la zone frontale, ce qui leur permet de soigner avec la voix. C'est un chant magique, un secret des anciens chamans mongols, un yoga sonore pratiqué par des moines tibétains pour atteindre l'illumination, un chant à pouvoirs, une vibration qui pénètre jusqu'aux cellules de l'organisme. C'est le fameux « chant qui guérit ».

Une démarche originale et féconde

Après plus de trois ans d'expériences personnelles en tant que chanteur, j'ai pu parvenir à la réalisation de cette technique vocale singulière, diffusée depuis 1972 dans le grand public. Dans les années 1980, et afin d'explorer les procédés physiologiques du chant diphonique, je me suis efforcé d'obtenir sur le sonagraphe des tracés de spectres semblables à ceux de chanteurs originaires de Mongolie, de Sibérie, du Rajasthan et d'Afrique du Sud. L'analyse comparée des spectrogrammes, à la lumière de ces expériences, a permis de classer pour la première fois les différents styles de chant diphonique d'Asie et d'Afrique du Sud en fonction des résonateurs, des contractions musculaires et des ornementations. Les recherches expérimentales ont en outre conduit :

1. à mettre en évidence le bourdon harmonique et la mélodie fondamentale,

2. L'article « Recherches expérimentales sur le chant diphonique » (Zemp & Trân Quang 1991) retrace toutes les étapes de cette recherche expérimentale.

ce qui va à l'encontre du principe initial du chant diphonique traditionnel ; 2. à croiser les deux mélodies (fondamentale et harmoniques) et à explorer le chant triphonique ;

3. à mettre en évidence les trois zones harmoniques sur la base d'un même son fondamental ;
4. à mettre au jour la possibilité de créer des sons fondamentaux (une octave au-dessous du son fondamental, voire une octave et une quinte, et deux octaves au-dessous du son fondamental) ;
5. à montrer en images les sept chakras du yoga par la présence des harmoniques selon les voyelles sélectionnées pour faire une pyramide de chakras.

J'ai parallèlement utilisé des moyens fibroscopiques, stroboscopiques et laryngoscopiques complétés par des analyses spectrales sur le sonagraphe, mené des études comparatives et pragmatiques de divers styles de chant diphonique chez différentes populations (Mongols, Touvains, Xhosas, Rajasthani, Tibétains), et ai débuté quelques explorations harmoniques préliminaires à travers le chant du millet *Pasi but but* des Bunun (Formose), des récitations bouddhiques *shômyô* (Japon), et des chants de gorge des Dani en Irian Jaya. Enfin j'ai utilisé la technique du chant diphonique dans diverses compositions musicales électro-acoustiques et avant-gardistes.

Pour conclure, mentionnons que ces recherches sont restituées par le film de Hugo Zemp (2005), *Le Chant des harmoniques*. Ce film montre la technique du chant diphonique du point de vue articulatoire et spectral. Le cinéma-radiologie, avec le traitement informatique de l'image en temps réel et son synchrone, permet de montrer les modifications de la cavité buccale grâce aux spectres sonores analysés par le sonagraphe de différentes techniques du chant diphonique, par des chanteurs de Mongolie, du Rajasthan, d'Afrique du Sud, du Tibet, de la République de Touva, et par moi-même.

Bibliographique indicative

Abitol, Jean, 2004. *L'Odyssée de la voix*, Paris, Robert Laffont.

Adachi, Seiji; Yamada, Masashi, 1999. « An acoustical study of sound production in biphonic singing, *xöömij* », *Journal of the Acoustical Society of America,* vol. 105, n° 5, pp. 2920-2932.

Aksenov, Aleksej Nikolaevich, 1973. « Tuvin folk music », *Journal of the Society for Asian Music*, vol. 4, n° 2, pp. 7-18. — 1964. *Tuvinskaja narodnaja muzyka*, Moscou.

— 1967. « Die Stile der Tuvinischen zweistimmigen Sologesanges », *in* Erich Stockmann (dir.), *Sowjetische Volkslied- und Volksmusikforschung*, Berlin, Akademie Verlag, pp. 293-308.

Badraa, Z., 1986. « L'art Xöömij », *Les Nouvelles de Mongolie*, n° 9, pp. 18-19.

— 1981. « *"Xöömij"* i *"urtyn duu"*, specificeskie Javienija Mongol'skoj tradicionnoj klassiceskoj muzyki », *Professional'naja muzyka ustoj tradicij narodov bliznevo vostoka i sovremennost*, Tachkent, pp. 116-119.

Batzengel, 1978. « *Urtyn duu, xöömii* and *morin xuur* », Yuki Minegishi & Richard Emmert (dir.), *Muscial Voices of Asia*, actes du colloque « Asian traditional performing arts (ATPA) », Tokyo, Heibonsha Ltd Publishers, pp. 52-53.

Belfer, Richard, 1986. « Chant harmonique : découvrez votre deuxième voix », *Médecines douces*, n° 77, pp. 50-53.

Bloothooft, Gerrit; Bringmann, Eldrid; Capellen, Marieke (van) ; Luipen, Jolanda B. (van) ; Thomassen, Koen P. , 1992. « Acoustic and Perception of Overtone Singing », *Journal of the Acoustical Society of America (JASA)*, vol. 92, n° 4, pp. 1827-1836.

Borel-Maisonny, Suzanne ; Castellengo, Michèle, 1976. « Étude radiographique des mouvements oro-pharyngée pendant la parole et le jeu instrumental », *Bulletin du Groupe d'acoustique musicale (GAM)*, n° 86.

Desjacques, Alain, 1993. « Chapitre 1. Le *xöömij* », *in* « Chants de l'Altaï Mongol », thèse de doctorat nouveau régime dirigée par les professeurs Manfred Kelkel et Jacques Legrand à l'université Paris-IV Sorbonne, pp. 7-108.

Dargie, Dave, 1988. *Xhosa Music. Its Techniques and Instruments, with a Collection of Songs*, Cape Town, David Philip.

— 1985. « Some recent discoveries and recordings in Xhosa music », *in* Collectif, *Symposium 5*, conférence donnée au cours du 5ᵉ « Ethnomusicology Symposia » (University of Cape Town, 1984), Grahamtown, International Library of African Music, pp. 29-35.

Dmitriev, L.; Chernov, B.; Maslow, V., 1983. « Functioning of the voice mechanism in double-voice Touvinian singing », *Folia Phoniatrica*, vol. 35, n° 5, pp. 193-197.

Fuks, Leonardo; Hammarberg, Britta; Sundberg, Johan, 1998. « A selfsustained vocal-ventricular phonation mode: acoustical, aerodynamic and glottographic evidences », *TMH-QPSR*, n° 3, pp. 49-59.

Gunji, Sumi, 1980. « An Acoustical Consideration of Xöömij », *in* The Japan Foundation (dir.), *Musical Voices of Asia*, Tokyo, Heibonsha Publishers, pp. 135-141.

Hamayon, Roberte, 1980. « Mongol Music », in Stanley Sadie (dir.), *New Grove's Dictionary of Music and Musicians*, vol. 12, Londres, MacMillan Publishers, pp. 482-485.

Harvilahti, Lauri, 1983. « A two voiced song with no word », *SuomalaisUgrilaisen Seuran Aikakauskirja* [*Journal de la Société finno-ougrienne*], vol. 78, pp. 43-56.

Harvilahti, Lauri; Kaskinen, Hannu, 1983. « On the application possibilities of overtone singing », *Suomen Antropologi*, vol. 4, pp. 249-255.

Laneri, Roberto, 1983. « Vocal techniques of overtone production », *NPCA Quarterly Journal*, vol. 12, n°s 2-3, pp. 26-30.

Leipp, Émile, 1971. « Considération acoustique sur le chant diphonique », *Bulletin du Groupe d'acoustique musicale (GAM)*, n° 58, pp. 1-10.

Lentin, Jean-Pierre, 1986. « Je fais chanter tout mon corps », *Actuel*, n°s 81-82, pp. 142- 145.

Léothaud, Gilles, 1989. « Considérations acoustiques et musicales sur le chant diphonique », *in* Collectif, *Le Chant diphonique*, Limoges, Institut de la voix, coll. « Dossiers », pp. 17-43.

Neuschaefer-Rube, Christiane; Saus, Wolfgang; Matern, Gabriele; Kob, Malte; Klajman, Stanislaw, 2002. « Sonographische und endoskopische Untersuchungen beim

Obertonsingen », *in* Hellmut K. Geissner (dir.), *Stimmkulturen*, vol. 3, *Stuttgarter Stimmtage 2000*, St. Ingbert (Allemagne), Röhrig Universitätsverlag, pp. 219-222.

Pailler, J.-P., 1989. « Examen vidéo du larynx et de la cavité buccale de Monsieur Trân Quang Hai », *in* Collectif, *Le Chant diphonique*, Limoges, Institut de la voix, coll. « Dossiers », pp. 11-13.

Pegg, Carole, 1992. « Mongolian conceptualizations of overtonesinging (*xöömii*) », *The British Journal of Ethnomusicology*, vol. 1, pp. 31-53.

Rachelle, Rollin, 1996. *Overtone Singing Study Guide*, Amsterdam, Cryptic Voices Productions.

Sauvage, J.-P., 1989. « Observation clinique de Monsieur Trân Quang Hai », *in* Collectif, *Le Chant diphonique*, Limoges, Institut de la voix, coll. « Dossiers », pp. 3-10.

Smith, Huston; Stevens, Kenneth N.; Tomlinson, Raymond S., 1967. « On an unusual mode of chanting of certain Tibetan lamas », *Journal of the Acoustical Society of America*, vol. 41, n° 5, pp. 1262-1264.

Tisato, Graziano ; Rici Maccarini, Andrea, 1991. « Analysis and synthesis of diphonic singing », *Bulletin d'audiophonologie*, vol. 7, n°s 5-6, « Nouvelles voies de la voix », pp. 619-648.

Tisato, Graziano ; Rici Maccarini, Andrea ; Trân quang, Hai, 2002. « Caratteristiche fisiologiche e acustiche del Canto Difonico », contribution au 2e « Convegno internazionale di foniatria e logopedia » (Ravenne, 2002). Disponible en ligne,

http://www.voicecentercesena.it/upload/
pdf/canto_difonico.pdf [consulté en juin 2010].

Tisato, Graziano; Cosi, Piero, 2003. « On the magic of
overtone singing », in Piero Cosi, Emanuela Magno
Caldognetto & Alberto Zamboni (dir.), *Voce, Canto, Parlato.
Studi in onore di Franco Ferrero*, Padoue/Rome,
Unipress/Istituto di scienze e tecnologie della cognizione
(Sezione di fonetica e dialettologia), pp. 83-100. Disponible en
ligne, http://www2.pd.istc.

cnr.it/Papers/PieroCosi/cp-MF2002-02.pdf [consulté en juin 2010].

Tisato Graziano, 1989. « Il canto degli armonici », *Culture
musicali. Quaderni di etnomusicologia*, vol. 15-16, « Nuove
tecnologie et documentazione etnomusicologica », pp. 44-68.

— 1979. « Analisi digitale dei suoni multifonici », *in* Giovanni
De Poli (dir.), *Atti del terzo colloquio di informatica musicale*,
Padoue, Universita di Padova, pp. 107-128.

Trân quang, Hai ; Guillou, Denis, 1980. « Original research
and acoustical analysis in connection with the *xöömij* style of
biphonic singing », *in* Yuki Minegishi & Richard Emmert
(dir.), *Muscial Voices of Asia*, actes du colloque « Asian
traditional performing arts (ATPA) », Tokyo, Heibonsha Ltd
Publishers, pp. 162-173.

Trân quang, Hai, 2002. « À la découverte du chant diphonique
», *in* Guy Cornut (dir.), *Moyens d'investigation et pédagogie
de la voix chantée*, actes du colloque organisé au Conservatoire
national de région de Lyon dans le cadre des Rencontres
vocales en région Rhône-Alpes (8-10 février 2001), Lyon,
Symétrie, pp. 117-132.

— 2002. « New experiments on overtone singing », *in* Hellmut K. Geissner (dir.), *Stimmkulturen*, vol. 3, *Stuttgarter Stimmtage 2000*, St. Ingbert (Allemagne), Röhrig Universitätsverlag, pp. 65-70.

— 1997. « Recherches introspectives sur le chant diphonique et leurs applications », *La Licorne*, n° 41, « Penser la Voix », pp. 95-210.

— 1995. « Survey of overtone singing style », *Dokumentation 1994*, actes du congrès de l'European Voice Teachers Association (Detmold, 1994), Detmold, EVTA, pp. 49-62.

— 1995. « Le chant diphonique : description, historique, styles, aspect acoustique et spectral », *EM. Annuario degli archivi di etnomusicologia dell'Accademia nazionale di Santa Cecilia*, n° 2, pp. 123-150.

— 1991. « New experimental about the overtone singing style », *Bulletin d'audiophonologie*, vol. 7, n°s 5-6, « Nouvelles voies de la voix », pp. 607-618.

— 1990. « Les musiques vocales », *in* Jean-Marc Alby, Catherine Alès & Patrick Sansoy (dir.), *L'Esprit des voix. Études sur la fonction vocale*, Grenoble, La Pensée sauvage, coll. « Corps et psychisme », pp. 43-52.

— 1975. « Technique de la voix chantée mongole : *xöömij* », *Bulletin du CEMO*, n°s 14-15, pp. 32-36.

Van Tongeren, Mark, 2002. *Overtone Singing. Physics and Metaphysics of Harmonics in East and West*, Amsterdam, Fusica, coll. « The Harmonic Series ».

— 1995. « A Tuvan perspective on throat singing », *in* Wim Van Zanten and Marjolijn Van Roon (dir.), *Oideion*, vol. 2, *The Performing Arts World-Wide*, Leyde, Leiden University, coll. « CNWS Publications », pp. 293-312.

— 1994. « *Xöömij* in Tuva : new developments, new dimensions », mémoire de maîtrise sous la direction de Ernst Heins soutenue à l'Ethnomusicologisch Centrum « Jaap Kunst » de l'Université d'Amsterdam.

Vargyas, Lajos, 1968. « Performing styles in Mongolian chant », *Journal of the International Folk Music Council*, vol. 20, pp. 70-72.

Vlachou, Evangelia, 1985. « Recherches vocales contemporaines : chant diphonique », mémoire de maîtrise soutenue à l'université Paris-VIII Saint Denis.

Walcott, Ronald, 1974. « The *chöömij* of Mongolia. A spectral analysis of overtone singing », *Selected Reports in Ethnomusicology*, vol. 2, n° 1, pp. 55-59.

Zarlino, Gioseffo, 1558. *Le Istitutioni harmoniche di M. Gioseffo Zarlino da Chiogga, nelle quali oltra le materie appartenti alla musica, si trovano dichiarati molti luoghi vedere*, Venise.

Zemp, Hugo; Trân quang, Hai, 1991. « Recherches expérimentales sur le chant diphonique », *Cahiers de musiques traditionnelles*, vol. 4, « Voix », pp. 27-68.

Discographie indicative

Touva

Bois, Pierre (prod.), 1996. *Chants épiques et diphoniques. Touva, Tadjikistan, Kalmoukie, Chor (Asie centrale et Sibérie)*, Paris, INÉDIT/Maison des cultures du monde, n° W 260 067.

Shu-de, 1994. *Voices from the Distant Steppe*, Londres, Realworld, n° CDRW 41.

Tumat, Gennadi ; Kuular, German ; Kuular Oleg *et al.,* 1993. *C''oomej : ThroatSinging from the Center of Asia*, Frankfort, World Network, n° 55.838.

Huun-Huur-Tu, 1993. *Sixty Horses In My Herd. Old Songs and Tunes of Tuva*, New Jersey, Shanachie Records, n° 64050.

Tuva Ensemble, 1992. *Echoes from the Spirit World*, Leyde, Pan Records, n° PAN 2013 CD.

Ondar, Kongar-ool; Khovalig, Kaigal-ool; Tumat, Gennadi, 1991. *Tuva. Voices from the Land of Eagles*, Leyde, Pan Records, n° PAN 2005 CD.

Ozum, [Sprouts], 1991. *Young Voices of Ancient Tuva*, Amsterdam, Window to Europe, n° SUM 90 008.

Levin, Ted; Alexeev, Eduard; Kirgiz, Zoya (prod.), 1990. Tuva. *Voices from the Center of Asia*, Washington DC/Cambridge (USA), Smithsonian Folkways/ Rounder Records, n° CD SF 40017.

Mongolie

Melodies of the Steppes, 1992. White Moon (Tsagaan Sar). *Traditional and Popular Music from Mongolia*, Leyde, Pan Records, coll. « Ethnic Series », n° PAN 2010 CD.

Bois, Pierre (prod.), 1989. *Mongolie. Musique vocale et instrumentale*, Paris, INÉDIT/Maison des cultures du monde, n° W 260 009.

Collectif, 1986. *Mongolie. Musique et chants de tradition populaire*, Paris, Groupe de recherches et d'études des musiques (GREM), n° G 7511.

Bashkirie, Altaï, Touva

Mongush, Boris ; Kuular, Sergei ; Khunashtaar-ool, Oorzhak *et al.*, 1993. Uzlyau. Gutteral Singing from the Sayan, Altai And Ural Mountains, Leyde, Pan Records, n° PAN 2019 CD.

Afrique du Sud

The Ngqoko Women's Ensemble, 1996. *Le Chant des femmes Xhosa (Afrique du Sud)*, Genève, VDE-Gallo Records, n° VDE 879.

Collectif, 1996. *Les Voix du monde. Une anthologie des expressions vocales*, Paris, CNRS/Musée de l'Homme, coll. « Le chant du monde », n° CMX 374 1010.12.

Filmographie indicative

Béguinet, Christian, 2004. *Le Chant diphonique*, écrit par Trân Quang Hai & Luc Souvet, Saint-Denis de la Réunion, CRDP de la Réunion, DVD, vidéo, 27 min.

Zemp, Hugo, 2005 [1989]. *Le Chant des Harmoniques*, écrit par Trân Quang Hai & Hugo Zemp, Paris, CNRS Audiovisuel/Société française d'ethnomusicologie, DVD, 16 mm, 38 min.

Kersalé, Patrick, 2006. *La Voix,* Lyon, Éditions musicales Lugdivine, coll. « Thèm'Axe », DVD, vidéo, 100 min.

Tran Quang Hai et le sonagraph, 2000

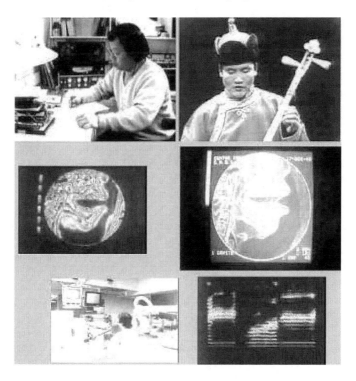

Extraits d'images du film Le Chant des Harmoniques avec Tran Quang Hai, 1998

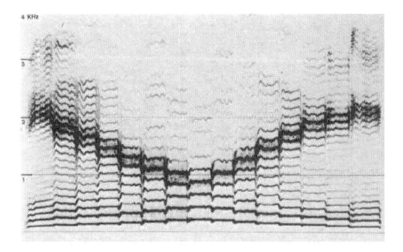

Analyse spectrale de la voix diphonique de Tran Quang Hai ,2002

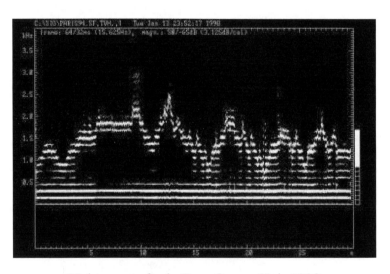

Voix spectrale de Tran Quang Hai, 1998

Original Research and Acoustical Analysis in connection with the Xöömij Style of Biphonic Singing

Tran Quang Hai, Centre National de la Recherche Scientitique, Paris 1980.

Denis GUILLOU, Conservatoire. National des Arts et Métiers, Paris.

The present article is limited in its scope to our own original research and to acoustical analysis of biphonic singing, this is preceded by a summary of the various terms proposed by different researchers. The first half the article concerning xöömij technique was written by Tran Quang Hai. Guillou has written the second half concerning acoustical analysis.

Until the present time it has not been possible to confirm that the centre, of biphonic singing within Turco-Mongol culture is in fact Mongolia. Biphonic singing is also employed by neighbouring peoples such as the Tuvins (Touvins), Oirats, Khakass, Gorno-Altais and Baschkirs; it is called kai by the Altais, uzliau by the Baschkirs, and the Tuvins possess four different styles called, *sygyt, borbannadyr, ezengileer* and kargyraa. A considerable amount of research is at present being carried out throughout the world into this vocal phenomenon, particularly as it is practised in Mongolia.

Research can be carried out in various ways: by means of observation of native performers after one or more visits to the country concerned, or by means of practical instrumental or vocal studies aimed at a better understanding of the musical structure employed by the population being studied. My own research does not belong to either of these two categories since I have never been to Mongolia and I have never learned the xöömij style of biphonic singing from a Mongolian teacher. What 1 shall describe in this article is the result of my own experience which will enable anybody to produce two simultaneous sounds similar to Mongolian biphonic singing.

Definition

Simultaneous two-part singing by a single person is known in the Mongol language as xöömij (literally "pharynx"). The manner in which the Mongol word is transcribed is by no means uniform; *ho-mi, ho-mi,* (Vargyas 1968), *khomi, khöömii,* (Bosson 1964: 11), *xomej, chöömej,* (Aksenov 1964) *chöömij,* (Vietze 1969:15-16. Walcott 1974) *xöömij,* (Hamayon 1973). French researchers have used other terms to describe this particular vocal technique such as *chant biphonique* or *diphonique (Leipp* 1971, Tran Quang Hai 1974). *voix guimbarde. voix dédoublee* (Heitfer 1973, Hamayon 1973), and *chant diphonique* solo (Marcel-Dubois 1979). Several terms exist in English such as split-tone singing, throat singing and overtone singing, and in German*sweistimmigen Sologesang.*

For convenience 1 have employed in this article the term biphonic singing to describe a style of singing realized by a single person producing simultaneously a continuous drone and another sound at a higher pitch issuing from a series of partials or harmonies resembling the sound of the flute.

Origin of My Research

In 1971, the date of my first contact with Mongolian music in the form of recordings made in Mongolia between 1967 and 1970 by Mrs. Roberte Hamayon, researcher at the Centre National de la Recherche Scientifique and especially after listening to a tape on which were recorded three pieces in the biphonic singing style, I was struck by the extraordinary and unique nature of this vocal technique.

For several months I carried out bibliographical research into articles concerned with this style of singing with the aim of obtaining information on the practice of biphonic singing, but received little satisfaction. Explanations of a merely theoretical and sometimes ambiguous nature did nothing so much as to create and increase the confusion with which my research was surrounded. In spite of my complete ignorance of the training methods for biphonic singing practised by the Mongols, the Tuvins and other peoples, I was not in the least discouraged by the negative results at the beginning of my studies after even several months of effort.

Working Conditions

According to Hamayon, the xöömij, which exists throughout Mongolia but is gradually dying out, is practised exclusively by men. It represents an imitation, by means of a single voice of two instruments, the flute and the Jew's harp.

The xöömij refers to the simultaneous production of two sounds, one similar to the fundamental produced on the Jew's harp (produced at the back of the throat), and the other resulting from a modification of the buccal cavity without moving the lips which remain only slightly open; positioning the lips as for a rear vowel results in a low sound, whereas front vowel positioning produces a high sound (Hamayon 1973), a technique similar to that used by the Tuvins (Aksenov 1964). The cheeks are tightened to such a degree that the singer breaks out into a sweat. It is the position of the tongue which determines the melody. Anybody who possesses this technique is able to copy any tune (Hamayon 1973).

I worked entirely alone groping my way through the dark for two years, listening frequently to the recordings made by Hamayon stored in the sound archives of the ethnomusicology department of the Musee de l'Homme. My efforts were however to no avail. Despite my efforts and knowledge of Jew's harp technique, the initial work was both difficult and discouraging. 1 also tried to whistle while producing a low sound as a drone. However, checking on a sonograph showed that this was not similar to the xöömij technique. At the end of 1972 I got to the stage that I was able to produce a very weak harmonic tone which when recorded on tape, showed that 1 was still a long way from my goal. Then, one day in November 1973, in order to calm my nerves in the appalling traffic congestion of Paris, I happened to make my vocal chords vibrate in the pharynx with my mouth half open while reciting the alphabet. When I arrived at the letter L and the tip of my tongue was about to touch the top of my mouth, I suddenly heard a pure harmonic tone, clear and powerful. I repeated the operation several times and each time I obtained the same result. I then tried to modify the position of the tongue in relation to the foot of the mouth while maintaining the low fundamental. A series of partials resonated in disorder inside my ears.

At the beginning I obtained the harmonics of a perfect chord. Slowly but surely, after a week of intensive work, by changing the fundamental tone upwards or downwards, 1 had managed to discover all by myself a vocal jaw's harp technique or biphonic singing style which appeared to be similar to that used by the Mongols and the Tuvins.

Basic Techniques

After two months of research and numerous experiments of all kinds I was able to establish some of the basic rules for the realization of what I call biphonic singing.

1) Half open the mouth.

2) Emit a natural sound on the letter A without forcing the voice and remaining in the middle part of the vocal range (between F and A below middle C for men, and between F and A above middle C for women).

3) Intensify the vocal production while vibrating the vocal chords.

4) Force out the breath and hold it for as long as possible.

5) Produce the letter L. Maintain the position with the tip of the tongue touching the roof of the mouth.

181

6) Intensify the tonal volume while trying to keep the tongue stuck firmly against the palate in order to divide the mouth into two cavities, one at the back and one at the front, so that the air column increases in volume through the mouth and the nose.

7) Slowly pronounce the sounds represented by the phonetic signs "ï" anti *"u"* while varying the position of the lips.

8) Modify the buccal cavity by changing the position of the tongue inside the mouth without interrupting or changing the height of the fundamental already amplified by the vibration of the vocal chords.

9) In this way it is possible to obtain both the drone arid the partials or harmonics either in ascending or descending order according to the desire of the singer.

For beginners the harmonics of the perfect chord (C. E. G. C) are easy to obtain. However, a considerable amount of hard work is necessary, especially to obtain a pentatonic anhemitonic scale. Every person has his favourite note which permits him to produce a large range of partials. This favourite fundamental tone varies according to the tonal quality of the singer's voice and his windpipe. It often happens that two people using the same fundamental tone do riot necessarily obtain the same series of partials.

Regular practice and the application of the basic techniques which 1 have just described above permitted me to acquire a range of between an eleventh and a thirteenth according to the choice of the drone. Biphonic singing can also be practised by women and children, and several successful experiments have been carried out in this connection.

Other experiments which I have been carrying out recently indicate that it is possible to obtain two simultaneous sounds in two other ways. In the first method, the tongue may be either flat or slightly curved without actually at any stage touching the root of the mouth, and only the mouth and the lips move. Through such variation of the buccal cavity, this time divided into a single cavity it is possible to hear the partials faintly.

In the second method the basic technique described above is used. However instead of keeping the mouth half open it is kept almost completely shut with the lips pulled back and very tight. To make the partials audible, the position of the lips is varied at the same time as that of the tongue. The partials are very clear and distinctive, but the technique is rather exhausting and it is not possible to sing for a long time using it.

In the northeast of Mongolia in the borderland area between Mongolia and Siberia live the Tuvins, a people of Turkish origin numbering one hundred thousand. The Tuvins possess not only the biphonic singing style used by the Mongols, but four other different styles within this genre, called svgyt, *ezengileer. kargyraa* and *borbannadyr.* Table 1 will facilitate comparison between these four styles.

Biphonic singing is also practised by a number of ethnic groups in the republics of the Soviet Union bordering on Mongolia.

The late John Levy made a recording in Rajasthan in 1967 on which can be heard an example of biphonic singing similar to that practised by the Mongols and the Tuvins (1). The virtuoso performer in the recording imitates the double flute called the satara (an instrument producing simultaneously a drone and a melody) or the Jew's harp with his voice. However, this may well be an exceptional example in that no mention is ever made of biphonic singing techniques in the musical traditions of Rajasthan or elsewhere in India.

183

Tibetan monks, particularly those in the monasteries of Gyume and Gyuto (2), make use of a technique using two simultaneous voices, although this technique is far less developed than that used by the Mongols and the Tuvins. The low register of the drone makes it impossible to produce harmonics as clear and resonant as those emitted by the Mongols and the Tuvins, and furthermore the production of harmonics is not the aim of Tibetan Buddhist chant.

In Western contemporary music groups of singers have also succeeded in emitting two voices at the same time and vocal pieces have been created in the context of avant-garde music (3) and in recent years of electronic music (4).

An X-ray film was mode for the first time in 1974 at the Centre Medico-chirurgical of the Porte do Choisy in Paris at the request of Professor S. Borel-Maisonny, speech therapist and of Professor Emile Leipp, acoustician. This film which was made with the cooperation of the present author made it possible to examine closely the internal functioning and placement of the tongue during biphonic singing, and was thus of great interest. Thanks to this film the author has improved his biphonic singing technique as a result of which he has been able to decrease the volume of the drone and increase that of the harmonics.

Table 1: Characteristics of the biphonic singing styles of the Tuvins

Pitch of the drone or fundamental

SYGYT: changes in the course of singing

EZENGILEER: no change

KARGYRAA: no change, althouth sometimes lowered by a minor third

BORBANNADYR: no change

Tonality

SYGYT: more intense and higher than that of the Kargyraa style

EZENGILEER: same as Sygyt

KARGYRAA: low

BORBANNADYR: soft

Position of the mouth

SYGYT: half open

EZENGILEER: half open

KARGYRAA: half open

BORBANNADYR: almost closed

Harmonics or partials

SYGYT: 8,9,10 for uneven verses, 8,9,10,12 for even verses

EZENGILEER: (6), 8,9,10, 11,12,13

KARGYRAA: (6), 8,9,10,11,12

BORBANNADYR: 6,7,8,9,10,12,13

Special features

SYGYT: Harmonics used as an ostinato accompaniment, thus resulting in a narrow range in the course of a song, at the end of each phrase a note is held (fundamental for uneven verses or a descending tone for an even verses)

EZENGILEER: Alternation of strong and weak accents like a gallop rhythm

KARGYRAA: Each vowel corresponds to a partial – Psalmodic recitation with or without special text on two pitches or drone in two positions rising and descending by a minor third – Called Borbannadyr in cases when the Borbannadyr is named Khomei

BORBANNADYR: -Occasionally three voices with two used as a drone: tonic & fifth (in exceptional cases) and third voice producing melodic harmonics – Called Khomei in certain areas.

Acoustical Analysis-introduction

The present study is concerned with biphonic singing its understanding and interpretation, and does not constitute a complete and definitive piece of research. In fact, the discovery of certain phenomena permits us only to imagine what might be the reality, this being particularly true in relation to the mechanism involved in the production of biphonic singing. Thus, it will be necessary to carry out further research in the following areas: psycho -acoustics and particularly the perception of pitch and phonatory acoustics.

Biphonic singing differs from so-called natural singing on account of its sonority as well as of course the vocal technique involved. As its name indicates it consists of two sounds. On the basis of simple aural observation, it is possible to distinguish a first sound whose pitch is constant and which we shall call the drone and a second sound which takes the form of a melody which the singer can

186

produce at will. It is basically possible for anybody to produce this biphonic sonority but to make the second voice dominate and to trace a melody with it depends upon the talent of the artist.

Firstly, we shall examine the concept of pitch perception in terms of acoustics and psycho-acoustics. Secondly, we shall try to define biphonic singing, to differentiate it from other vocal techniques and to specify its scope. It will then be worthwhile to formulate several hypotheses concerning the mechanism whereby this style of singing is produced and finally to present a few examples of such a technique.

Pitch Perception

It is first of all necessary to comprehend exactly what is meant by the pitch of sounds or tonality. This concept presents a considerable amount of ambiguity and does not correspond to the simple principle of the measurement of the frequencies produced. The pitch of sounds is related more to psycho-acoustics than to physics.

Our own proposals are based partially on the recent discoveries of certain researchers, and partially on observations which we have made ourselves with the help of a sonagraph machine.

The sonagraph makes it possible for us to obtain the image of the sound which we wish to study. On a single piece of paper is given information concerning time and frequency, and, in accordance with the thickness of the line traced information concerning intensity.

The classical manuals on acoustics tell us that the pitch of harmonic sounds, that is sounds with, for example a fundamental with the frequency F and a series of harmonic, F1, F2. F3.... multiples of F. is determined by the frequency of the first fundamental F. This is not entirely correct in that it is possible to suppress electronically this fundamental without thereby changing the subjective pitch of the actually perceived sound. If this theory were correct an electro-acoustic chain not reproducing the lowest sound would change the pitch of the sounds. This is evidently not the case since the tonal quality changes but not the pitch. Certain researchers have proposed a theory which would appear to be more coherent: the pitch of sounds is determined by the separation of the harmonic lines or the difference in frequency between two harmonic lines. What is the pitch of the sounds, in this case for sonic spectra with "partials" (harmonics are not complete multiples of the fundamental)? In this case, the individual perceives an average of the separation of the lines in the zone which interests him. This in fact corresponds with the differences in perception which may be observed from one individual to the other (Fig. 1).

Fig. 1 Sonagram representation of three types of sound

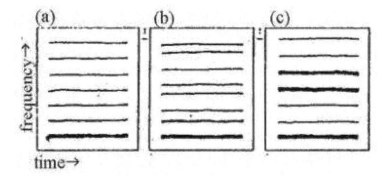

a)   Harmonic spectrum: the harmonics are whole multiples of the fundamental.

b) Partials spectrum: the harmonics are no longer whole multiples of the fundamental.

c) Formant spectrum: two harmonics are intense and constitute a formant in the harmonic spectrum.

Formant spectrum: the accentuation in intensity of a group of harmonics constitutes a formant and is thus a zone of frequencies in which there is a large amount of energy.

Taking this formant into consideration a second concept of the perception of pitch comes to light. It has in effect been established that the position of the formant in the sonic spectrum results in the perception of a new pitch. In this case it is no longer a matter of the separation of the harmonic lines in the formant zone but of the position of the formant in the spectrum. This theory should be qualified however, since conditions also have to be considered.

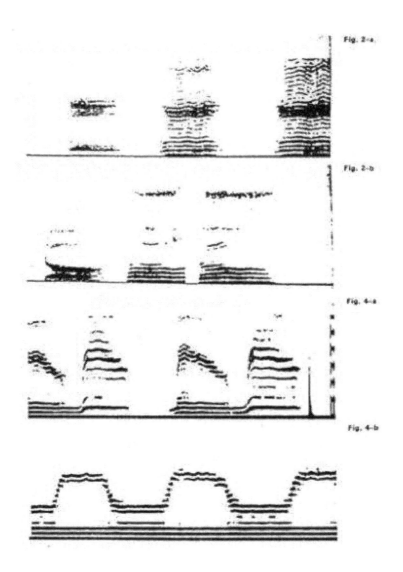

Experiment: Tran Quang Hai sang two C's an octave apart making his voice carry as if he were addressing a large audience. We observed, using a sonagram, that the maximum energy was situated in the zone perceptible by the human car (3, 4 KHz) and that the formant was situated between 2 and 4 KHz. We then recorded two C's an octave apart in the same tonality, but this time he used his voice as it addressing a small audience, and we observed the disappearance of this formant (Fig. 2-a. 2-b).

In this case the disappearance of the formant does not change the pitch of the sounds. We then rapidly observed that the perception of pitch through the position of the formant was only possible it the formant was very acute for knowing that the sonic energy was only divided on two or three harmonics. Thus, if the energy density of the formant is large and the formant is narrow the formant gives information concerning the pitch as well as the overall tonality of the sonic item. Through this expedient we arrive at the biphonic vocal technique.

Fig. 4 Normal singing and biphonic singing

a) Sonagraph representation of normal singing. An octave passage is equivalent to a doubling of the gap between the harmonic lines and to a drone of double frequency, (The first bar represents the base line of the sonagram, and the drone is represented by the second bar.)

b) Sonagraph representation of biphonic singing. An octave passage is represented by a displacement of the formant. The harmonic lines of the formant are displaced in a zone in which the frequency is doubled.

Comparison between Biphonic Technique and Classical Technique

It may be said that biphonic singing consists as its name indicates, of the production of two sounds, one a drone which is low and constant, and the other at a higher pitch consisting of a formant which displaces itself in the spectrum in order to produce a certain melody. The concept of pitch given by the second voice is moreover somewhat ambiguous. The Western ear may need a certain amount of training before becoming accustomed to the sound quality.

Evidence concerning the drone is relatively easy to obtain thanks to the sonagram: it can be seen clearly and is also very clear on an auditory level. The device in Fig. 3 also makes it possible to see a pure amplitude frequency of a constant nature.

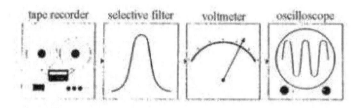

Fig. 3 Device for providing evidence of perfect constancy of the drone in intensity and frequency.

After having examined the fundamental tone we compared two spectra, one of biphonic singing and the other of the so-called classical singing style, the two being produced by the same singer. The sonagrams of these two types of singing are shown in Fig. 4. Classical singing is characterized by a doubling of the separation of the harmonic lines when an octave is exceeded (a). Biphonic singing is characterized on the other hand by the fact that the separation of the lines remains constant (this was foreseeable since the drone is constant), and that the formant is displaced by an octave (b). In fact, it is easy to measure the distance between the lines for each sound. In this case, the perception of the melody in biphonic singing works through the expedient of the displacement of the formant in the sonic spectrum.

It should be stressed that this is only really possible if the formant is high, and this is obviously so in the case of biphonic singing. The sonic energy is divided principally between the drone and the second voice consisting of two or at the most three harmonics.

It has sometimes been stated that it is possible to produce a third voice. Using the sonagrarn we have in actual fact established that this third voice exists (see sonograms of Tuvin techniques), but it is impossible to state that it can be controlled. In our opinion this additional voice results more from the personality of the performer than from any particular technique.

As a result of our work we have been able to establish a parallel between biphonic singing and the technique of the Jew's harp. As in the case of biphonic singing the Jew's harp produces several different voices, the drone, the main melody and a counter melody. We may consider this third voice as a counter melody which may be produced on a conscious level but can presumably not be controlled. As far as possibility of variation is concerned, biphonic singing is the same as normal singing except in connection with pitch range.

The time of execution is evidently a function of the thoracic cage of the singer and thus of breathing, since the intensity is related to the output of air. Possibility of variation with regard to intensity is on the other hand relatively restricted and the level of the harmonics is connected to the level of the drone. The singer has to try and retain a suitable drone and produce the harmonics as strongly as possible. We have already observed that the clearer the harmonics the more the formant is narrow and intense. We are able furthermore to observe connections between intensity, time and clarity. Possibility of variation in relation to tone quality may pass without comment, since the resulting sound is in the majority of cases formed from a drone and one or two harmonics. The most interesting question is that of pitch range.

Table 2   Pitch range of biphonic singing for several tonalities

Tonality	Notes	Range	No. of harmonics
C_2	E_4 G_4 A_4 C_5 D_5 E_5 G_5 A_5 C_6	thirteenth	9
D_2	D_4 $F^{\sharp}_4 A_4$ B_4 D_5 E_5 $F^{\sharp}_5 A_5$ B_5	thirteenth	9
E_2	E_4 $G^{\sharp}_4 B_4$ $C^{\sharp}_5 E_5$ $F^{\sharp}_5 G^{\sharp}_5 B_5$	twelfth	8
F_2	F_4 A_4 C_5 D_5 F_5 G_5 A_5 C_6	twelfth	8
G_2	D_4 G_4 B_4 D_5 E_5 G_5 A_5 B_5	thirteenth	8
A_2	E_4 A_4 $C^{\sharp}_5 E_5$ $F^{\sharp}_5 A_5$ B_5	twelfth	7
B_2	$F^{\sharp}_4 B_4$ $D^{\sharp}_5 F^{\sharp}_5 G^{\sharp}_5 B_5$	eleventh	6
C_3	G_4 C_5 E_5 G_5 A_5 C_6	eleventh	6

(Table drawn up by Trần Quang Hải and verified acoustically)

It is generally accepted that, for a sensible tonality (in consideration of the performer and of the piece to be performed a singer may modulate or choose between harmonics 5 and 13. This is true but should be stated more precisely. The range is a function of the tonality. If the tonality is on C2, the range represents nine harmonics from the fifth to the thirteenth, this involving a range of a major thirteenth. If the tonality is raised for example to C3 the choice is made between six harmonics, numbers 3 to 8 (see Table 2), representing an interval of an seventh. The following remarks should be made in this context. Firstly, the pitch range of biphonic singing is more restricted than that of normal singing. Secondly, the singer theoretically selects the tonality which he wishes between C2 and C3. In practice however, he instinctively produces a compromise between the clarity of the second voice and the pitch range of his singing, since the choice of the tonality is also a function of the musical piece to be performed. Thus, if the tonality is raised, for example to C3, the choice of harmonics is restricted but the second voice is very clear. In the case of a tonality on C2 the second voice is more indistinct while the pitch range is at a maximum. The clarity of the sounds can be explained by the fact that in the first case, the singer is only able to select a single harmonic, whereas in the second case, he may select almost two (see Fig.5). As far as pitch range is concerned, it is known that the movement of the buccal resonators is independent of the tonality of the sounds produced by

194

the vocal chords, or, put in another way. The singer always selects harmonics in the same zone of the spectrum whether the harmonics are broad or narrow.

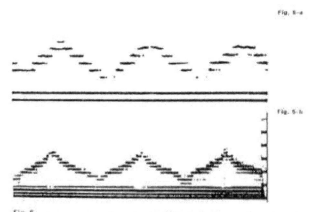

Fig. 5
a) Ascending and descending scale—G, C, E, G, A, C. The drone (second bar) is C_3. The pitch range is narrow (an eleventh) but the harmonics are clearly audible.
b) Ascending and descending scale—E, G, A, C, D, E, G, A, C, in the tonality C_2 (a thirteenth). The pitch range is the maximum but the harmonics seem less clear than before.

It results from all this that the singer chooses the tonality instinctively in order to have the maximum range and clarity. For Tran Quang Hai, the best compromise exists between C2 and A2. He can thus obtain a range of between an octave and a thirteenth.

Mechanism for the Production of Biphonic Singing

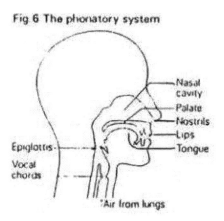

Fig 6 The phonatory system

It is always very difficult to know what is taking place inside a machine when we are placed outside it and can only watch it in operation. This is the case with the phonatory mechanism. The following remarks are only approximate and of a schematic nature and should not be assumed to be the final word on the subject. In dealing by analogy with the phonatory system we can get an idea of the mechanisms but surely not a complete explanation. Fig. 6 is a representation of the phonatory system which can be compared with Fig. 7, showing an excitation system producing harmonic sounds and a series of resonating systems amplifying certain parts of this spectrum.

Fig. 7 Schematic functioning of the phonatory system

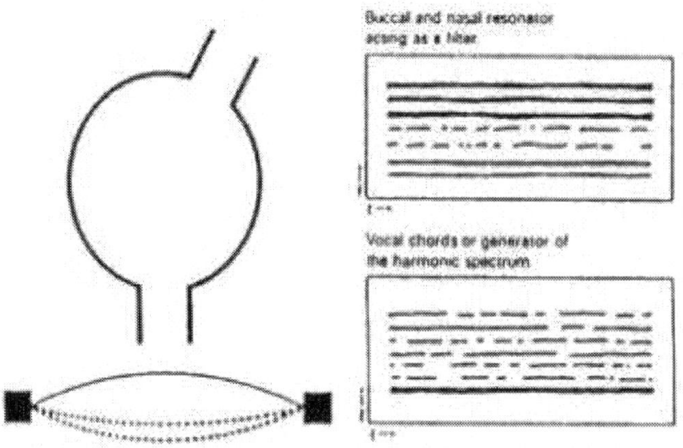

A resonator is a cavity equipped with a neck capable of resonating in a certain range of frequencies. The excitation system, i.e., the pharynx and the vocal chords emits a harmonic spectrum consisting of the frequencies F1, F2. F3. F4 ... of resonators which select certain frequencies

$$\text{fo} = \frac{c}{2\pi}\sqrt{\frac{s}{lv}}$$

and amplify them. The choice of these frequencies evidently depends upon the ability of the singer. This is the case when a singer projects his voice within a large hail in that he instinctively adapts his resonators in order to produce the maximum energy within the area in which the ear is sensitive.

It should be noted that the amplified frequencies are a function of the volume of the cavity, the section of the opening and the length of the neck constituting the opening:

Through this principle it is possible to see already the action of the size of the buccal cavity, of the opening of the mouth, and of the position of the lips during singing.

However, this does not tell us anything about biphonic singing. In practice we need two voices. The first, the drone, is given to us simply by virtue of the fact that its production is intense, and that in any case, it does not undergo filtering by the resonators. Its intensity, higher than that of the harmonics, permits it to survive on account of buccal and nasal diffusion. We have observed that as the nasal cavity was closed, so the drone diminished in intensity. This occurs for two reasons, firstly that a source of diffusion is closed through the nose and secondly, by closing the nose the flow of air is reduced, as is the sonic intensity produced at the level of the vocal chords.

The possession of several cavities is of prime importance. In practice, we have established that only coupling between several cavities has enabled us to have a sharp formant such as is required by biphonic singing.

For the purposes of this research we initially carried out investigations into the principle of resonators in order to determine the influence of the fundamental parameters. It was observed that the tonality of the sound rises if the mouth is opened wider. In order to investigate the formation of a sharp formant, we carried out the following experiment. Tran Quang Hai produced two kinds of biphonic singing, one with the tongue at rest. i.e., not dividing the mouth into two cavities and the other with the mouth divided into two cavities. The observation which we made is as follows (an observation which could have been foreseen on the basis of the theory of coupled resonators).

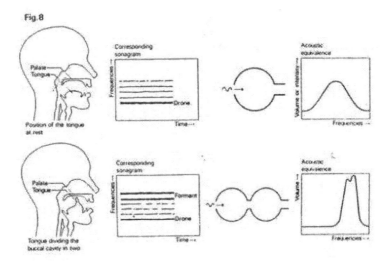

Fig. 8

In the first case the sounds were not clear: the drone could be heard distinctly but the second voice was difficult to bear. There was no clear distinction between the two voices, and, furthermore, the melody was indistinct. The corresponding sonagrams bore this out: with a single buccal cavity the energy of the formant is dispersed over three or four harmonics and so the sense of a second voice is very much on the weak side. On the other hand, when the tongue divides the mouth into two cavities, the formant reappears in a sharp and intense manner. In other words, the harmonic sounds produced by the vocal chords are filtered and amplified in a rough manner with a single buccal cavity and the biphonic effect disappears. Biphonic singing thus necessitates a network of very selective resonators which filters only the harmonics required by the singer. Fig. 8 shows the responses in frequencies of the resonators, both simple and coupled. In the case of a tight coupling between the two cavities, these produce a single and very sharp resonance. If the coupling is loose, the formant has less intensity and the sonic energy in the spectrum is stemmed. If the cavities are transformed into a single cavity, the pointed eee becomes even rounder, and one ends up with the first example with a very blurred type of biphonic singing (tongue at rest). The conclusion can be drawn that the mouth along with the position of the tongue plays the major role, and it can be compared roughly to a pointed filter which changes its place in the spectrum with the sole aim of selecting the interesting harmonics.

We should like to express our gratitude and sincere thanks to Research Team 165 of the Centre National de la Recherche Scientifique directed by Mr. Gilbert Rouget, who allowed us access to valuable documents concerning biphonic singing stored in the sound archives of his department. Our thanks go also to Professor Claudie Marcel-Dubois, Head of the Department of Ethnomusicology at tile Musee National des Arts et Traditions Populaires, who gave us a great deal of help and encouragement. We should like also to thank Professor Emile Leipp, Dr. Michele Castellengo and Professor Solange Borel-Maisonny, who made it possible for us to examine the internal functioning of biphonic singing by means of the production of a radiographic film.

(Translated from French by Robin THOMPSON)

NOTES

1. This tape is preserved in the Ethnomusicology Department of the Musee de L'Homme. Paris. Archive number BM 78 2, 1.

2. See the record "The Music of Tibet." recorded by Peter Crossley-Holland, Anthology Records (30133) AST 4005, New York, 1970.

3. See the record "The tail of the Tiger." Ananda 2.

4. An example is the electronic music composition entitled "Ve nguon" (Return to the Source), composed by Nquyen Van Tuong, with Tran Quang Hai as soloist. The first performance was given in France in 1975. The third movement (25 minutes) uses biphonic singing.

http://soundtransformations.co.uk/tranquanghaiguillouacouticalan alysisxoomij.htm

Recherches expérimentales sur le chant diphonique

Hugo Zemp et Trần Quang Hải

National Center for Scientific Research, France.

Ces recherches ont été effectuées dans le cadre de l'Unité Propre de Recherche n° 165 du CNRS, au Département d'ethnomusicologie du Musée de l'Homme

La dénomination « chant diphonique » désigne une technique vocale singulière selon laquelle une seule personne chante à deux voix : un bourdon constitué par le son fondamental, et une mélodie superposée formée par des harmoniques.

Les détails de la réalisation de ce film – dont la première a eu lieu le 27 juillet 1989 lors du Congrès international de l'ICTM à Schladming en Autriche.

Recherche menée en étroite collaboration par les deux co-auteurs. Cet article est issu de deux approches complémentaires : une recherche pragmatique par l'apprentissage et l'exercice du chant diphonique que Trân Quang Hai mène depuis 1971, et une recherche de visualisation conduite sur le plan physiologique et acoustique pour la préparation et la production du film *Le chant des harmoniques*, réalisé par Hugo Zemp en 1988-89. Dans ce film, Trân Quang Hai est l'acteur principal, tour à tour chanteur et ethnomusicologue : enseignant le chant diphonique lors d'un atelier, interviewant des chanteurs mongols, se prêtant à la radiocinématographie avec traitement informatique de l'image, et chantant dans le microphone du spectrographe pour analyser ensuite sa propre technique vocale[2]. Les images spectrographiques que nous avons découvertes pratiquement en même temps que nous les filmions – le dernier modèle de Sona-Graph permettant l'analyse du spectre sonore en temps réel et son synchrone était arrivé au Département d'ethnomusicologie du Musée de l'Homme quelques jours avant le tournage – nous ont encouragés à poursuivre ces investigations et à les conduire dans une direction que nous n'aurions probablement pas envisagée sans la réalisation du film.

Paru dans une nouvelle publication : le Dossier n° 1 de l'Institut de la Voix, Limoges. Outre deux brefs rapports relatant des examens cliniques et paracliniques de l'appareil phonatoire et de l'émission diphonique de Trân Quang Hai, examens effectués l'un par un médecin O.R.L. (Sauvage, 1989) et l'autre par un phoniâtre (Pailler, 1989), ce dossier contient la bibliographie et la discographie les plus complète à ce jour concernant le chant diphonique.

L'utilisation des outils spectrographiques pour l'analyse des chants diphoniques n'est pas nouvelle : Leipp (1971), Hamayon (1973), Walcott (1974), Borel-Maisonny et Castellengo (1976), Trân Quang Hai et Guillou (1980), Gunji (1980), Harvilahti (1983), Harvilahti et Kaskinen (1983), Desjacques (1988), Léothaud (1989). Il n'est pas question, dans le cadre de cet article, d'évaluer ces travaux, d'en résumer les résultats ou d'en faire l'historique. Dans l'étude la plus récente, G. Léothaud (1989 : 20-21) résume excellemment ce qu'il appelle la « genèse acoustique du chant diphonique » :

L'appareil phonatoire, comme tout instrument de musique, se compose d'un système excitateur, ici le larynx, et d'un corps vibrant chargé de transformer l'énergie reçue en rayonnement acoustique, le conduit pharyngo-buccal.
Le larynx délivre un spectre harmonique, le son laryngé primaire, déterminé en fréquence, d'allure homogène, c'est-à-dire dénué de formants notables – donc de couleur vocalique – et dont la richesse en harmoniques varie essentiellement en fonction de la structure vibratoire des cordes vocales.

Cette fourniture primaire traverse les cavités pharyngo-buccales, y subissant d'importantes distorsions : le pharynx et la bouche se comportent donc comme des résonateurs de Helmholtz, et cela pour toutes les fréquences dont la longueur d'onde est supérieure à la plus grande dimension de ces cavités.
Les paramètres déterminant la fréquence propre des cavités phonatoires peuvent varier dans des proportions considérables grâce au système articulateur, notamment par la mobilité de la mâchoire, l'ouverture de la bouche et la position de la langue. Celle-ci, surtout, peut diviser la cavité buccale en deux résonateurs de plus petit volume, donc de fréquence propre plus élevée. En d'autres termes, les cavités buccales peuvent continuer à se comporter en résonateurs de Helmholtz même pour des harmoniques très aigus du spectre

laryngé, ceux dont la longueur d'onde est petite, et en tout cas inférieure à la longueur du conduit pharyngo-buccal.

L'émission diphonique consiste pour le chanteur à émettre un spectre riche en harmoniques, puis à accorder très finement une cavité phonatoire sur l'un des composants de ce spectre, dont l'amplitude augmente ainsi fortement par résonance ; par déplacement de la langue, le volume buccal peut varier, donc la fréquence propre, et sélectionner de cette façon différents harmoniques.

Il propose une grille d'analyse, axée sur quatre niveaux et douze critères pertinents. *1°* Caractéristiques du spectre vocal ; *2°* Nature du formant diphonique ; *3°* Caractéristiques de la mélodie d'harmoniques ; *4°* Champ de liberté de la fluctuation diphonique. L'application de cette grille permet d'approfondir et de systématiser l'analyse spectrale du chant diphonique qui peut maintenant s'appuyer sur de nombreux nouveaux documents sonores publiés récemment sur des disques, s'ajoutant aux anciens bien connus. Cependant, tel n'est pas notre but.

La translittération change selon les auteurs *xöömij*, *khöömii*, *chöömij*, *ho-mi*.

Nous nous proposons d'examiner comment les différents styles ou variantes stylistiques du chant diphonique – appelé chez les Mongols *khöömii*[5] (« pharynx, gorge ») et chez les Touvains de l'URSS *khoomei* (du terme mongol) – sont produits sur le plan physiologique. Dans ce domaine, les descriptions sont rares et peu détaillées, alors qu'on connaît depuis de nombreuses années les noms vernaculaires désignant ces styles chez les Touvains dont Aksenov (1973 : 12) pense qu'ils forment le centre de la culture turco-mongole du chant diphonique, puisqu'ils ne pratiquent pas seulement une mais quatre variantes stylistiques (*kargiraa*, *borbannadir*, *sigit*, *ezengileer* ; un cinquième nom, *khoomei* qui est en même temps le nom générique du chant diphonique, remplaçant dans certains lieux le terme *borbannadir*). Implicitement, les peuples voisins qu'il cite – Mongols, Oirats, Kharkass, Gorno-Altaïs et Bashkirs – n'en connaîtraient qu'un seul style. En tout cas, pour les Mongols et pour les Altaï de l'URSS, montagnards habitant la chaîne du même nom, cela n'est pas exact. Les derniers utilisent trois styles nommés sur la notice d'un disque *sibiski*, *karkira*, *kiomioi* (Petrov et Tikhonurov). Le chanteur diphonique le plus connu en Mongolie et à l'étranger, D. Sundui, a énuméré cinq styles lors du festival *Musical Voices of Asia* au Japon : *xarkiraa xöömij* (*xöömij* narratif), *xamrijn xöömij* (*xöömij* de nez), *bagalzuurijn xöömij* (*xöömij* de gorge), *tseedznii xöömij* (*xöömij* de poitrine), *kevliin xöömij* (*xöömij* de ventre), les deux derniers n'étant généralement pas différenciés (Emmert et Minegishi 1980 : 48). Dans l'interview du film *Le chant des harmoniques*, T. Ganbold indique les même cinq noms. Il présente brièvement les quatres premiers styles, en ajoutant qu'il ne sait pas faire le « *khöömii* de ventre », le distinguant par là du « *khöömii* de poitrine ». Mais il n'explique pas comment il produit ces différents styles. Il est vrai que l'interview avait dû être réalisé en très peu de temps, en économisant de la pellicule, et avec l'aide d'un traducteur, fonctionnaire du Ministère des Affaires étrangères de Mongolie, probablement peu familier avec les subtilités du chant. T. Ganbold et G. Iavgaan avaient également dirigé plusieurs ateliers à la Maison des cultures du monde à Paris ; cette fois-ci la traduction était assurée par un ethnomusicologue, Alain Desjacques, mais les deux chanteurs n'en étaient pas plus explicites. Quant à D. Sundui, à qui un musicologue japonais demandait comment faire pour apprendre le chant diphonique, il répondait simplement qu'il fallait savoir tenir son souffle aussi longtemps que possible, l'utiliser efficacement, puis écouter des enregistrements sonores et essayer (Emmert et Minegushi 1980 : 49).

Malgré le fait que son pays d'origine (le Vietnam) et son pays d'accueil (la France) ne connaissent pas traditionnellement le chant diphonique – ou peut-être grâce à cela – Trân Quang Hai réussit à reproduire différents styles ou variantes stylistiques, ou du moins à s'en approcher. Ayant appris sans recevoir d'instructions ou de conseils de chanteurs chevronnés, et sans pouvoir s'appuyer sur des descriptions publiées, il a été obligé de procéder par tâtonnement. Cette recherche empirique, mais néanmoins systématique, lui a permis de prendre conscience de ce qui se passe au niveau de la cavité buccale. Conduire depuis de nombreuses années des ateliers d'introduction au chant diphonique l'a amené à savoir l'expliciter.

L'originalité des nouvelles recherches présentées ici consiste en 3 points :

1. Trân Quang Hai essaie d'imiter le mieux possible des chants reproduits sur les enregistrements sonores dont nous disposons. Pour cela, il s'appuie à la fois sur la perception auditive et visuelle, en essayant d'obtenir, sur le moniteur du Sona-Graph, des tracés de spectres semblables à ceux de chanteurs originaires de Mongolie, de Sibérie, du Rajasthan et d'Afrique du Sud.
2. Il décrit subjectivement ce qu'il fait et ressent sur le plan physiologique, quand il obtient ces tracés.
3. Afin de mieux comprendre le mécanisme des différents styles et d'en explorer toutes les possibilités – même si elles ne sont pas exploitées dans les chants diphoniques traditionnels –, il effectue des expériences que nul n'a probablement jamais tentées.

Cette recherche ne pouvait être effectuée avec des spectrographes de facture ancienne utilisés jusqu'en 1989 par les auteurs mentionnés plus haut. Il fallait pour cela un appareil capable de restituer le spectre sonore en temps réel et son synchrone, le DSP Sona-Graph Model 5500 que notre équipe de recherche acquit en décembre 1988. Si l'on change, en chantant, les paramètres de l'émission vocale, on voit immédiatement se modifier le tracé des harmoniques. Grâce au feed-back du nouveau tracé, l'émission vocale peut de nouveau être modifiée. Ainsi, la recherche est proprement expérimentale.

Dans la première étude sur l'acoustique du chant diphonique, E. Leipp reproduit un schéma théorique de l'appareil phonatoire, figurant cinq cavités principales comme résonateurs : *1°* la cavité pharyngienne ; *2°* la cavité buccale postérieure ; *3°* la cavité buccale antérieure, la pointe de la langue dirigée vers le palais séparant les cavités 2 et 3 ; *4°* la cavité située entre les dents et les lèvres ; *5°* la cavité nasale (Leipp 1971). Le rôle exact de ces différentes cavités semble difficile à définir.

Grâce à son expérience pragmatique de chanteur et de pédagogue, Trân Quang Hai a été amené à distinguer deux techniques de base utilisant essentiellement une cavité buccale ou deux cavités buccales (Trân et Guillou 1980 : 171), les deux techniques pouvant être plus ou moins nasalisées. Dans la technique à une cavité, la pointe de la langue reste en bas, comme lorsqu'on prononce des voyelles. Trân Quang Hai a trouvé cette technique parfaite pour mieux faire sentir aux débutants la modification du volume buccal avec la prononciation des voyelles. Il dit aux stagiaires qu'il faut « laisser la langue en position de repos » (cf. le film *Le chant des harmoniques*). Les images radiologiques du film montrent cependant que l'arrière de la langue se lève pendant la prononciation successive des voyelles o, ɔ, a (ceci n'est pas lié au chant diphonique). Le radiologue F. Besse parle de « l'ascension de la langue ». La métaphore du « repos de la langue » reste pourtant valable dans le sens où la pointe de la langue reste en bas. L'image radiologique montre que dans cette technique, il y a un contact entre le voile du palais et la partie postérieure de la langue, séparant la cavité buccale de la zone pharyngienne.

Dans la technique à deux cavités, la pointe de la langue est appliquée contre la voûte du palais, divisant ainsi le volume buccal en une cavité antérieure et une cavité postérieure. Ici, il n'y a pas de contact entre l'arrière de la langue et le voile du palais ; la cavité buccale postérieure et la cavité pharyngienne étant reliées par un large passage. La sélection des différents harmoniques pour créer une mélodie peut se faire de deux manières : *a)* la pointe de la langue se déplace de l'arrière à l'avant, l'harmonique le plus aigu étant obtenu dans la position le plus en avant ; la cavité buccale antérieure est alors réduite au maximum (cf. les images radiologiques du film *Le chant des harmoniques*) ; *b)* la pointe de la langue reste collée au palais sans se déplacer, les harmoniques étant sélectionnés en fonction de l'ouverture plus ou moins grande des lèvres : de l'ouverture la plus petite quand on prononce la voyelle o (harmonique grave) jusqu'à l'ouverture la plus grande quand on prononce la voyelle i (harmonique aigu). Cette deuxième manière ne semble pas être utilisée par les chanteurs mongols que nous avons pu observer, et Trân Quang Hai ne l'emploie que pour son intérêt pédagogique (comparaison avec la technique à une cavité) lors de ses ateliers d'initiation.

Afin d'explorer toutes les possibilités des deux techniques principales, Hai a chanté des échelles d'harmoniques à partir de différentes hauteurs du fondamental. Pour la technique à une cavité, on s'aperçoit sur la figure 1 que les harmoniques utilisables pour créer une mélodie ne dépassent que de peu la limite supérieure de 1000 Hz, quel que soit le fondamental. Mais plus le fondamental est grave, plus les harmoniques sont nombreux. Ainsi, pour le fondamental le plus grave (90 Hz, approximativement un fa1) de la fig. 1, les harmoniques exploitables sont H4 (360 Hz), 5, 6, 7, 8, 9, 10, 11, 12 (1080 Hz), ce qui donne l'échelle (transposée) do, mi, sol, si ♭ -, do, re, mi, fa#-, sol. Pour le fondamental le plus aigu (180 Hz) de la fig. 1, seuls les harmoniques 3, 4, 5 et 6 sont exploitables, et l'échelle résultante, sol, do, mi, sol, est beaucoup plus pauvre en possibilités mélodiques.

13Avec la technique à deux cavités (fig. 2), et le fondamental le plus grave (110 Hz = La1), Trân Quang Hai arrive à faire ressortir les harmoniques entre H6 (660 Hz) et H20 (2200 Hz). Pour créer une mélodie dans la zone la plus aiguë, il faut sélectionner des harmoniques pairs ou impairs (cf. plus loin fig. 11 et 12), puisque les harmoniques sont trop rapprochés pour une échelle musicale. L'émission du fondamental le plus aigu (220 Hz) de la fig. 2 permet de sélectionner de H4 (880 Hz) à H10 (2200 Hz).

14Un rapide coup d'œil permet de constater qu'en fait, les harmoniques obtenus par la technique à une cavité se situent essentiellement dans une zone jusqu'à 1 KHz, alors que les harmoniques obtenus par la technique à deux cavités sont placés surtout dans la zone de 1 à 2 KHz.

15Dans la tradition, les femmes mongoles et tuva ne pratiquaient pas le chant diphonique. Selon le chanteur D. Sundui, cette pratique nécessiterait trop de force, mais il n'y aurait pas d'interdit à ce sujet chez les Mongols (Emmert et Minegushi 1980 : 48). Chez les Tuva de l'Union soviétique, le chant diphonique serait presque exclusivement réservé aux hommes ; un tabou basé sur la croyance qu'il causerait l'infertilité à la femme qui le pratiquerait serait progressivement abandonné, et quelques jeunes filles l'apprendraient maintenant (Alekseev, Kirgiz et Levin 1990). Ces auteurs disent encore que « les femmes sont capables de produire les même sons, bien qu'à des hauteurs plus élevés », ce qui n'est que partiellement vrai. C'est vrai si on parle « des sons » du bourdon qui sont plus élevés pour une voix de femme que pour une voix d'homme, mais c'est faux en ce qui concerne la mélodie d'harmoniques qui ne peut monter plus haut que chez les hommes. On peut déjà le déduire en examinant les fig. 1 et 2 où la limite supérieure des harmoniques obtenus à partir des fondamentaux les plus aigus (180 et 220 Hz) n'est pas plus élevée que la limite supérieure des harmoniques obtenus à partir du fondamental le plus grave, une octave plus bas (90 et 110 Hz). On peut trouver la confirmation en examinant les fig. 3 et 4, reproduisant la voix de Minh-Tâm, la fille de Trân Quang Hai6. Avec la technique à une cavité et un fondamental de 240 Hz, le nombre d'harmoniques est très restreint H3 à H5 (1200 Hz). Avec la technique à deux cavités et un fondamental à 270 Hz, les harmoniques 4 (1080 Hz) à 8 (2160 Hz) peuvent être utilisés pour créer une mélodie, ce qui donne une échelle plus riche (transposée do, mi, sol, sib -, do). Il s'en suit qu'une voix aiguë de femme ne permet pas de créer des mélodies selon la technique à une cavité. La femme xhosa d'Afrique du Sud enregistrée par le R.P. Dargie, qui utilise cependant cette technique (comme le montrent les fig. 7 et 8), a une voix grave, dans le registre des voix d'hommes (100 et 110 Hz = Sol1 et La1).

• 6 Elle avait dix-sept ans quand cet enregistrement fut fait, mais son père lui avait enseigné le chant diphonique dès l'âge de six ans.

16Si les conclusions que nous avons tirées de ces expérimentations (fig. 1 à 4) sont justes – et nous pensons qu'elles le sont – on devrait pouvoir en déduire que les styles du chant diphonique dont les sonagrammes présentent une mélodie d'harmoniques ne dépassant pas pour l'essentiel 1 KHz sont obtenus selon la technique à une cavité, alors que ceux dont la mélodie d'harmoniques se situe essentiellement entre 1 et 2 KHz sont obtenus selon la technique à deux cavités. Les expériences faites par Trân Quang Hai, en essayant d'imiter les différentes variantes stylistiques, le confirment. Dans les lignes qui suivent, nous allons examiner les caractéristiques physiologiques des différentes variantes stylistiques du chant diphonique, en dégageant trois critères : le(s) résonateur(s) ; les contractions musculaires ; les procédés d'ornementation.

G. YAVGAAN. Photogramme extrait du film « Le chant des harmoniques » de H. Zemp.

Agrandir Original (jpeg, 80k)

T. GANBOLD. Photogramme extrait du film « Le chant des harmoniques » de H. Zemp.

Agrandir Original (jpeg, 84k)

211

Le(s) résonateur(s)

Selon Alekseev, Kirgiz et Levin (1990), la pièce que nous avons représentée dans les fig. 9 et 10 est une variante du kargiraa, appelée « steppe kargiraa » et rappelle les chants tantriques des moines tibétains

Les harmoniques de cette deuxième zone enrichissent sans doute le timbre, mais ils ne sont pas perçus par l'oreille comme formant une mélodie séparée de la mélodie d'harmoniques de la premirère zone

Folkways/Smithsonian n° 1, 8, 9, 17, 18. Melodia, face A, plage 9. Le Chant du Monde, face A, plage 5

Selon Aksenov, le style *kargiraa* des Touvains se caractérise par un fondamental grave situé sur l'un des quatre degrés les plus bas de la grande octave, et pouvant descendre une tierce mineure pendant un court instant. Le changement mélodique d'un harmonique à l'autre est accompagné d'un changement de voyelles (Aksenov 1973 : 13). Les deux chants reproduits ici (fig. 5, 9 et 10) ont des fondamentaux de 62 Hz et 67 Hz (momentanément 57 Hz). La mélodie d'harmoniques atteint dans le premier cas 750 Hz (H12), dans le second cas 804 Hz (H12)7. Au dessus de la mélodie d'harmoniques on aperçoit une deuxième zone, à l'octave quand les voyelles postérieures sont prononcées (fig. 5 et 9), ou plus haut avec les voyelles antérieures (fig. 10)8. En imitant le tracé de la fig. 5, Trân Quang Hai utilise la technique à une cavité, la bouche semi-ouverte ; à la différence des chants touvains, la mélodie d'harmoniques est à bande large, et H1 est très marqué (fig. 6). Tous les sept enregistrements identifiés sur les notices des disques comme faisant partie du style *kargiraa* chez les Touvains et *karkira* chez les Altaï ont été vérifiés au Sona-Graph. La fréquence du fondamental se situe entre 62 et 95 Hz ; les mélodies d'harmoniques de toutes les pièces sans exception se situent en dessous de 1 KHz.

212

18 Ce n'est que depuis les travaux récents concernant la musique du peuple xhosa d'Afrique du Sud effectués par le R.P. Dargie (1989), et les enregistrements qu'il avait confiés en 1984 à Trân Quang Hai pour les archives sonores du Musée de l'Homme, que l'on connaît l'existence du chant diphonique pratiqué loin d'Asie centrale. La pièce chantée par une femme xhosa (fig. 7), caractérisée par l'alternance de deux fondamentaux de 100 et 110 Hz et d'une mélodie d'harmoniques ne dépassant pas 600 Hz, est sans doute faite selon la technique à une cavité, comme le montre l'imitation de Trân Quang Hai aussi imparfaite qu'elle soit (fig. 8).

Cela semble être un phénomène récent. Selon Alekseev, Kirgiz et Levin (1990), les chanteurs tuva étaient autrefois spécialistes en un ou deux styles paarentés, mais aujourd'hui les jeunes utilisent plusieurs styles et arrangent fréquemment des segments mélodiques en des mélanges polystylistiques.

Qu'en est-il du style *kargiraa khöömii*10 du chanteur mongol T. Ganbold (fig. 11), dont nous avons placé le sonagramme à dessein en face d'un *kargiraa* tuva (fig. 9 et 10) ? Le fondamental est grave (85 Hz) et peu marqué comme dans les pièces tuva, mais la mélodie d'harmoniques se situe dans la zone de 1 à 2 KHz et non pas au-dessous de 1 KHz. Pour obtenir un tracé semblable, Trân Quang Hai a dû employer la technique à deux cavités. Comment expliquer cette différence par rapport au style équivalent chez les Tuva ? A l'arrivée de l'Ensemble de Danses et de Chants de la R.P. de Mongolie à Paris, l'Ambassade de Mongolie a organisé une réception à laquelle nous avons eu l'honneur et le plaisir d'assister. Comme d'autres artistes de la troupe, T. Ganbold y faisait une démonstration de son art, et nous avons pensé qu'il serait intéressant d'inclure dans notre film la pièce qu'il avait composée, « Liaisons de *khöömii* », pour présenter au public trois variantes stylistiques du chant diphonique. La pièce ne figurait pas dans le programme des concerts à la Maison des Cultures du Monde, parce que T. Ganbold, l'ayant composée récemment, ne la maîtrisait pas encore complètement. En accord avec le directeur de la troupe, il a néanmoins accepté de la chanter sur scène hors concert pour le tournage du film, puis lors d'un concert, en bis (afin que nous puissions filmer son entrée sur scène ainsi que les applaudissements), et de faire une courte démonstration des différents styles lors de l'interview. En l'absence d'enregistrements d'autres chanteurs mongols, on ne peut dire si T. Ganbold s'est trompé de technique, ou si en Mongolie il est considéré comme juste de chanter le style *khöömi kargiraa* selon la technique à deux cavités. On peut aussi considérér que les frontières entre les différents styles ne sont pas rigides, que les chanteurs utilisent les possibilités techniques comme ils veulent (ou peuvent), qu'ils emploient les dénominations avec plus ou moins de rigueur. Chez les Touvains aussi, nous le verrons dans le paragraphe suivant, une même dénomination de style peut désigner des chants exécutés selon les deux techniques différentes.

Folkways/Smithsonian, n° 11 et 14.

Melodia, face 1, plage 5. Folkways/Smithsonian, n° 12 et 13.

Selon Aksenov, le style *borbannadir* tuva se caractérise par un fondamental un peu plus élevé que celui du *kargiraa*, utilisant l'un des trois degrés au milieu de la grande octave. Les lèvres sont presque complètement fermées, le son en serait plus doux (*soft*) et résonnant. Le style *borbannadir* serait considéré par les Touvains comme techniquement similaire au style *kargiraa*, ce qui permettrait un changement subit de l'un à l'autre au sein d'une même pièce (1973 : 14). L'examen des cinq pièces identifiées sur les notices de disques comme faisant partie du style *borbannadir* montre que dans deux pièces, le fondamental est à 75 et à 95 Hz, et la mélodie d'harmoniques au-dessous de 1 KHz[12] (cf.fig. 13). Ces deux pièces sont donc effectivement très proches du style *kargiraa*, chanté selon la technique à une cavité. Les trois autres enregistrements de

214

borbannadir ont un fondamental plus aigu (120, 170 et 180 Hz) et une mélodie d'harmoniques au-dessus de 1 KHz, donc obtenue par la technique à deux cavités. Nous en reproduisons un exemple (fig. 15), et son imitation par Hai (fig. 16).

L'analyse sonagraphique montre (mais la simple écoute aussi) que dans un enregistrement dénommé *borbannadir* par les auteurs de la notice du disque, et dont nous avons déjà parlé brièvement (fig. 13), trois styles sont chantés en alternance. L'extrait à gauche présente toutes les caractéristiques du style *kargiraa*, qui est suivi manifestement, après une interruption d'une seconde, par le style *borbannadir* avec le même fondamental et la mélodie d'harmoniques au-dessous de 1 KHz. Le sonagramme de la fig. 14, montrant un autre extrait du même enregistrement, présente également à gauche le style *kargiraa*, suivi cette fois-ci sans interruption par un très court fragment (2 secondes) de *borbannadir* avec le même fondamental. Puis, après une courte interruption, le fondamental fait un saut d'octave de 95 Hz à 190 Hz, et la mélodie d'harmoniques est située au-dessus de 1 KHz, dépassant même à certains endroits les 2 KHz (cf. aussi les imitations de Hai, fig. 16 et 17). A l'écoute et sur le tracé du sonagramme, cette dernière partie ressemble beaucoup au style « khöömi de ventre » du chanteur mongol D. Sundui (fig. 20), et il n'est pas douteux qu'elle soit chantée selon la technique à deux cavités.

Folkways/Smithsonian, nº 7.

Folkways/Smithsonian, nº 5, 6, 8. Le Chant du Monde, face A, plage 4.

D'après Aksenov, dans certains lieux tuva, le nom de *khomei* remplace le nom de *borbannadir*. Parmi les six exemples de *khomei* tuva (dans le sens restreint) et le seul exemple de *kiomioi* altaï que nous connaissons, l'un a un fondamental grave de 90 Hz et des harmoniques ne dépassant pas 1 KHz, les quatre autres ont des fondamentaux entre 113 Hz et 185 Hz (fig. 18, et l'imitation fig. 19) et sont proches du *borbannadir* à fondamental aigu (cf. fig. 15 et *22*) chanté selon la technique à deux cavités.

23Le style *ezengileer* – dont un seul enregistrement est connu (fig. 21) – semble également proche du *borbannadir* à fondamental aigu (fig. 15 et 22).

24Tous les enregistrements de *borbannadir*, *khomei* et *ezengileer* tuva que nous avons pu examiner ont en commun une pulsation rythmique que nous examinerons plus loin sous la rubrique des procédés d'ornementation. Il semble donc que pour le *borbannadir*, l'usage actuel permette deux variantes : un fondamental relativement grave (75 à 95 Hz) et une mélodie d'harmoniques au-dessous de 1KHz, donc chantée selon la technique à une cavité, et un fondamental plus aigu (120 à 190 Hz) avec une mélodie d'harmoniques au-dessus de 1 KHz, chantée selon la technique à deux cavités, le trait commun étant la pulsation rythmique.

Le style tuva qui s'oppose le plus clairement au *kargiraa* et au *borbannadir* (à fondamental grave) est le *sigit*. Selon Aksenov, il se caractérise par un fondamental plus tendu et plus élevé, la hauteur se situant au milieu de la petite octave. Le fondamental peut changer à l'intérieur d'une pièce et peut constituer la voix mélodique sans mélodie d'harmoniques au début des vers. A la différence des autres styles tuva, la voix supérieure ne constitue pas une mélodie bien caractérisée, mais reste longtemps sur une seule hauteur avec des ornements rythmiques (Aksenov 1973 : 15-16). Cf. *infra* notre analyse des procédés d'ornementation.

Folkways/Smithsonian, n° 2, 3, 4, 8, 16, 17. Melodia, face A, plages 1, 2, 6, 7, 8. Le Chant du Monde.

Dans les onze enregistrements de *sigit* tuva et le seul exemple de *sibiski* altaï que nous connaissons, le fondamental se situe entre 160 et 210 Hz. Nous avons choisi d'en reproduire trois sonagrammes (fig. 23, 24 et un bref extrait fig. 18). Pour l'imitation (fig. 26), Trân Quang Hai emploie la technique à deux cavités.

Tangent TGS 126, face B, plage 1 Tangent TGS 127, face B, plage 3. Victor, face A, plages 5, 6 et 7.

De nombreux chants mongols connus par des enregistrements ont une sonorité proche de celle du *sigit*. Le tracé des harmoniques est semblable, mais le style musical est différent en ce que les harmoniques font une véritable mélodie. C'est le cas des chants de D. Sundui (fig. 25), le spécialiste du chant diphonique mongol apparaissant probablement le plus souvent sur des disques. Les notices de ces différents disques n'indiquent que le terme général (*khöömii*), mais on sait par ailleurs qu'il chante surtout le *kevliin khöomii* (« *khöömii* de ventre ») ; ce dernier style et le *tseedznii khöomii* (« *khöömii* de poitrine ») étant pour lui « en général la même chose » (Emmert et Minegushi 1980 : 48).

Selon Alain Desjacques qui a assumé la traduction, le terme *kholgoï* est synonyme de *bagalzuuliin.*

Cf. la notice du CD Maison des cultures du monde, n° 4 et 6.

Un autre chanteur mongol a indiqué le nom de *khooloin khöömii* (« *khöömii* de gorge ») pour une pièce, et tseesni khend (traduit par « technique ventrale ») pour une autre, alors que la plus simple écoute montre, et l'analyse spectrographique le confirme, qu'il s'agit d'un même style (CD GREM , n° 32 et 33), en l'occurrence le style que D.Sundui appelle kevliin khöömii (« khöömi du ventre »)~~ (...)~~

Vogue, face B, plage 3. Hungaroton, face A, plage 5, et face B, plage 7. ORSTOM-SELAF, face B, plage 2. Maison des Cultures du Monde, n° 4,5,6.

Dans l'interview du film *Le chant des harmoniques*, T. Ganbold appelle son style favori, dont un court exemple est reproduit en fig. 29, *kholgoï khöömii* (« *khöömii* de gorge ») ; alors que pour l'enregistrement d'un disque effectué trois jours auparavant, il a nommé ce même style *tseedznii khöömii* (« *khöömii* de poitrine »). S'est-il trompé lors de l'enregistrement du disque ou lors du tournage du film ? Quoi qu'il en soit, le fait de se tromper confirme ce que nous avons déjà suggéré plus haut, à savoir que l'attribution d'une dénomination à un style ou à une technique ne semble pas être une préoccupation majeure pour certains chanteurs. Cependant, T. Ganbold ayant été un élève de D. Sundui qui pratique le « *khöömii* de ventre » (ou de poitrine), nous sommes enclins à penser que « *khöömii* de poitrine » est le terme juste. L'examen des différences relatives aux contractions musculaires confirme cette hypothèse (cf. *infra*). Les autres enregistrements publiés de chant diphonique mongol, dont nous ne reproduisons pas ici des sonagrammes parce que le style n'est pas nommé sur les notices des disques, apparaissent appartenir à ce même style que D. Sundui appelle (rappellons-le) « *khöömii* de ventre », et qui semble être le plus répandu en Mongolie.

Très proche du sonagramme du chant de D. Sundui est le tracé de l'enregistrement que John Levy a effectué en 1967 au Rajasthan (fig. 27). Aucune documentation concernant le lieu exact, le nom du chanteur et les circonstances de l'enregistrement n'accompagnant la bande magnétique déposée aux archives sonores du Musée de l'Homme, on en est réduit aux conjectures. Il est troublant qu'aucun enregistrement d'un autre chanteur du Rajasthan ne soit connu et qu'aucune publication ne mentionne le chant diphonique dans cette région. Lors de sa visite au Musée de l'Homme en 1979, Komal

Kothari, directeur du *Rajasthan Institute of Folklore*, affirma à Trân Quang Hai qu'il avait entendu parler de ce phénomène vocal sans avoir pu l'écouter lui-même.

L'unique exemple de « *khöömii* de nez » dont nous disposons est un très court fragment de six secondes enregistrées lors de l'interview avec T. Ganbold. La seule différence avec le « *khöömii* de poitrine » (?) (cf. fig. 29 et 31) tient au fait que le chanteur ferme complètement la bouche ; la mélodie d'harmoniques est alors moins marquée, « noyée » en quelque sorte dans les harmoniques présents sur toute l'étendue du spectre (fig. 30 et 32).

Un dernier style reste à examiner le « *khöömii* de gorge » (nous corrigeons la dénomination, cf. *supra*) chanté par T. Ganbold (fig. 33, et son imitation par Trân Quang Hai, fig. 34). Il fait clairement partie des styles utilisant la technique à deux cavités. Nous en reparlerons sous la rubrique des contractions musculaires.

Le tableau 1 classe les différents styles selon les résonateurs.

Tableau 1 : Classement des styles en fonction des résonateurs.

1 cavité	*kargiraa* (tuva)
	khargyraa khöömii (mongol)
	karkira (altaï)
	umngqokolo ngomqangi (xhosa)
	chants bouddhiques tibétains (monastère Gyüto)
	borbannadir et *khomei grave* (tuva)
2 cavités	*sigit* (tuva)
	sibiski (altaï)
	chant du Rajasthan
	khöömii de poitrine (mongol)
	khöömii de ventre (mongol)
	khöömii de nez (mongol)

khöömii de gorge (mongol)
borbannadir et *khomei* aigu (tuva)
kiomioi (altaï)
ezengileer (tuva)

Contractions musculaires

Lors des tournées européennes de chanteurs diphoniques mongols et touvains, Trân Quang Hai a souvent assisté aux concerts dans les coulisses ou rejoint les artistes dans les vestiaires. Il a pu constater que ceux-ci revenaient essoufflés et fatigués, le visage marqué par l'afflux du sang. Ce n'est certainement pas sans raisons que les pièces sont très courtes, et qu'un même chanteur n'interprète généralement pas plus de deux ou trois chants diphoniques lors d'un même programme.

En essayant de reproduire la sonorité des chants ainsi que le tracé des sonagrammes des différents styles du chant diphonique, Trân Quang Hai a remarqué qu'il devait employer différents degrés de contraction des muscles abdominaux et sterno-cléido-mastoïdiens (muscles du cou), et plus particulièrement au niveau du pharynx.

Trân Quang Hai était directeur artistique pour la section de musique asiatique au festival de musique asiatique au festival de musique de chambre à Kuhmo en 1984 et à ce titre avait invité le chanteur D. Sundui à se produire en Finlande.

Dans le style *kargiraa* touvain et mongol, les muscles abdominaux et le pharynx sont relaxés (fig. 6 et 12). A première vue, cela n'a rien d'étonnant, puisque le kargiraa est le style dans lequel le fondamental est le plus grave (entre 57 et 95 Hz), et pour produire un son grave il semble plus naturel de relâcher les muscles que de les contracter. Cependant, pour imiter le mieux possible le chant xhosa d'Afrique du Sud qui utilise également un fondamental grave

(100 et 110 Hz), Trân Quang Hai a dû contracter très fortement les muscles abdominaux et le pharynx (fig. 8). Pour les chants mongols et touvains caractérisés par des fondamentaux plus aigus (entre 160 et 220 Hz), l'expérience montre des degrés variables de la tension musculaire. Ainsi, la plus forte contraction apparaît dans le style *sigit* touvain (fig. 26), avec un conduit d'air étroit. En sont très proches le chant du Rajasthan (fig. 28), le style « *khöömii* de poitrine » mongol de T. Ganbold (fig. 29) et le « *khöömii* de ventre » de D. Sundui (fig. 25). Ce dernier, lors d'un festival de musique asiatique en Finlande, a pris la main de Trân Quang Hai pour la poser successivement sur son ventre et sur sa gorge, afin de lui faire ressentir les différences de contraction. Pour le *khargiraa khöömii*, les muscles abdominaux étaient relâchés ; pour le « *khöömii* de ventre » (la spécialité de D. Sundui), le ventre était dur comme de la pierre. Est-ce la raison de cette dénomination ? Si, comme dit D. Sundui, « *khöömii* de ventre » et « *khöömii* de poitrine » sont en général la même chose (*op. cit.*), comment expliquer les deux expressions ? Quand Trân Quang Hai imite ce style, il ressent une vibration en haut de la poitrine, au niveau du sternum. La dénomination « *khöömii* de ventre » se référerait alors à la très grande tension des muscles abdominaux ; la dénomination « *khöömii* de poitrine » indiquerait plutôt la vibration que le chanteur ressent au niveau du sternum. L'autre style utilisé par T. Ganbold, dont il faudrait alors corriger l'appellation en « *khöömii* de gorge » (et non pas « de poitrine » comme il dit dans le film), est caractérisé par une mélodie d'harmoniques beaucoup moins marquée, « noyée » en quelque sorte dans les harmoniques couvrant toute l'étendue du spectre (fig. 33). En essayant de l'imiter (fig. 34), Trân Quang Hai contracte moins les muscles abdominaux et le pharynx, et quand on pose les doigts sur la gorge au-dessus du cartilage thyroïde (pomme d'Adam), on perçoit effectivement une vibration plus forte à ce niveau-là.

Dans le *borbannadir* à fondamental aigu (fig. 20) et le *khomei* (fig. 19), les contractions musculaires semblent plus faibles que dans le *sigit*, mais plus fortes que dans le *kargiraa*.

Nous devons cette question à Gilles Léothaud qui l'a posée au séminaire de notre équipe de recherche lorsque nous avons exposé nos travaux.

La contraction musculaire est-elle un facteur déterminant du style ou de la manière de chanter d'un individu ? Trân Quang Hai réussit à imiter les caractéristiques stylistiques du *sigit* tuva ou du « *khöömii* de ventre » mongol sans contraction abdominale et pharyngienne excessive, mais la puissance de la mélodie d'harmoniques est nettement moindre et la sonorité plus matte (fig. 37). Pour produire une plus grande puissance et un son ressemblant aux enregistrements des chanteurs touvains et mongols, il contracte à l'extrême les muscles abdominaux et sterno-cléido-mastoïdiens du cou. En bloquant le pharynx pour obtenir un conduit d'air très resserré, il obtient une mélodie d'harmoniques plus « détachée » des autres harmoniques du spectre (fig. 35). En contractant un peu moins le pharynx et en laissant un conduit d'air plus large, il a l'impression d'avoir davantage de résonance dans les cavités buccales ; le résultat est une mélodie d'harmoniques plus large et un tracé plus foncé de l'ensemble des harmoniques (fig. 36). A titre comparatif, nous avons reproduit un sonagramme montrant l'émission diphonique à bouche fermée (fig. 38).

Le premier à avoir suggéré une relation entre la tension de certaines parties corporelles et la brillance des sons harmoniques dans le chant diphonique est S. Gunji. S'appuyant sur un texte de l'acousticien allemand F. Winckel, il rappelle que les parois intérieures des cavités corporelles sont molles et peuvent être modifiées par tension ; si la tension est élevée, les hautes fréquences ne seront pas absorbées et le son sera très brillant, et le contraire survient si le degré de tension est bas (Gunji 1980 : 136). Il faudrait poursuivre les recherches dans ce domaine – y compris avec des chanteurs d'opéra qui obtiennent de la puissance et des sons brillants apparemment sans tension musculaire excessive – avant de pouvoir tirer des conclusions définitives.

Le tableau 2 classe les styles en fonction de leur contraction musculaire.

Tableau 2 : Classement des styles en fonction de la contraction musculaire.

Relaxation pharyngienne et abdominale	*kargiraa* (fig. 5, 9, 10, imitation 6)
	kargiraa khöömii (Ganbold, fig. 11, imitation fig. 12) *karkira* (altaï)
	chant bouddhique tibétain (monastère Gyütö)
	borbannadir grave (fig. 13, imitation fig. 16).
	borbannadir aigu (fig. 15 et 22, imitation fig. 20)
	khomei (fig. 18, imitation fig. 19)
	khöömii de gorge (?) Ganbold, fig. 33, imitation fig. 34)
Contraction pharyngienne et abdominale	*sigit* (fig. 23 et 24, imitation fig. 26)
	sibiski (altaï)
	khöömii de poitrine (?) (Ganbold fig. 29)
	khöömii de ventre (fig. 25)

223

khöömii de nez (fig. 30)

umngqokolo ngomqangi (fig. 7,
imitation fig. 8)

Procédés d'ornementation

Les enregistrements sonores dont nous disposons présentent plusieurs procédés d'ornementation qui enrichissent la texture rythmique et harmonique du chant diphonique. La réduction du format des sonagrammes – nécessaire pour cette publication – rend la lecture des ornements difficile. Nous avons choisi de reproduire à une plus grande échelle huit extraits de chants déjà analysés : cette fois-ci l'analyse de la fréquence est limitée à 2 KHz (et non pas à 4 KHz), et l'axe temporel est deux fois plus grand (fig. 39 à 42).

« *an ornamented trilling and punctuating rhythm principally on two pitches (the ninth and tenth partials of the two fundamentals* "

1) Dans le style *sigit* touvain et *sibiski* altaï, il ne s'agit pas d'une ornementation ajoutée à la mélodie, mais de l'élément principal du style musical. Comme le dit Aksenov, à la différence des autres styles touvains, la voix supérieure du *sigit* ne constitue pas une mélodie bien caractérisée mais plutôt un rythme ponctué principalement sur deux hauteurs, le 9e et le 10e harmoniques des deux fondamentaux (Aksenov 1973 : 15-16). Ces ponctuations se succèdent à un rythme régulier une fois par seconde ou un peu plus rapproché (fig. 23, 24 et 39).

Logiquement, pour obtenir une ponctuation sur l'harmonique immédiatement supérieur à la ligne mélodique principale, il faut diminuer le volume de la cavité buccale antérieure en avançant la pointe de la langue. Avancer très rapidement et reculer une fois par seconde la pointe de la langue, qui est dirigée verticalement contre

224

le palais, est assez inconfortable. Hai a trouvé une autre possibilité en aplatissant légèrement la pointe de la langue contre le palais, la cavité buccale antérieure est également raccourcie, et en revenant rapidement dans la position initiale, le mouvement de la langue est plus confortable (fig. 26). On ne sait pas comment les chanteurs du *sigit* procèdent, si c'est la première ou la deuxième solution qu'ils adoptent, mais selon la loi du moindre effort, on peut supposer qu'ils utilisent le second procédé. Sur le sonagramme, cette ponctuation est le très marquée sur l'harmonique immédiatement supérieur de la ligne mélodique, et plus faiblement sur le deuxième et le troisième harmoniques au dessus, mais pas sur les harmoniques inférieurs, notamment ceux du bourdon.

GREM, n° 2.

2) Un autre procédé de pulsation rythmique est effectué sans aucun doute par des coups de langue dirigés verticalement contre le palais. Nous en connaissons deux exemples, l'un provenant de Mongolie, l'autre du Rajasthan (fig. 27 et 40). Cette fois-ci, l'accentuation est visible sur toute l'étendue du spectre sonore, et en particulier sur H2 et 3 par des traits verticaux. La langue n'est pas avancée horizontalement ou aplatie contre le palais comme corrigera de lui-même cette mauvdans le *sigit*, mais elle fait un mouvement de va-et-vient vertical (imitation fig. 28).

Le tracé de la partie droite de la fig. 15, représentant un *borbannadir*, montre sur H13 une ponctuation rythmique proche de celle du *sigit*, et une accentuation sur les harmoniques inférieurs, notamment sur H3, ce qui laisse supposer qu'elle est faite par des coups de langue (fig. 20) comme dans le cas du chant du Rajasthan.

In the broken singing of this style the intoning of v is interrupted by the full closing of the lips followes by opening either on x the plosive voiced consonant b or on the nasal consonant m (Aksenov 973 : 14)

225

Les trois auteurs écrivent que la mélodie d'harmoniques est produite par de rapides vibrations de lèvres (*In ezengileer, soft, shimmering harmonic melodies produced by rapide vibrations of the lips, are sung over a low fundament drone*). Le lecteur corrigera de lui même cette mauvaise formulation, car bien entendu ce n'est pas la mélodie d'harmoniue qui est produite par la vibration des lèvres, mais le rythme pulsé.

3) Selon Aksenov, dans le style *ezengileer*, caractérisé par des accents irréguliers (*agogic*), on entend dans la mélodie des harmoniques et dans le fondamental les pulsations dynamiques ininterrompues du rythme du galop, la dénomination de ce style venant du terme « étrier » (1973 : 16). Aksenov mentionne ailleurs que le chant du *borbannadir* peut être ininterrompu ou brisé ; dans ce dernier cas, l'intonation du v̱ est interrompue par la fermeture des lèvres suivie par leur ouverture, ou bien sur x̱, la consonne occlusive ḇ ou la consonne nasale m̱. Alekseev, Kirgiz et Levin (1990) écrivent que ce rythme pulsé et asymétrique du *ezengileer* est produit par de rapides vibrations des lèvres, et que le terme de *borbannadir* – « utilisé métaphoriquement pour signifier "roulant" » – est caractérisé par le même rythme pulsé.

Cette pulsation est visible sur les sonagrammes du *khoomei* et du *ezengileer* par un tracé sur une ou deux hauteurs d'harmoniques, alternativement au-dessus et au-dessous de la ligne horizontale. Dans l'exemple *khoomei* (fig. 18 et 45), il y a cinq battements par seconde ; dans l'exemple *ezengileer* (fig. 21 et 46), les battements sont plus rapprochés : neuf par seconde. Pour obtenir un tracé semblable, Trân Quang Hai fait de rapides mouvements de la lèvre inférieure vers la lèvre supérieure (fig. 19). Sur les sonagrammes du *borbannadir* à fondamental grave (fig. 13 et 43), la pulsation à huit battements/seconde est reproduite en forme de « zigzag » ; pour l'imiter, Trân Quang Hai fait des mouvements rapides de la langue d'avant en arrière (fig. 16).

C'est ainsi qu'on peut traduire l'expression « with finger strokes across the lips ». On peut supposer qu'un doigt (l'index ?) est mis horizontalement entre les lèvres et qu'un rapide va-et vient vertical imprime la pulsation à l'émission diphonique.

4) Si les ornements et procédés rythmiques décrits dans les paragraphes 1 à 3 sont exclusivement rléalisés par l'appareil phonatoire, un autre procédé utilise une intervention extérieure : le frappement d'un doigt (des doigts) entre (contre) les lèvres (Alekseev, Kirgiz et Levin 1990), marqué sur les sonagrammes (fig. 22 et 44) par une sorte de « hachure » sur H2. Comme ces auteurs ne donnent pas plus de précisions, Trân Quang Hai a essayé toutes les variantes possibles de frappement, avec un ou plusieurs doigts, en position horizontale ou verticale, contre ou entre les lèvres. Mais aucun de ces essais ne permettait de différencier le rythme irrégulier du frappement de(s) doigt(s) sur H2, de la pulsation régulières des harmoniques supérieurs.

5) Il n'est peut-être pas orthodoxe d'inclure le vibrato dans les procédés d'ornementation (encore que certains musicologues le font), mais il nous semble intéressant de l'étudier ici précisément pour dégager les différences mais aussi les similitudes avec les autres techniques. En fin de compte, c'est un procédé comme les autres pour enrichir la sonorité du chant diphonique et structurer le temps.

Communication verbale de D. Sundui à Trân Quang Hai lors du festival en Finlande, 1984.

Pour ce qui est du chant d'opéra et de concert, l'ondulation du vibrato est décrit comme presque sinusoidale, avec un ambitus de l'ordre de +50 Hz (Sundberg 1980 : 85), c'est-à-dire de quart de ton.

Le vibrato en modulation de fréquence est caractérisé sur le sonagramme par une fluctuation plus ou moins forte de la mélodie d'harmoniques principale ainsi que des autres harmoniques figurant sur le tracé, dessinant quatre à cinq « ondulations » par seconde. Le vibrato le plus fort que nous avons entendu et vu sur un sonagramme est fait par le chanteur mongol D. Sundui, dont le chant diphonique se caractérise par ailleurs par l'emploi d'une mélodie d'harmoniques à large bande : à certains endroits, le « sommet de la vague » d'un harmonique touche presque le « bas de la vague » de l'harmonique supérieur (fig. 25 et 41). Sur H8 par exemple, le vibrato oscille entre 1620 et 1790 Hz, l'ambitus du vibrato étant de 170 cents, c'est-à-dire entre le trois-quart de ton et le ton entier. Cet artiste ayant étudié le chant classique occidental au conservatoire de Moscou[29] – il chante d'ailleurs aussi selon la technique du chant diphonique des airs de compositeurs comme Tchaikovsky et Bizet (Batzengel 1980 : 52) – on serait tenté de supposer que son vibrato très marqué ait été acquis lors de ses études au conservatoire[30]. Le chanteur du Rajasthan (fig. 27), dont on ne sait rien, a aussi un vibrato très fort, également combiné avec une mélodie d'harmoniques à large bande.

Le vibrato peut être combiné avec d'autres procédés d'ornementation, comme les coups de langue contre le palais dans le chant du Rajasthan (fig. 27), ou l'aplatissement rythmique de la langue contre le palais dans le *sigit* (fig. 26). Dans ce dernier exemple, on peut compter quatre oscillations de vibrato pour un accent rythmique par seconde. Le sonagramme de la fig. 18 est particulièrement intéressant puisqu'il permet de comparer le tracé du vibrato (à droite pour le *sigit*) avec la pulsation rythmique (à gauche pour le *khomei*), les deux procédés étant utilisés successivement par le même chanteur dans la même pièce.

Le tableau 3 résume ces différents procédés d'ornementation.

Tableau 3 : Procédés d'ornementation.

Coups de langue contre le palais	Chant du Rajasthan (fig. 27, 40, imitation fig. 28) *borbannadir* (fig. 15, imitation fig. 20)
Aplatissement rythmique de la pointe de la langue contre le palais	*sigit* tuva (fig. 18, 23, 24, 39, imitation fig. 26) *sibiski* altaï
Mouvements rapides de fermeture et d'ouverture des lèvres	*khoomei* (fig. 18 et 45, imitation fig. 19)
Mouvements de va et vient horizontal de la langue	*borbannadir* à fondamental grave (fig. 13 et 43, imitation fig. 16)
Frappements de(s) doigts entre (contre) les lèvres	*borbannadir* (fig. 22 et 44)
Vibrato	plus ou moins présent dans la plupart des chants les plus marqués :fig. 5 et 42, 9 et 10, 25 et 41, 27

A quel point l'analyse spectrographique montre-t-elle des différences individuelles de l'émission vocale entre des chanteurs utilisant le même style ? Cette question mériterait une analyse approfondie, mais avec beaucoup plus d'enregistrements d'un même style chanté plusieurs fois par le même chanteur, et par des chanteurs différents. L'examen des sonagrammes que nous avons effectués permet néanmoins de donner une première réponse : il apparaît qu'il y a en effet des différences individuelles (que l'on peut supposer être du même ordre que les différences de style et de voix des chanteurs d'opéra, par exemple). Nous avons vu que pour les quatre styles chantés par T. Ganbold, le spectre sonore est caractérisé par une zone importante d'harmoniques au-dessus de 4 KHz, ce qui n'est pas le cas chez les autres chanteurs dont nous publions des sonagrammes. Deux sonagrammes du style *sigit* chanté par deux chanteurs différents montrent chez l'un une sorte de « bourdon harmonique » au-dessus de la mélodie d'harmoniques (fig. 23), absent chez l'autre (fig. 24). De même, le « bourdon harmonique » est très marqué chez un chanteur de *kargiraa* (fig. 5), et absent chez un autre (fig. 9 et 10). Bien entendu, il faut être prudent et ne pas tirer des conclusions définitives avec si peu d'exemples, car surtout dans les zones aigües, certaines différences peuvent résulter également des conditions d'enregistrement (équipement, environnement).

Mais des différences se remarquent aussi dans des zones plus graves : sur beaucoup de sonagrammes, l'harmonique 1 est très faible (fig. 5, 7, 9, 10, 11, 13, 18, 22), alors que sur d'autres, il est au contraire très marqué (fig. 15, 21, 25, 27, 29, 30, 33). L'intensité de H1 est-elle fonction du style ? Nous ne le pensons pas : en tout cas, le style *sigit* peut manifestement comporter un H1 faible (fig.18) ou fort (fig. 23 et 24). L'intensité de l'harmonique 1 semble être plutôt une caractéristique individuelle des chanteurs. Chez T. Ganbold, H1 est très marqué quel que soit le style (rappelons qu'il est le seul chanteur pour qui nous disposons d'enregistrements de quatre styles : fig. 11, 29, 30, 33). De même, tous les sonagrammes de chants de Trân Quang Hai ont l'harmonique 1 très marqué. Cependant, nous avons au moins un sonagramme montrant d'un même chanteur un H1 faible pour un style et un H1 fort pour un autre (fig. 14). Là encore, les recherches devraient être poursuivies.

Traduction de la notice de B. Tchourov par Philippe Mennecier (communication personnelle). Le même chanteur a exécuté deux pièces de styles sigit et deux pièces de style khöömei qui ne comportent pas ce « bourdon à la quinte » (Mélodia, face 1, plages à 4).

Faut-il parler de « chant triphonique » quand des chanteurs font ressortir un deuxième bourdon soit dans l'aigu avec l'harmonique 18 (fig. 23) ou l'harmonique 44 (fig. 5), soit dans le grave avec l'harmonique 3 (fig. 15) ? Dans le premier cas, le sifflement aigu de ce « bourdon harmonique » peut difficilement être qualifié de troisième voix. Dans le deuxième cas, l'auteur de la notice en tout cas pense que dans le *borbannadir* en question, cette quinte qu'on entend très clairement au-dessus de l'octave du fondamental « fait naître comme résultat un chant à trois voix »[31]. Cependant, dans les deux cas, il n'y a pas de troisième voix indépendante du fondamental et de la mélodie d'harmoniques. Il s'agit manifestement de variantes individuelles que, pour ce qui est du bourdon à la quinte (H3), Trân Quang Hai imite bien (fig. 20). Ces chants sont de même nature que tous les autres analysés dans cet article, et nous ne pensons pas qu'il y ait lieu de changer de terminologie.

Nous avons gardé pour la fin deux sonagrammes représentant des exercices de style (et non pas des styles traditionnels !), où Trân Quang Hai fait preuve de toute sa virtuosité.

Dans la fig. 47, il inverse le dessin habituel d'un bourdon grave et d'une mélodie d'harmoniques dans l'aigu, pour en faire à partir de fondamentaux changeants une hauteur fixe dans l'aigu. Ainsi, le « bourdon harmonique » de 1380 Hz est réalisé successivement par H12, 9, 8, 6, 8, 9, 12, alors que les fondamentaux changent en montant La1, Re2, Mi2, La2 et en redescendant au La1.

Dans la fig. 48, l'exercice est encore plus difficile, puisqu'il présente simultanément une échelle ascendante pour les fondamentaux et une échelle descendante pour les harmoniques, et vice versa.

Reproduites ici pour l'intérêt scientifique (et le plaisir) qu'apporte l'exploration des limites physiologiques de la voix humaine, ces possibilités techniques ne sont pas exploitées dans les traditions d'Asie centrale et d'Afrique du Sud. Ne doutons pas qu'elles le seront bientôt par des compositeurs de musique contemporaine en Occident dont certains, depuis *Stimmung* (1968) de Stockhausen, cherchent à enrichir les techniques vocales par les moyens du chant diphonique.

Bibliographie

AKSENOV A. N., 1973, « Tuvin Folk Music ». *Asian Music* 4(2) : 7-18. (Extraits traduits de *Tuvinskaia narodnaia muzyka*, Moskou 1964)

ALEKSEEV Eduard, Zoya KIRGIZ et Ted LEVIN, 1990, Notice du disque *Tuva-Voices from the Center of Asia*.

BATZENGEL, 1980, « *Urtiin duu, xöömij*, and *morin xuur* ». *In* R. Emmert et Y. Minegushi (ed.), *Musical Voices of Asia* 52-53. Tokyo Heibonsha Publishers.

BOREL-MAISONNY Suzanne et Michèle CASTELLENGO, 1976, « Étude radiographique des mouvements oro-pharyingés pendant la parole et le jeu instrumental », *Bulletin du Groupe d'Acoustique Musicale* 86 (Université de Paris VI).

DARGIE David, 1988, *Xhosa Music. Its techniques and instruments, with a collection of songs.* Cape Town et Johannesburg David Philip.

DESJACQUES Alain, 1988, « Une considération phonétique sur quelques techniques vocales diphoniques mongoles ». *Bulletin du Centre d'Études de Musique Orientale* 31 : 46-45 (Paris).

EMMERT Richard et Yuki MINEGUSHI (ed.) , 1980, *Musical Voices of Asia.* Tokyo Heibonsha Publishers.

GUNJI Sumi, 1980, « An Acoustical Consideration of Xöömij ». *In* R. Emmert et Y. Minegushi (ed.), *Musical Voices of Asia* 135-141. Tokyo Heibonsha Publishers.

HAMMAYON Roberte, 1973, Notice du disque *Chants mongols et bouriates.* Collection Musée de l'Homme. Vogue LDM 30138.

HARVILAHTI Lauri, 1983, « A two voiced-song with no words ». *Suomalais-ugrilaisen seuran aikakauskirja* 78 : 43-56 (Helsinki).

HARVILAHTI Lauri et KASKINEN H., 1983, « On the Application Possibilities of Overtone Singing ». *Suomen Antropologi* i Finland 4 : 249-255 (Helsinki).

LEIPP Émile, 1971, « Le problème acoustique du chant diphonique ». *Bulletin du Groupe d'Acoustique Musicale* 58 : 1-10. Université de Paris VI.

LEOTHAUD Gilles, 1989, « Considérations acoustiques et musicales sur le chant diphonique », *Institut de la voix, Dossier n° 1* : 17-44. Limoges.

PAILLER Jean-Pierre, 1989, « Examens vidéo de Monsieur Trân Quang Hai ». *Institut de la voix, Dossier n° 1* : 11-14. Limoges.

PETROV Valérii et Boris TIKHOMIROV, 1985, Notice du disque *Voyage en URRS vol. 10 Sibérie, Extrême Orient, Extrême Nord.*

SAUVAGE Jean-Pierre, 1989, « Observation clinique de Monsieur Trân Quang Hai ». *Institut de la voix, Dossier n° 1* : 3-10. Limoges.

SUNDBERG Johan, 1980, « Acoustics, IV The voice ». *In* Stanley Sadie (ed.), *The New Grove Dictionary of Music and Musicians* 1 : 82-87. Londres Macmillan.

TRÂN Quang Hai, 1989, « Réalisation du chant diphonique ». *Institut de la voix, Dossier n° 1* : 15-16. Limoges.

TRÂN Quang Hai et Denis GUILLOU, 1980, « Original Research and Acoustical Analysis in connection with the *Xöömi* Style of Biphonic Singing ». In R. Emmert et Y. Minegushi (ed.), *Musical Voices of Asia* : 162-173. Tokyo Heibonsha Publishers.

WALCOTT Ronald, 1974, « The Chöömij of Mongolia A Spectral Analysis of Overtone Singing ». *Selected Reports in Ethnomusicology* 2(1) : 55-60.

ZEMP Hugo, 1989, « Filming Voice Technique : The Making of "The Song of Harmonics" ». *The World of Music* 31(3) : 56-85.

Discographie

(Pour des raisons de commodité, les références dans le texte et dans les légendes concernent les éditeurs plutôt que les titres des disques dont plusieurs se ressemblent.)

GREM, G 7511. *Mongolie. Musique et chants de tradition populaire.* 1 disque compact. Enregistrements et notice de X. Bellenger. 1986.

Hungaroton, LPX 18013-14. *Mongol Nepzene* (Musique populaire mongole). 2 disques 30 cm. Enregistrements et notice de Lajos Vargyas. Unesco Co-operation, ca. 1972. (Réédition *Mongolian Folk Music*, 2 disques compacts, HCD 18013-14, 1990).

Le Chant du Monde, LDX 74010. *Voyage en URRS vol. 10 : Sibérie, Extrême Orient, Extrême Nord.* 1 disque 30 cm. Notice de V. Petrov et B. Tikhomirov. 1985.

Maison des Cultures du Monde, W 260009. *Mongolie. Musique vocale et instrumentale.* 1 disque compact, série « Inédit ». Notice de P. Bois. 1989.

Melodia, GOCT 5289-68. *Pesni i instrumental'nye melodii tuvy* (Chants et mélodies instrumentales des Touva). 1 disque 30 cm. Notice de B. Tchourov.

ORSTOM-SELAF, Ceto 811. *Mongolie. Musique et chants de l'Altaï.* 1 disque 30 cm. Enregistrements et notice de Alain Desjacques. 1986.

Smithsonian/Folkways SF 40017. *Tuva-Voices from the Center of Asia.* 1 disque compact. Enregistrements et notice de E. Alekseev, Z. Kirgiz et T. Levin. 1990.

Tangent TGS 126 et 127. *Vocal Music from Mongolia ; Instrumental Music from Mongolia.* 2 disques 30 cm. Enregistrements et notices de Jean Jenkins. 1974.

Victor Records, SJL 209-11. *Musical Voices of Asia (Asian Traditional Performing Arts 1978).* 3 disques 30 cm. Enregistrements de S. Fujimoto et T. Terao, notice de F. Koizumi, Y. Tokumaru et O. Yamaguchi. 1979.

Vogue LDM 30138. *Chants mongols et bouriates.* 1 disque 30 cm. Enregistrements et notice de Roberte Hamayon. Collection Musée de l'Homme. 1973.

Filmographie

Le chant des harmoniques (version anglaise *The Song of Harmonics*). 16 mm, 38 min. Auteurs : Trân Quang Hai et Hugo Zemp. Réalisateur : Hugo Zemp. Coproduction CNRS Audiovisuel et Société Française d'Ethnomusicologie, 1989. Distribition CNRS Audiovisuel, 1, place Aristide Briand, F-92195 Meudon.

Lecture des sonagrammes

Dans le film *Le chant des harmoniques*, les sonagrammes en temps réels sont reproduits selon une échelle de couleurs qui nous semblait la plus lisible. Pour l'impression en noir et blanc de cette revue, nous avons choisi de photographier l'inscription sur papier continu que fournit le Sona-Graph, où les degrés de noirceur correspondent aux degrés d'intensité des harmoniques.

Les mélodies d'harmoniques ne dépassant jamais la limite supérieure de 3000 Hz, l'analyse spectrographique dans cet article a été limitée à 4 KHz. Cependant, pour être sûr que d'éventuelles zones de formants dans des fréquences supérieures n'échappent à l'analyse, nous avons examiné tous les exemples choisis avec une grille jusqu'à 8 KHz. Seul le chanteur mongol T. Ganbold dépasse 4 KHz, non pas avec la mélodie d'harmoniques, mais avec une troisième zone de formants (affectant sans doute le timbre, mais non pas le contour de la mélodie d'harmoniques). Nous reproduisons les sonagrammes de deux enregistrements analysés d'abord à 4 KHz (fig. 29 et 30), puis à 8 KHz (fig. 31 et 32).

Les modèles précédents du Sona-Graph ne permettaient d'imprimer qu'une inscription correspondant à 2,4 secondes, respectivement à 4,8 secondes si la bande magnétique était lue à moitié vitesse. Le DSP Sona-Graph 5500 peut analyser et inscrire sur du papier continu jusqu'à 3 minutes. Pour reproduire les sonagrammes sur une page de revue, il nous a fallu choisir la durée maximale de l'enregistrement, l'étalement du signal en fonction du temps, tout en faisant attention à ce que les différents harmoniques soient lisibles. En imprimant, pour des raisons d'économie, deux sonagrammes sur une même page, complétés par des légendes substantielles, nous avons pensé qu'une durée maximale de 14 secondes constituait le meilleur compromis. Bien sûr, une reproduction plus grande donnerait une lisibilité accrue, mais étant donné qu'il ne fallait pas augmenter le nombre de pages de l'article ni les frais de photogravure, la réduction choisie nous a semblé acceptable. Pour faciliter la comparaison, la majorité des sonagrammes (fig. 3 à 38, 47 et 48) ont été reproduits à la même échelle. Si l'inscription couvre toute la largeur du « satzspiegel », il s'agit donc d'un signal de 14 secondes ; si deux sonagrammes de longueur sensiblement égale se partagent la même surface, le signal est évidemment de moitié plus court, c'est-à-dire de 7 secondes environ. Par contre, l'inscription des deux premiers sonagrammes a dû être comprimée afin de pouvoir reproduire la totalité de l'échelle des fondamentaux (20 secondes pour la fig. 1, 28 secondes pour la fig. 2).

Pour des raisons de lisibilité, nous avons reproduit, à une échelle plus grande, huit extraits de chants déjà analysés (fig. 39 à 46) : cette fois-ci l'analyse de la fréquence est limitée à 2 KHz (et non pas à 4 KHz), et l'axe temporel est deux fois plus grand, ce qui représente pour chaque sonagramme une durée de 3 secondes environ.

Fig. 1 : Échelles d'harmoniques avec différentes hauteurs du fondamental (90 à 180 Hz selon une échelle diatonique), par Trân Quang Hai. Technique à une cavité.

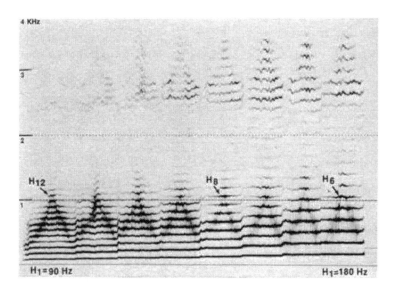

Agrandir Original (jpeg, 128k)

Voix fortement nasalisée. Prononciation marquée de voyelles. H1, 2 et 3 du bourdon très marqués. Avec le fondamental le plus grave (90 Hz), les harmoniques 4 (360 HZ) à 12 (1080 Hz) peuvent être utilisés pour créer une mélodie. Avec le fondamental le plus aigu (180 Hz), seuls les harmoniques 3 à 6 (1080 Hz) ressortent. Deuxième zone d'harmoniques entre 2500 et 4000 Hz, séparée des harmoniques utilisables par une « zone blanche » sur le sonagramme.

Fig. 2 : Échelles d'harmoniques avec différentes hauteurs du fondamental (110 à 220 Hz, selon une échelle diatonique), par Trân Quang Hai. Technique à deux cavités.

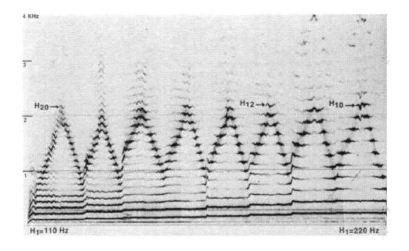

Agrandir Original (jpeg, 144k)

Voix nasalisée. H1 et 2 du bourdon très marqués. Les harmoniques bien tracés sur le sonagramme atteignent la limite supérieure de 2200 Hz avec H10 dans le cas du fondamental le plus aigu à 220 Hz, et H20 dans le cas du fondamental le plus grave, à l'octave inférieure (110 Hz). Les harmoniques exploitables pour une mélodie sont dans le premier cas H4 (880 Hz) à H10 (2200 Hz), et dans le deuxième cas H6 (660 Hz) à H20 (2200 Hz).

Fig. 3 : Échelles d'harmoniques avec bourdon stable, par Minh-Tâm, fille (17 ans) de Trân Quang Hai. Technique à une cavité.

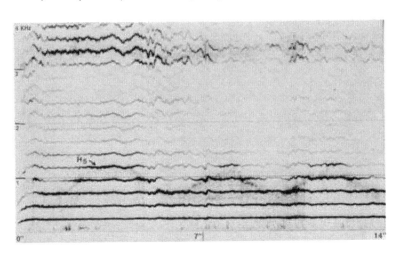

Agrandir Original (jpeg, 128k)

H1 (240 Hz), 2 et 3 du bourdon très marqués. Harmoniques utilisables pour une mélodie H3, 4 et 5 (1200 Hz). Pour une voix de femme, à cause de la hauteur du fondamental plus élevé (ici 240 Hz), le nombre d'harmoniques exploitables pour une mélodie est très limité.

Fig. 4 : Échelles d'harmoniques avec bourdon stable, par Minh-Tâm, fille (17 ans) de Trân Quang Hai. Technique à deux cavités.

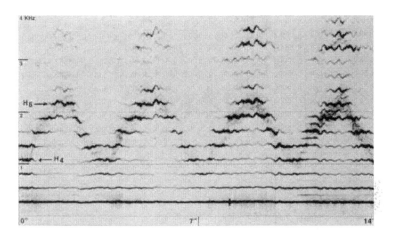

Agrandir Original (jpeg, 132k)

Voix nasalisée. H1 (270 Hz). Harmoniques exploitables pour une mélodie H4 (1080 Hz), 5, 6, 7, 8 (2160 Hz). H8 fait apparaître H12 et 13 dans la zone aiguë.

Fig. 5 : Tuva (URSS). CD Smithsonian/Folkways, n° 18. Style *kargiraa*, pièce « Artii-sayir » par Vasili Chazir.

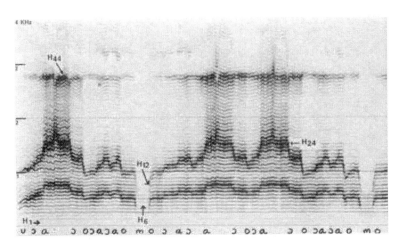

Agrandir Original (jpeg, 140k)

Prononciation marquée de voyelles. H1 (62 Hz), 2 et 3 du bourdon très faibles. Mélodie d'harmoniques H6 (375 Hz), 8, 9, 10, 12 (750 Hz). Deuxième zone de mélodie d'harmoniques à l'octave, entre H12 (750 Hz) et H24 (1500 Hz). « Bourdon harmonique » aigu H44 (2690 Hz), plus marqué quand la voyelle a est prononcée (avec une sorte de « colonne grisée » entre 1500 et 2700 Hz. (Transcription musicale de cette pièce dans la notice du CD).

Fig. 6 : Imitation par Trân Quang Hai du style *kargiraa* tuva de la fig. 5.

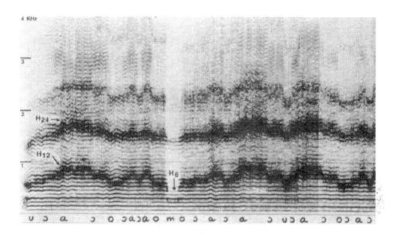

Agrandir Original (jpeg, 176k)

Technique à une cavité, prononciation marquée de voyelles. Bouche ouverte, sauf quand la mélodie d'harmoniques descend à H6 (alors bouche fermée avec prononciation de la consonne m). Relaxation pharyngienne et abdominale. H1 (70 Hz), 2, 3 et 4 du bourdon très marqués, H2 et 4 un peu plus que H1 et 3. Mélodie d'harmoniques à large bande H6 (420 Hz), 8, 9, 10, 12 (840 Hz). Deuxième zone de mélodie d'harmoniques à l'octave, entre H18 (1260 Hz) et H24 (1680 Hz). Troisième zone de mélodie d'harmoniques très faible, entre 2100 et 2400 Hz.

Fig. 7 : Xhosa (Afrique du Sud). Enreg. D. Dargie, Phonothèque Musée de l'Homme BM 87.4.1. Style imitant le jeu de l'arc musical *umrhubhe*, par Nowayilethi.

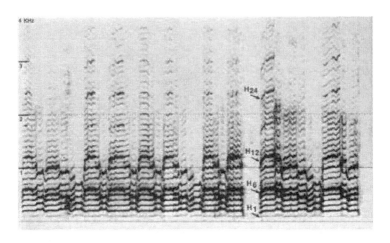

Agrandir Original (jpeg, 148k)

Alternance de deux fondamentaux à l'intervalle d'un ton. H1 (100Hz et 110 Hz), très faible ; H2, 3 et 4 du bourdon marqués. Mélodie d'harmoniques H4 (400 Hz), 5, 6 (600 Hz) quand le fondamental est à 100 Hz ; et H4 (440 Hz) et H5 (550 Hz) quand le fondamental est à 110 Hz. Deuxième zone de mélodie d'harmoniques entre 800 et 1200 Hz. Troisième zone plus faible à 2400 Hz ; par exemple, lorsque la mélodie d'harmoniques est sur H6, les harmoniques 10 et 12, ainsi que H24 sont très marqués. (Notation musicale dans Dargie 1988 : 59)

Fig. 8 : Imitation par Trân Quang Hai du chant xhosa de la fig. 7.

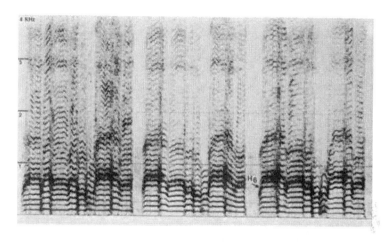

Agrandir Original (jpeg, 176k)

Technique à une cavité. Voix peu nasalisée, bouche moins ouverte que dans le style *kargiraa*. Contraction pharyngienne et abdominale. H1 (100 et 110 Hz), 2, 3 et 4 marqués. Mélodie d'harmoniques H4 (400Hz), 5, 6, 8 (800 Hz). Technique mal maîtrisée. Absence de deuxième et troisième zone dans l'aigu.

Fig. 9 : Touva (URSS). CD Smithsonian/Folkways, n° 1. Style « Steppe » *kargiraa*, par Fedor Tau. Début du chant.

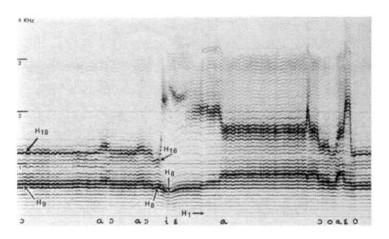

Agrandir Original (jpeg, 148k)

Prononciation marquée de voyelles. H1 (67 Hz) très faible ; H1 est abaissé d'une tierce mineure (57 Hz) au moment où la voyelle i̱ est prononcée. Paralellement, la mélodie d'harmoniques baisse également d'une tierce mineure, l'harmonique restant le même (H8). Mélodie d'harmoniques à large bande H8 (536 Hz) et 456 Hz), 9, 10, 12 (804 Hz). Deuxième zone de mélodie d'harmoniques entre H16 (1072 Hz) et H30 (2010 Hz). Pour les voyelles postérieures o̱, ɔ̱, a̱, la deuxième zone de mélodie d'harmoniques est à l'octave H8 — H16, H9 — H18, H10 — H20, H12 — H24.

246

Fig. 10 : Reprise du chant de fig. 9. Même mélodie d'harmoniques, mais différence de la deuxième zone en raison de la différence des voyelles. Pour les voyelles antérieures i̱, e̱, la deuxième zone de mélodie d'harmoniques est plus haute la voyelle e au début de la reprise (fig. 10) H8 — H32 (= double octave) ; la voyelle i̱ H9 — large bande de H28 à 30.

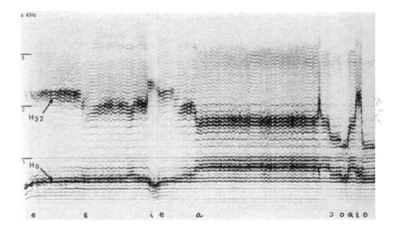

Agrandir Original (jpeg, 148k)

Fig. 11 : Mongolie. Film *Le chant des harmoniques*. Style *khargiraa khöömii*, démonstration pour l'interview, par T. Ganbold.

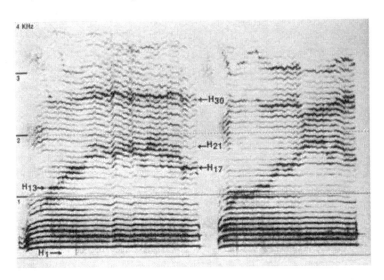

Agrandir Original (jpeg, 144k)

H1 (85 Hz) très faible ; H2, 3, 4, 5 et 6 du bourdon très marqués. Mélodie d'harmoniques faible, avec des harmoniques impairs H13 (1105 Hz), 15, 17, 19, 21 (1785 Hz). Dans l'aigu, une zone d'harmoniques faible entre H28 et H 30 (2630 à 2800 Hz).

Fig. 12 : Imitation par Trân Quang Hai du style *khargiraa khöömii* mongol de la fig. 11.

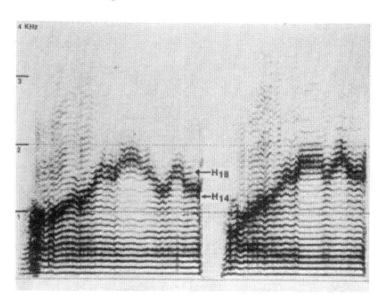

Agrandir Original (jpeg, 104k)

Technique à deux cavités. H1 (90 Hz) de même que H2, 3, 4 et 5 très marqués. Mélodie d'harmoniques avec des harmoniques paires H12 (1080 Hz), 14, 16, 18, 20 (1800 Hz). Relaxation pharyngiennee et abdominale.

Fig. 13 : Touva (URSS). CD Smithsonian/Folkways, n° 14. Pièce intitulée *borbannadir*, par Anatolii Kuular.

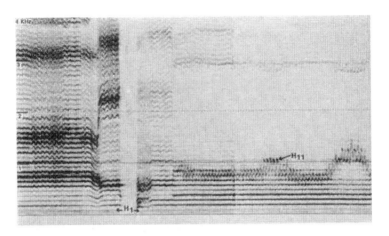

Agrandir Original (jpeg, 144k)

Manifestement les styles *kargiraa* et *borbannadir* se succèdent. Tracé caractéristique de *kargiraa*, avec vibrato six battements/seconde en forme d'ondulations. H1 (95 Hz) faible. Dans la partie *borbannadir*, H1 (95 Hz) faible ; H2, 3 et 4 marqués. Pulsation à huit battements/seconde « en zigzag » sur la mélodie d'harmoniques à bande large H7 (685 HZ), 8, 9 et 11 (1045 Hz).

Fig. 14 : Même pièce que fig. 13, un peu plus loin.

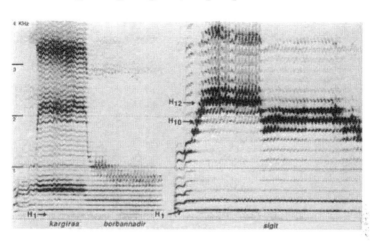

Agrandir Original (jpeg, 144k)

Manifestement trois styles. Dans le premier segment, styles *kargiraa* et *borbannadir* enchainés, avec H1 (95 Hz) faible. Après une courte interruption, deuxième segment de style différent, avec un saut d'octave du fondamental, H1 (190 Hz) et H2 bien marqués. Mélodie d'harmoniques à bande large, avec pulsation à sept battements/seconde « en zigzag », H9 (1710 Hz), 10 et 12 (2280 Hz).

Fig. 15 : Touva (URSS). Disque Melodia, face A, plage 5. Style *borbannadir*, pièce « *Boratmoj, Spoju Borban* », par Oorzak Xunastar-ool.

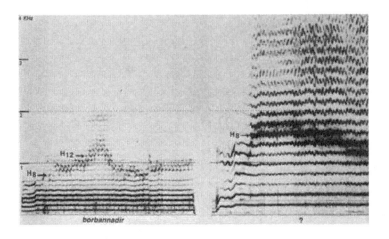

Agrandir Original (jpeg, 152k)

H1 (120 Hz) et 2 marqués. H3 du bourdon très marqué (on entend bien ce deuxième bourdon à la quinte). Mélodie d'harmoniques H8 (980 Hz), 9, 10 et 12 (1440 Hz). Accents rythmiques visibles surtout sur H3, 12 et 13.

Fig. 16 : Imitation par Trân Quang Hai du style *borbannadir* de la fig. 13.

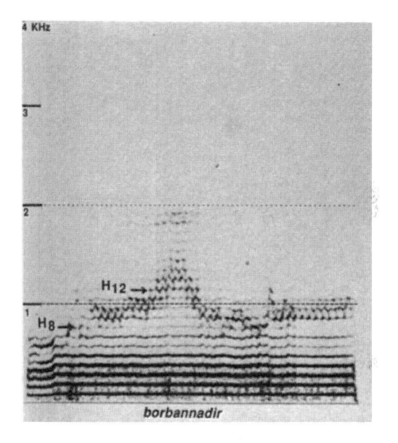

Agrandir Original (jpeg, 124k)

Technique à une cavité. Émission nasalisée, bouche presque fermée, prononciation de la voyelle o. H1 (95Hz), 2 à 5 très marqués. Mouvements rapides de la langue en avant et en arrière pulsation « en zigzag » sur la mélodie d'harmoniques à bande large H9 (855 Hz) à 13 (1235 Hz).

Fig. 17 : Imitation par Trân Quang Hai du style non identifié de la fig. 14.

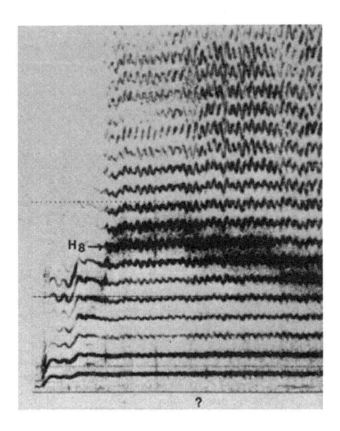

Agrandir Original (jpeg, 132k)

Technique à 2 cavités. Forte nasalisation, contraction pharyngienne et abdominale. H1(190Hz) et 2 très marqués. Rapides aplatissements de la pointe de la langue contre le palais, et simultanément tremblement de la mâchoire inférieure pulsation « en zigzag » sur la mélodie d'harmoniques à bande large H6 (1140 Hz) et 8 (1520 Hz).

Fig. 18 : Touva (URSS). CD Smithsonian/Folkways, n° 8. Styles *khoomei* et *sigit*, par Tumat Kara-ool.

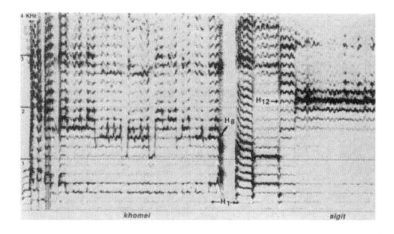

Agrandir Original (jpeg, 164k)

H1 (175 Hz). Pour le *khoomei*, H1 faible ; H2 et 3 marqués. Mélodie d'harmoniques à bande large H6 (1050 Hz), 8, 9, 10 (1750 Hz). Pulsation rythmique visible sous forme de traits verticaux dirigés alternativement vers le haut et le bas à partir de la ligne horizontale indiquant la mélodie d'harmoniques. Pour le *sigit* (cf. aussi fig. 21 et 22), H1, 2 et 3 du bourdon faible. Mélodie d'harmoniques H12 (2050 Hz) et ornement H13 ; les autres harmoniques n'apparaissant pas sur l'extrait de ce sonagramme.

Fig. 19 : Imitation par Trân Quang Hai du style *khoomei* touvain de la fig. 18.

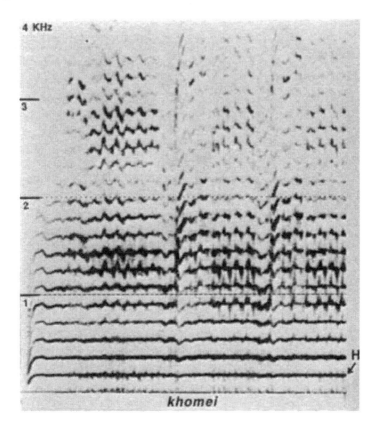

Agrandir Original (jpeg, 128k)

Technique à deux cavités. Voix peu nasalisée. Contraction pharyngienne modérée. Bouche moins ouverte que pour le *sigit*. Mouvements rythmiques de la lèvre inférieure vers la lèvre supérieure : pulsation rythmique visible sous forme de traits verticaux alternativement au-dessus et au-dessous de la ligne horizontale.

Fig. 20 : Imitation par Trân Quang Hai du style *borbannadir* touvain de la fig. 15.

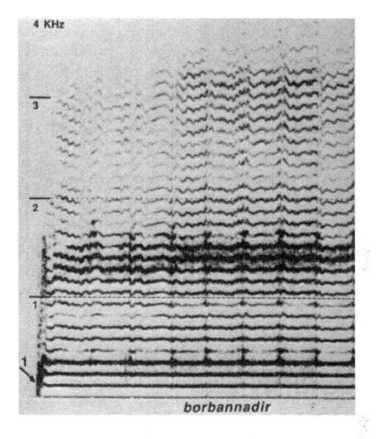

Agrandir Original (jpeg, 132k)

Technique à deux cavités. Voix nasalisée. Contraction pharyngienne modérée comme pour la fig. 18a, mais la bouche encore moins ouverte, arrondie. Coups de langue rythmiques contre le palais, bien marqués sur H3 du bourdon et sur les harmoniques supérieurs. H1 (175 Hz), 2 et 3 très marqués ; mélodie d'harmoniques H10 (1750 Hz) et H 12 (2050 Hz).

Fig. 21 : Touva (URSS). CD Smithsonian/Folkways, n° 15. Style *ezengileer*, par Marzhimal Ondar.

257

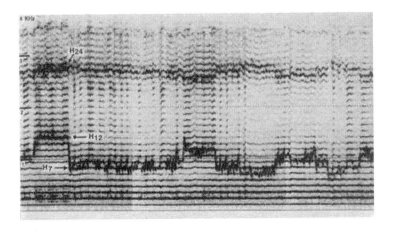

<u>Agrandir</u> <u>Original (jpeg, 180k)</u>

H1 (120 Hz), 2, 3, 4 du bourdon très marqués. Mélodie d'harmoniques H6 (720 Hz), 7, 8, 9, 10, 12 (1440 Hz). Le tracé est caractérisé par des accents rythmiques « en zigzag » sur 2 ou 3 harmoniques (l'extrait choisi ne comporte pas le frappement de doigts sur un bol de thé, indiqué sur la notice du CD). Dans l'aigu, une deuxième zone d'harmoniques entre H22 et H24 (2880 Hz).

Fig. 22 : Touva (URSS). CD Smithsonian/Folkways, n° 13. Pièce intitulée « *Borbannadir* with finger strokes », par Tumat Kara-ool.

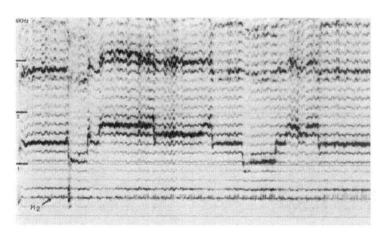

Agrandir Original (jpeg, 156k)

H1 (180 Hz) faible. « Hachures » irrégulieres sur H2, rythmiquement différentes du vibrato en forme d'ondulations marqué sur les harmoniques supérieurs. Mélodie d'harmoniques H6 (1080), 8, 9, 10 (1800 Hz). Deuxième zone de mélodie d'harmoniques à l'octave, sauf H10 — H18.

Fig. 23 : Touva (URSS). CD Smithsonian/Folkways, n° 3. Style *sigit*, pièce « *Alash* » par Mergen Mongush.

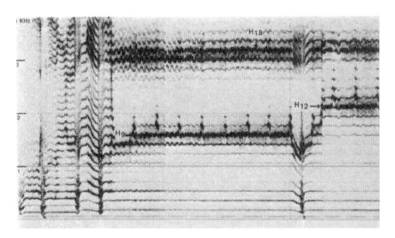

Agrandir Original (jpeg, 152k)

Début chanté avec des paroles en voix naturelle. Abaissement momentané du fondamental à une tierce mineure. H1 (190 Hz), 2 et 3 du bourdon marqués. Mélodie d'harmoniques H8 (1520 Hz), 9, 10 et 12 ; ornements rythmiques sur H10 et 13. Dans l'aigu, « bourdon harmonique » à l'octave de la mélodie d'harmoniques (H9 — H18) et à la quinte (H12 — H18). Zone de rejection d'harmoniques entre le bourdon (H1 à H3) et la mélodie d'harmoniques, et entre celle-ci et le bourdon aigu (H18).

Fig. 24 : Touva (URSS). Disque Melodia, face A, plage 1. Style *sigit*, pièce « *Reka Alas* » (même pièce que fig. 23).

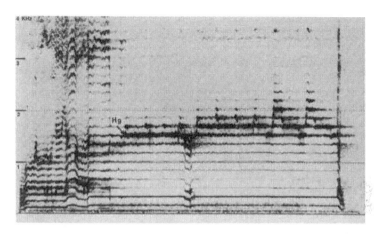

Agrandir Original (jpeg, 148k)

Début chanté avec des paroles en voix naturelle. Abaissement momentané du fondamental d'une tierce mineure. H1 (170 Hz) et 2 marqués. Mélodie d'harmoniques H9 (1530 Hz), 10, 12 (2030 Hz) ; ornements rythmques sur H10 et 11. Absence de deuxième zone dans l'aigu.

Fig. 25 : Mongolie. Disque Tangent, face B, plage 1. Pièce intitulé « *Mouth music* », par Sundui (cf. aussi le film *Le chant des harmoniques*). Style non nommé sur la notice du disque, mais sans doute « *khöömi* de ventre », le style préféré de Sundui.

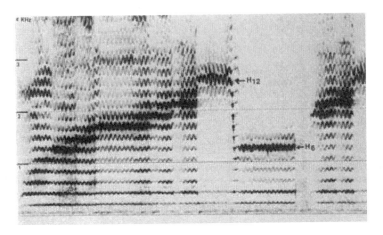

Agrandir Original (jpeg, 156k)

H1 (210 Hz) et 2 marqués, sauf quand la mélodie d'harmoniques est sur H12. Mélodie d'harmoniques à bande large H5 (1050 Hz), 6, 7, 8, 9, 10 et 12 (2510 Hz). Vibrato en forme d'ondulations.

Fig. 26 : Imitation par Trân Quang Hai du style *sigit* touvain de la fig. 23.

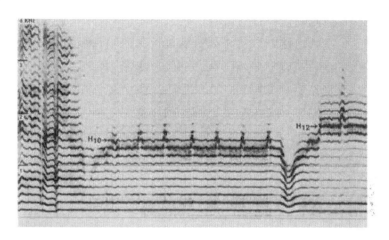

Agrandir Original (jpeg, 140k)

Technique à deux cavités. Forte nasalisation. Contraction abdominale et pharyngienne. Rétrécissement de la colonne d'air. Pour obtenir les ornements rythmiques (H10 à partir de la ligne mélodique H9, et H13 à partir de la ligne mélodique H12), la pointe de la langue est légèrement aplatie contre le palais. H1 (145 Hz) et H2 très marqués. Même mélodie d'harmoniques que fig. 23 et 24. Absence de deuxième zone dans l'aigu, comme fig. 24.

Fig. 27 : Rajasthan. Enregistrement J. Levy. Phonothèque du Musée de l'Homme BM78.2.1.

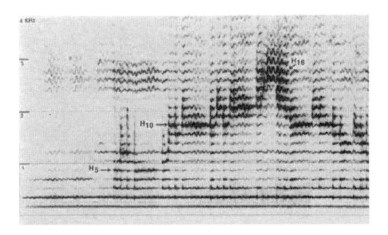

Agrandir Original (jpeg, 152k)

H1 (170 Hz) et 2 très marqués. Mélodie d'harmoniques H5 (850 Hz), 6, 8, 9,10, 11, 12, 13, 16 (2720 Hz), à large bande. Accents rythmiques, sans doute pour imiter le jeu de la guimbarde. Plus grand ambitus de toutes les pièces analysées dans cet article.

Fig. 28 : Imitation par Trân Quang Hai du chant du Rajasthan de la fig. 27.

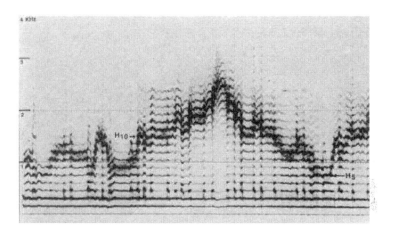

Agrandir Original (jpeg, 144k)

Technique à deux cavités. Voix fortement nasalisée. Forte contraction pharyngienne et abdominale (comme pour le *sigit*). Coups de langue rythmiques contre le palais, ce qui donne sur le tracé des lignes verticales comme sur la fig. 27. H1 (150 Hz), H5 (750 Hz) à H 16 (2400 Hz).

Fig. 29 : Mongolie. Probablement style *tzeedznii khöömii* (« *khöömii* de poitrine »), appelé dans le film Le chant des harmoniques par erreur *bagalzuuriin khöömi*, (« *khöömi* de gorge »). Démonstration pour l'interview, par T. Ganbold.

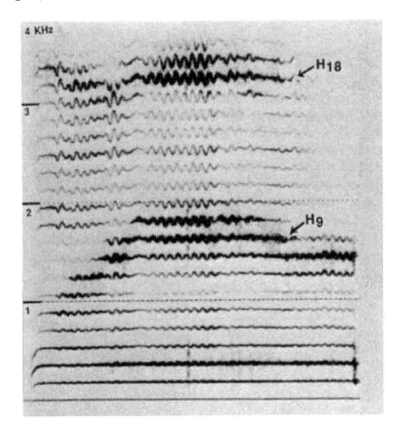

Agrandir Original (jpeg, 136k)

H1 (180 Hz) marqué, H2 très marqué. Mélodie d'harmoniques H8 (1440 Hz), 9, 10 (1800 Hz). Dans l'aigu, 2ᵉ zone à l'octave (H18 à 3240 Hz).

Fig. 30 : Même chanteur. Style *khamryn khöömii* (« *khöömii* de nez »).

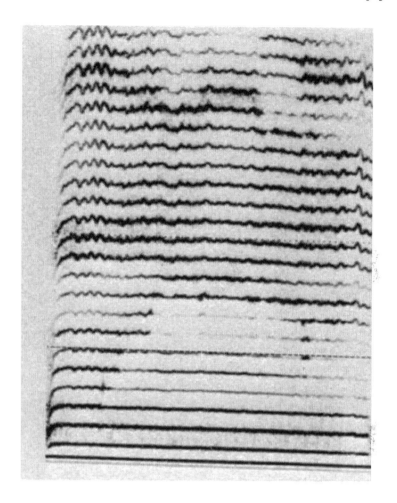

Agrandir Original (jpeg, 120k)

H1 (170 Hz), 2 et 3 marqués. Mélodie d'harmoniques très faible H8, 9 et 10, « noyée » dans les harmoniques couvrant toute l'étendue du spectre.

Fig. 31 : Même signal que fig. 29.

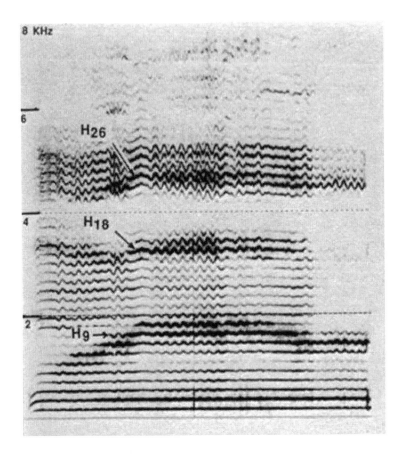

Agrandir Original (jpeg, 144k)

Analyse à 8 KHz, montrant une troisième zone à large bande au dessus de 4000 Hz.

Fig. 32 : Même signal que fig. 30.

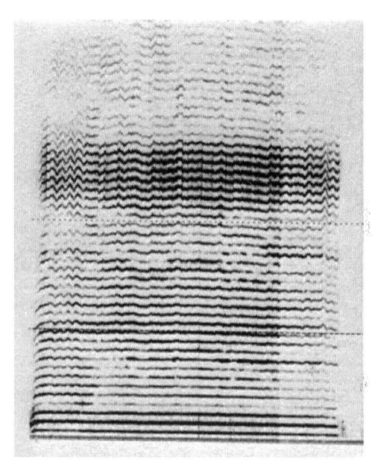

Agrandir Original (jpeg, 136k)

Analyse à 8 KHz, montrant une troisième zone à large bande au dessus de 4000 Hz.

Fig. 33 : Mongolie. Probablement style *bagalzuuliin khöömii*, (« *khöömii* de gorge »), appelé dans le film *Le chant des harmoniques* par erreur *tseedznii khöömi* (« *khöömi* de poitrine »). Démonstration pour l'interview, par T. Ganbold.

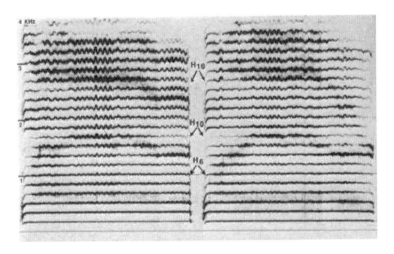

Agrandir Original (jpeg, 164k)

Bouche grande ouverte. H1 (170 Hz), 2, 3, 5, 6 du bourdon très marqués. Mélodie d'harmoniques H8 (1360 Hz), 9, 10 (1700 Hz). Dans l'aigu, une deuxième zone d'harmoniques à bande large H16 à 20 (2720 à 3400 Hz). Une analyse à 8000 Hz (non reproduite ici) montre une troisième zone très marquée au-dessus de 4000 Hz.

Fig. 34 : Imitation par Trân Quang Hai du style de la fig. 33.

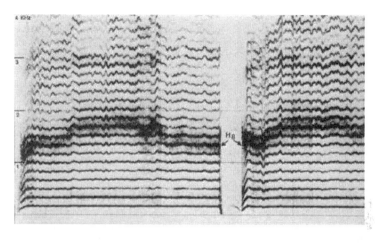

Agrandir Original (jpeg, 176k)

Technique à deux cavités avec l'arrière de la langue mordue par les molaires. Contraction pharyngienne avec une rétrécissement de la colonne d'air, musculature du cou « remontée ». Bouche grande ouverte, lèvres légèrement étirées comme pour prononcer la voyelle i. H1 (170 Hz), 2, 3, 4, 5, 6 du bourdon très marqués. Mélodie d'harmoniques H8 (1360 Hz), 9, 10 (1700 Hz).

Fig. 35 : Essai par Trân Quang Hai.

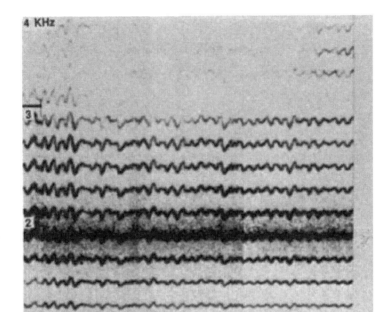

Agrandir Original (jpeg, 128k)

H1 (220 Hz) ; mélodie d'harmoniques H8. Forte contraction abdominale et pharyngienne. Conduit d'air très reserré. La vibration est ressentie plus fortement au-dessus de la pomme d'Adam.

Fig. 36 : Essai par Trân Quang Hai.

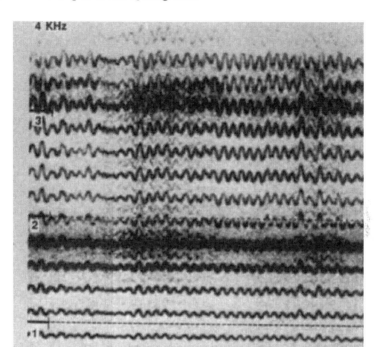

Agrandir Original (jpeg, 140k)

H1 (220 Hz) ; mélodie d'harmoniques H8. Forte contraction abdominale et pharyngienne. Conduit d'air plus large. La vibration est ressentie plus fortement au-dessous de la pomme d'Adam.

Fig. 37 : Essai par Trân Quang Hai.

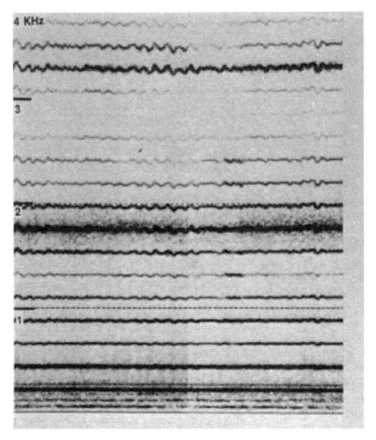

Agrandir Original (jpeg, 120k)

H1 (220 Hz) ; mélodie d'harmoniques H8. Relaxation abdominale et pharyngienne. Intensité faible ; pour obtenir un tracé noir, il fallait compenser en augmentant le niveau d'entrée du Sona-Graph.

Fig. 38 : Essai par Trân Quang Hai.

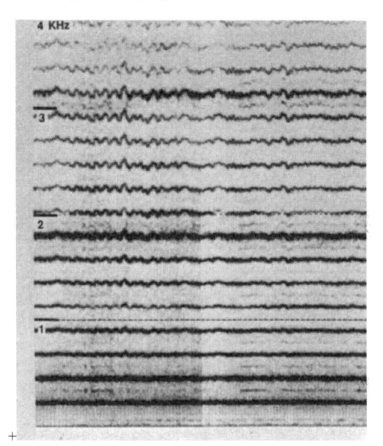

Agrandir Original (jpeg, 128k)

H1 (220 Hz) ; mélodie d'harmoniques H8.
Bouche fermée. Contractions comme pour la fig. 36. Intensité faible ; pour obtenir un tracé noir, il fallait compenser en augmentant le niveau d'entrée du Sona-Graph.

Fig. 39 : *Sigit* touvain (cf. fig. 23). Ornements rythmiques « en ponctuations » sur H10, combinés avec du vibrato.

275

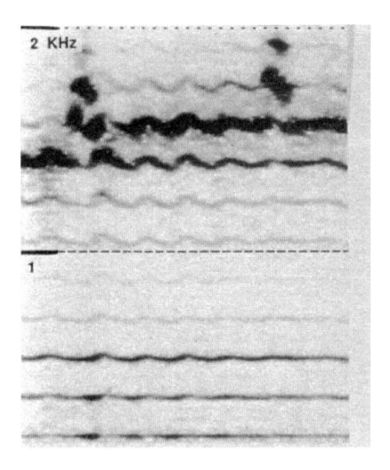

Agrandir Original (jpeg, 108k)

Fig. 40 : Chant du Rajasthan (cf. fig. 27). Accents rythmiques marqués par des lignes verticales sur toute l'étendue du spectre.

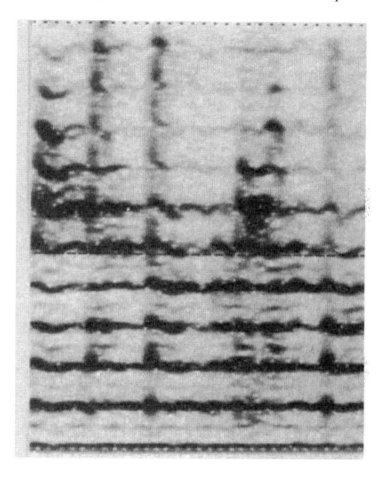

Agrandir Original (jpeg, 116k)

Fig. 41 : « *Khöömii* de ventre » mongol (cf. fig. 25). Vibrato « en ondulations ».

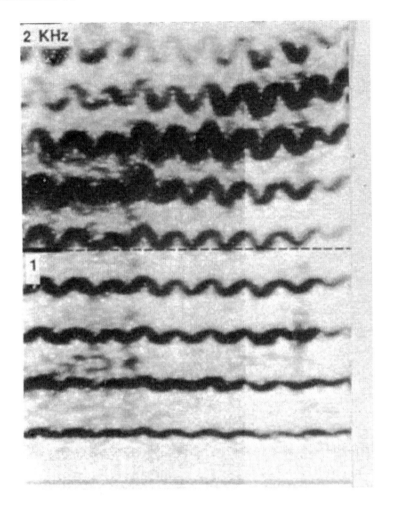

Agrandir Original (jpeg, 124k)

Fig. 42 : *Kargiraa* touvain (cf. fig. 5). Vibrato « en ondulations ».

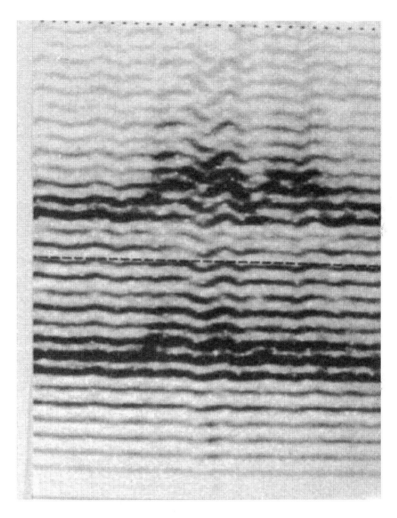

Agrandir Original (jpeg, 128k)

Fig. 43 : *Borbannadir* touvain à fondamental grave (cf. fig. 13). Pulsation « en zigzag » sur la mélodie d'harmoniques à bande large.

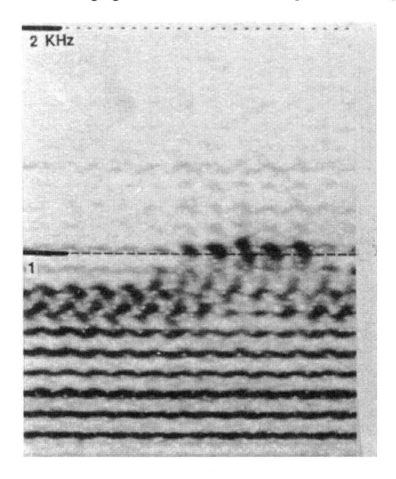

Agrandir Original (jpeg, 120k)

Fig. 44 : *Borbannadir* touvain à fondamental aigu (cf. fig. 22). Accents rythmiques « en hachures » sur H2 par frappement de doigt(s) sur les lèvres.

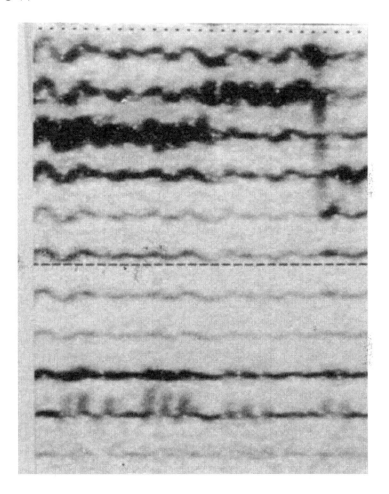

Agrandir Original (jpeg, 116k)

Fig. 45 : Khomei touvain (cf. fig. 18). Pulsation rythmique marquée par des traits verticaux alternativement au-dessus et au-dessous de la ligne horizontale.

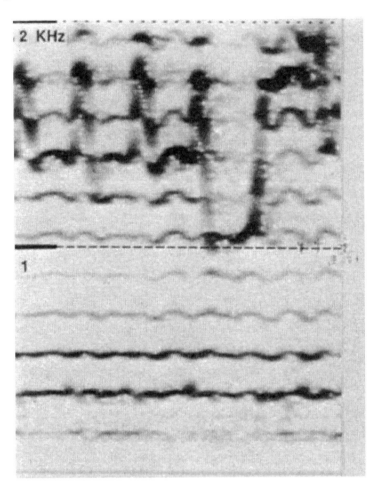

Agrandir Original (jpeg, 120k)

Fig. 46 : Ezengileer touvain (cf. fig. 21). Accents rythmiques marqués par des traits verticaux alternativement au-dessus et au-dessous de la ligne horizontale.

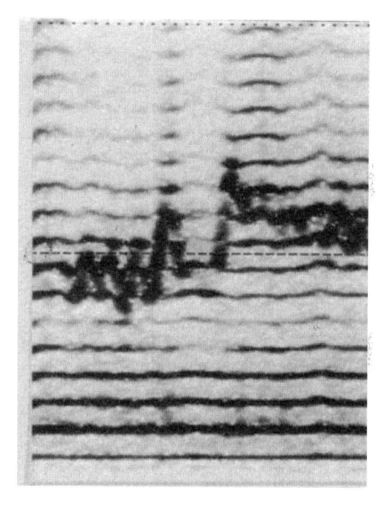

Agrandir Original (jpeg, 124k)

Fig. 47 : Expérimentation d'un « bourdon harmonique » dans l'aigu, avec variation du fondamental, par Trân Quang Hai.

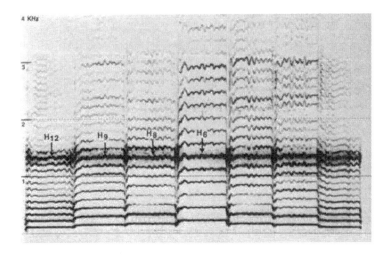

Agrandir Original (jpeg, 140k)

Technique à deux cavités. Voix fortement nasalisée. Contraction pharyngienne et abdominale. Échelle montante des fondamentaux La1 (135 Hz), Re2, Mi2, La2 (270 Hz), et redescendante au La1. « Bourdon harmonique » de 1380 Hz réalisé successivement par H12, 9, 8, 6, 8, 9, 12.

Fig. 48 : Expérimentation d'un mouvement contraire entre bourdon et mélodie d'harmoniques, par Trân Quang Hai.

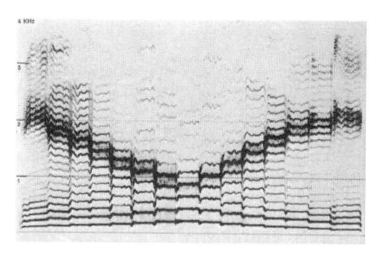

Agrandir Original (jpeg, 134k)

Technique à deux cavités. Voix fortement nasalisée. Contraction pharyngienne et abdominale. Échelle diatonique ascendante des fondamentaux du La1 (110 Hz) au La2 (220 Hz) et redescendante. Échelles d'harmoniques en mouvement contraire, descendante de H19 au H4 et remontante à H19.

Haut de page

285

Notes

1 Ces recherches ont été effectuées dans le cadre de l'Unité Propre de Recherche n° 165 du CNRS, au Département d'ethnomusicologie du Musée de l'Homme. Avant d'envoyer le manuscrit final à l'éditeur, nous avons pu présenter au séminaire de l'UPR un résumé de notre travail. Les questions et remarques nous ont aidé à corriger et préciser notre analyse. Gilles Léothaud et Gilbert Rouget nous ont alors fait l'amitié de relire le manuscrit et de nous faire part de leurs suggestions pour l'améliorer. Nous voudrions exprimer à tous notre gratitude.

2 Les détails de la réalisation de ce film – dont la première a eu lieu le 27 juillet 1989 lors du Congrès de l'International Council for Traditional Music à Schladming (Autriche) – sont décrits ailleurs (cf. Zemp 1989). Un livret, devant accompagner l'édition sous forme de vidéocassette, est actuellement en préparation.

3 Recherche menée en étroite collaboration par les deux co-auteurs qui chacun ont apporté – en plus de l'évaluation en commun de chaque étape du travail – des contributions spécifiques. Les sonagrammes, ainsi que les analyses détaillées ayant servi à rédiger les légendes des figures, sont de Trân Quang Hai qui, en plus, est en même temps « informateur privilégié » et chanteur de 26 enregistrements reproduits sur sonagrammes. La conception de la recherche, la mise en forme et la rédaction de l'article sont de Hugo Zemp.

4 Paru dans une nouvelle publication : le Dossier n° 1 de l'Institut de la Voix, Limoges. Outre deux brefs rapports relatant des examens cliniques et paracliniques de l'appareil phonatoire et de l'émission diphonique de Trân Quang Hai, examens effectués l'un par un médecin O.R.L. (Sauvage 1989) et l'autre par un phoniatre (Pailler 1989), et l'extrait d'un exposé sur la réalisation du chant diphonique

286

(Trân Quang Hai 1989), ce dossier contient également la bibliographie et la discographie les plus complètes à ce jour concernant le chant diphonique.

5 La translittération change selon les auteurs *xöömij*, *khöömii*, *chöömij*, *ho-mi*.

6 Elle avait dix-sept ans quand cet enregistrement fut fait, mais son père lui avait enseigné le chant diphonique dès l'âge de six ans.

7 Selon Alekseev, Kirgiz et Levin (1990), la pièce que nous avons représentée dans les fig. 9 et 10 est une variante du *kargiraa*, appelée « Steppe *kargiraa* », et rappelle les chants tantriques des moines tibétains. Pour notre part, nous n'avons pas remarqué de différence avec les autres pièces de style *kargiraa* tuva, et la mélodie d'harmoniques très caractéristique n'a que peu d'éléments en commun avec les harmoniques qui apparaissent dans les chants tibétains des monastères Gyüto et Gyümë.

8 Les harmoniques de cette deuxième zone enrichissent sans doute le timbre, mais ils ne sont pas perçus par l'oreille comme formant une mélodie séparée de la mélodie d'harmoniques de la première zone.

9 Folkways/Smithsonian n° 1, 8, 9, 17, 18. Melodia, face A, plage 9. Le Chant du Monde, face A, plage 5.

10 La dénomination *xaarkiraa xöömij* est « traduite » dans Emmert et Minegushi (1980 48) par « narrative *xöömij* », sans doute pour rendre compte du fait que dans ce style la partie diphonique peut être précédée par une partie narrative chantée avec la voix naturelle. Dans le film *Le chant des harmoniques*, la dénomination *kargiraa khöömii* a été traduite par Alain Desjaques par « *khöömii* grue noire », *khargiraa* désignant en mongol cet oiseau dont la voix grave

et enrouée aurait pu donner le nom à ce style. A moins que les Mongols aient emprunté le terme *kargiraa* aux Tuva pour qui, selon Alekseev, Kirgiz et Levin (1990), il proviendrait d'un mot onomatopéique signifiant « respirer péniblement », « parler d'une voix rauque ou enrouée ». Nous ne pouvons trancher entre les deux interprétations. Il est aussi possible que les uns aient emprunté le terme aux autres, tout en lui trouvant postérieurement une signification dans leur propre langue.

11 Cela semble être un phénomène récent. Selon Alekseev, Kirgiz et Levin (1990), les chanteurs tuva étaient autrefois spécialisés en un ou deux styles apparentés, mais aujourd'hui les jeunes utilisent plusieurs styles et arrangent fréquemment des ségments mélodiques en des mélanges polystylistiques.

12 Folkways/Smithsonian, n° 11 et 14.

13 Melodia, face 1, plage 5. Folkways/Smithsonian, n° 12 et 13.

14 Folkways/Smithsonian, n° 7.

15 Folkways/Smithsonian, n° 5, 6, 8. Le Chant du Monde, face A, plage 4.

16 Folkways/Smithsonian, n° 2, 3, 4, 8, 16, 17. Melodia, face A, plages 1, 2, 6, 7, 8. Le Chant du Monde, face A, plage 3.

17 Tangent TGS 126, face B, plage 1 Tangent TGS 127, face B, plage 3. Victor, face A, plages 5, 6 et 7.

18 Selon Alain Desjacques qui a assumé la traduction, le terme *kholgoï* est synonyme de *bagalzuuliin*.

19 Cf. la notice du CD Maison des cultures du monde, n° 4 et 6.

20 Un autre chanteur mongol a indiqué le nom de *khooloin khöömii* (« *khöömii* de gorge ») pour une pièce, et *tseesni khendi* (traduit par « technique ventrale ») pour une autre, alors que la simple écoute montre, et l'analyse spectrographique le confirme, qu'il s'agit d'un même style (CD GREM, n° 32 et 33), en l'occurrence le style que D. Sundui appelle *kevliin khöömii* (« *khöömii* de ventre »).

21 Vogue, face B, plage 3. Hungaroton, face A, plage 5, et face B, plage 7. ORSTOM-SELAF, face B, plage 2. Maison des Cultures du Monde, n° 4, 5, 6.

22 Trân Quang Hai était directeur artistique pour la section de musique asiatique au festival de musique de chambre à Kuhmo en 1984, et à ce titre avait invité le chanteur D. Sundui à se produire en Finlande.

23 Nous devons cette question à Gilles Léothaud qui l'a posée au séminaire de notre équipe de recherche lorsque nous avons exposé nos travaux.

24 « *an ornamented trilling and punctuating rhythm principally on two pitches (the ninth and tenth partials of the two fundamentals)* »

25 GREM, n° 2.

26 *In the broken singing of this style the intoning of v is interrupted by the full closing of the lips followed by opening either on x the plosive voiced consonant b or on the nasal consonant m.* (Aksenov 1973 : 14)

27 Les trois auteurs écrivent que la mélodie d'harmoniques est produite par de rapides vibrations de lèvres *(In* ezengileer, *soft, shimmering harmonic melodies produced by rapide vibrations of the lips, are sung over a low fundamental drone)*. Le lecteur corrigera

de lui-même cette mauvaise formulation, car bien entendu ce n'est pas la mélodie d'harmoniques qui est produite par la vibration des lèvres, mais le rythme pulsé. De même, la formulation disant que le style « *borbannadir* est utilisé métaphoriquement pour signifier "roulant" » (borbannadir, *used metaphorically to signify "rolling"*) n'est pas très heureuse.

<u>28</u> C'est ainsi qu'on peut traduire l'expression « with finger strokes across the lips ». On peut supposer qu'un doigt (l'index ?) est mis horizontalement entre les lèvres, et qu'un rapide va-et-vient vertical imprime la pulsation à l'émission diphonique.

<u>29</u> Communication verbale de D. Sundui à Trân Quang Hai lors du festival en Finlande, 1984.

<u>30</u> Pour ce qui est du chant d'opéra et de concert, l'ondulation du vibrato est décrit comme presque sinusoïdale, avec un ambitus de l'ordre de +50 Hz (Sundberg 1980 : 85), c'est-à-dire du quart de ton.

<u>31</u> Traduction de la notice de B. Tchourov par Philippe Mennecier (communication personnelle). Le même chanteur a exécuté deux pièces de styles *sigit* et deux pièces de style *khomei* qui ne comportent pas ce « bourdon à la quinte » (Melodia, face A, plages 1 à 4).

Table des illustrations

Titre G. YAVGAAN. Photogramme extrait du film « Le chant des harmoniques » de H. Zemp.

URL http://journals.openedition.org/ethnomusicolo gie/docannexe/image/1572/img-1.jpg

Fichier image/jpeg, 80k

Titre T. GANBOLD. Photogramme extrait du film « Le chant des harmoniques » de H. Zemp.

URL http://journals.openedition.org/ethnomusicolo gie/docannexe/image/1572/img-2.jpg

Fichier image/jpeg, 84k

Titre Fig. 1 : Échelles d'harmoniques avec différentes hauteurs du fondamental (90 à 180 Hz selon une échelle diatonique), par Trân Quang Hai. Technique à une cavité.

Légende Voix fortement nasalisée. Prononciation marquée de voyelles. H1, 2 et 3 du bourdon très marqués. Avec le fondamental le plus grave (90 Hz), les harmoniques 4 (360 HZ) à 12 (1080 Hz) peuvent être utilisés pour créer une mélodie. Avec le fondamental le plus aigu (180 Hz), seuls les harmoniques 3 à 6 (1080 Hz) ressortent. Deuxième zone d'harmoniques entre 2500 et 4000 Hz, séparée des harmoniques utilisables par une « zone blanche » sur le sonagramme.

URL http://journals.openedition.org/ethnomusicolo gie/docannexe/image/1572/img-3.jpg

Fichier image/jpeg, 128k

Titre Fig. 2 : Échelles d'harmoniques avec différentes hauteurs du fondamental (110 à 220 Hz, selon une échelle diatonique), par Trân Quang Hai. Technique à deux cavités.

Légende Voix nasalisée. H1 et 2 du bourdon très marqués. Les harmoniques bien tracés sur le sonagramme atteignent la limite supérieure de 2200 Hz avec H10 dans le cas du fondamental le plus aigu à 220 Hz, et H20 dans le cas du fondamental le plus grave, à l'octave inférieure (110 Hz). Les harmoniques exploitables pour une mélodie sont dans le premier cas H4 (880 Hz) à H10 (2200 Hz), et dans le deuxième cas H6 (660 Hz) à H20 (2200 Hz).

URL http://journals.openedition.org/ethnomusicologie/docannexe/image/1572/img-4.jpg

Fichier image/jpeg, 144k

Titre Fig. 3 : Échelles d'harmoniques avec bourdon stable, par Minh-Tâm, fille (17 ans) de Trân Quang Hai. Technique à une cavité.

Légende H1 (240 Hz), 2 et 3 du bourdon très marqués. Harmoniques utilisables pour une mélodie H3, 4 et 5 (1200 Hz). Pour une voix de femme, à cause de la hauteur du fondamental plus élevé (ici 240 Hz), le nombre d'harmoniques exploitables pour une mélodie est très limité.

URL http://journals.openedition.org/ethnomusicologie/docannexe/image/1572/img-5.jpg

Fichier image/jpeg, 128k

Fig. 4 : Échelles d'harmoniques avec bourdon
Titre stable, par Minh-Tâm, fille (17 ans) de Trân
Quang Hai. Technique à deux cavités.

Légene Voix nasalisée. H1 (270 Hz). Harmoniques
exploitables pour une mélodie H4 (1080 Hz),
5, 6, 7, 8 (2160 Hz). H8 fait apparaître H12 et
13 dans la zone aiguë.

URL http://journals.openedition.org/ethnomusicolo
gie/docannexe/image/1572/img-6.jpg

Fichier image/jpeg, 132k

Fig. 5 : Tuva (URSS). CD
Titre Smithsonian/Folkways, n° 18. Style *kargiraa*,
pièce « Artii-sayir » par Vasili Chazir.

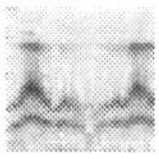

Légende Prononciation marquée de voyelles. H1 (62
Hz), 2 et 3 du bourdon très faibles. Mélodie
d'harmoniques H6 (375 Hz), 8, 9, 10, 12 (750
Hz). Deuxième zone de mélodie
d'harmoniques à l'octave, entre H12 (750 Hz)
et H24 (1500 Hz). « Bourdon harmonique »
aigu H44 (2690 Hz), plus marqué quand la
voyelle a est prononcée (avec une sorte de
« colonne grisée » entre 1500 et 2700 Hz.
(Transcription musicale de cette pièce dans la
notice du CD).

URL http://journals.openedition.org/ethnomusicolo
gie/docannexe/image/1572/img-7.jpg

Fichier image/jpeg, 140k

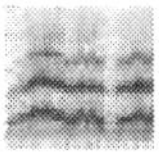

Titre **Fig. 6 :** Imitation par Trân Quang Hai du style
kargiraa tuva de la fig. 5.

Légene Technique à une cavité, prononciation
marquée de voyelles. Bouche ouverte, sauf

293

quand la mélodie d'harmoniques descend à H6 (alors bouche fermée avec prononciation de la consonne m). Relaxation pharyngienne et abdominale. H1 (70 Hz), 2, 3 et 4 du bourdon très marqués, H2 et 4 un peu plus que H1 et 3. Mélodie d'harmoniques à large bande H6 (420 Hz), 8, 9, 10, 12 (840 Hz). Deuxième zone de mélodie d'harmoniques à l'octave, entre H18 (1260 Hz) et H24 (1680 Hz). Troisième zone de mélodie d'harmoniques très faible, entre 2100 et 2400 Hz.

URL	http://journals.openedition.org/ethnomusicolo gie/docannexe/image/1572/img-8.jpg
Fichier	image/jpeg, 176k
Titre	Fig. 7 : Xhosa (Afrique du Sud). Enreg. D. Dargie, Phonothèque Musée de l'Homme BM 87.4.1. Style imitant le jeu de l'arc musical *umrhubhe*, par Nowayilethi.
Légen de	Alternance de deux fondamentaux à l'intervalle d'un ton. H1 (100Hz et 110 Hz), très faible ; H2, 3 et 4 du bourdon marqués. Mélodie d'harmoniques H4 (400 Hz), 5, 6 (600 Hz) quand le fondamental est à 100 Hz ; et H4 (440 Hz) et H5 (550 Hz) quand le fondamental est à 110 Hz. Deuxième zone de mélodie d'harmoniques entre 800 et 1200 Hz. Troisième zone plus faible à 2400 Hz ; par exemple, lorsque la mélodie d'harmoniques est sur H6, les harmoniques 10 et 12, ainsi que H24 sont très marqués. (Notation musicale dans Dargie 1988 : 59)

URL	http://journals.openedition.org/ethnomusicologie/docannexe/image/1572/img-9.jpg
Fichier	image/jpeg, 148k
Titre	Fig. 8 : Imitation par Trân Quang Hai du chant xhosa de la fig. 7.
Légende	Technique à une cavité. Voix peu nasalisée, bouche moins ouverte que dans le style *kargiraa*. Contraction pharyngienne et abdominale. H1 (100 et 110 Hz), 2, 3 et 4 marqués. Mélodie d'harmoniques H4 (400Hz), 5, 6, 8 (800 Hz). Technique mal maîtrisée. Absence de deuxième et troisième zone dans l'aigu.

URL	http://journals.openedition.org/ethnomusicologie/docannexe/image/1572/img-10.jpg
Fichier	image/jpeg, 176k
Titre	Fig. 9 : Touva (URSS). CD Smithsonian/Folkways, n° 1. Style « Steppe » *kargiraa*, par Fedor Tau. Début du chant.
Légende	Prononciation marquée de voyelles. H1 (67 Hz) très faible ; H1 est abaissé d'une tierce mineure (57 Hz) au moment où la voyelle i est prononcée. Paralellement, la mélodie d'harmoniques baisse également d'une tierce mineure, l'harmonique restant le même (H8). Mélodie d'harmoniques à large bande H8 (536 Hz) et 456 Hz), 9, 10, 12 (804 Hz). Deuxième zone de mélodie d'harmoniques entre H16 (1072 Hz) et H30 (2010 Hz). Pour les voyelles postérieures o, ɔ, a, la deuxième

zone de mélodie d'harmoniques est à l'octave H8 — H16, H9 — H18, H10 — H20, H12 — H24.

URL http://journals.openedition.org/ethnomusicolo gie/docannexe/image/1572/img-11.jpg

Fichier image/jpeg, 148k

Titre Fig. 10 : Reprise du chant de fig. 9. Même mélodie d'harmoniques, mais différence de la deuxième zone en raison de la différence des voyelles. Pour les voyelles antérieures i, e, , la deuxième zone de mélodie d'harmoniques est plus haute la voyelle e au début de la reprise (fig. 10) H8 — H32 (= double octave) ; la voyelle i H9 — large bande de H28 à 30.

URL http://journals.openedition.org/ethnomusicolo gie/docannexe/image/1572/img-12.jpg

Fichier image/jpeg, 148k

Titre Fig. 11 : Mongolie. Film *Le chant des harmoniques.* Style *khargiraa khöömii,* démonstration pour l'interview, par T. Ganbold.

Légen de H1 (85 Hz) très faible ; H2, 3, 4, 5 et 6 du bourdon très marqués. Mélodie d'harmoniques faible, avec des harmoniques impairs H13 (1105 Hz), 15, 17, 19, 21 (1785 Hz). Dans l'aigu, une zone d'harmoniques faible entre H28 et H 30 (2630 à 2800 Hz).

URL http://journals.openedition.org/ethnomusicolo gie/docannexe/image/1572/img-13.jpg

Fichier image/jpeg, 144k

Titre Fig. 12 : Imitation par Trân Quang Hai du style *khargiraa khöömii* mongol de la fig. 11.

Légende Technique à deux cavités. H1 (90 Hz) de même que H2, 3, 4 et 5 très marqués. Mélodie d'harmoniques avec des harmoniques paires H12 (1080 Hz), 14, 16, 18, 20 (1800 Hz). Relaxation pharyngiennee et abdominale.

URL http://journals.openedition.org/ethnomusicolo gie/docannexe/image/1572/img-14.jpg

Fichier image/jpeg, 104k

Titre Fig. 13 : Tuva (URSS). CD Smithsonian/Folkways, n° 14. Pièce intitulée *borbannadir*, par Anatolii Kuular.

Légende Manifestement les styles *kargiraa* et *borbannadir* se succèdent. Tracé caractéristique de *kargiraa*, avec vibrato six battements/seconde en forme d'ondulations. H1 (95 Hz) faible. Dans la partie *borbannadir*, H1 (95 Hz) faible ; H2, 3 et 4 marqués. Pulsation à huit battements/seconde « en zigzag » sur la mélodie d'harmoniques à bande large H7 (685 HZ), 8, 9 et 11 (1045 Hz).

URL http://journals.openedition.org/ethnomusicolo gie/docannexe/image/1572/img-15.jpg

Fichier image/jpeg, 144k

Titre Fig. 14 : Même pièce que fig. 13, un peu plus loin.

Légende Manifestement trois styles. Dans le premier segment, styles *kargiraa* et *borbannadir* enchainés, avec H1 (95 Hz) faible. Après une courte interruption, deuxième segment de style différent, avec un saut d'octave du fondamental, H1 (190 Hz) et H2 bien marqués. Mélodie d'harmoniques à bande large, avec pulsation à sept battements/seconde « en zigzag », H9 (1710 Hz), 10 et 12 (2280 Hz).

URL	http://journals.openedition.org/ethnomusicolo gie/docannexe/image/1572/img-16.jpg
Fichier	image/jpeg, 144k
Titre	Fig. 15 : Tuva (URSS). Disque Melodia, face A, plage 5. Style *borbannadir*, pièce « *Boratmoj*, *Spoju Borban* », par Oorzak Xunastar-ool.
Légen de	H1 (120 Hz) et 2 marqués. H3 du bourdon très marqué (on entend bien ce deuxième bourdon à la quinte). Mélodie d'harmoniques H8 (980 Hz), 9, 10 et 12 (1440 Hz). Accents rythmiques visibles surtout sur H3, 12 et 13.
URL	http://journals.openedition.org/ethnomusicolo gie/docannexe/image/1572/img-17.jpg
Fichier	image/jpeg, 152k
Titre	Fig. 16 : Imitation par Trân Quang Hai du style *borbannadir* de la fig. 13.
Lége nde	Technique à une cavité. Émission nasalisée, bouche presque fermée, prononciation de la voyelle o. H1 (95Hz), 2 à 5 très marqués. Mouvements rapides de la langue en avant et en arrière pulsation « en zigzag » sur la mélodie d'harmoniques à bande large H9 (855 Hz) à 13 (1235 Hz).

URL	http://journals.openedition.org/ethnomusicolo gie/docannexe/image/1572/img-18.jpg
Fichier	image/jpeg, 124k
Titre	Fig. 17 : Imitation par Trân Quang Hai du style non identifié de la fig. 14.
Légende	Technique à 2 cavités. Forte nasalisation, contraction pharyngienne et abdominale. H1(190Hz) et 2 très marqués. Rapides aplatissements de la pointe de la langue contre le palais, et simultanément tremblement de la mâchoire inférieure pulsation « en zigzag » sur la mélodie d'harmoniques à bande large H6 (1140 Hz) et 8 (1520 Hz).
URL	http://journals.openedition.org/ethnomusicolo gie/docannexe/image/1572/img-19.jpg
Fichier	image/jpeg, 132k
Titre	Fig. 18 : Tuva (URSS). CD Smithsonian/Folkways, n° 8. Styles *khoomei* et *sigit*, par Tumat Kara-ool.
Légende	H1 (175 Hz). Pour le *khoomei*, H1 faible ; H2 et 3 marqués. Mélodie d'harmoniques à bande large H6 (1050 Hz), 8, 9, 10 (1750 Hz). Pulsation rythmique visible sous forme de traits verticaux dirigés alternativement vers le haut et le bas à partir de la ligne horizontale indiquant la mélodie d'harmoniques. Pour le *sigit* (cf. aussi fig. 21 et 22), H1, 2 et 3 du bourdon faible. Mélodie d'harmoniques H12 (2050 Hz) et ornement H13 ; les autres harmoniques n'apparaissant pas sur l'extrait de ce sonagramme.

URL	http://journals.openedition.org/ethnomusicolo gie/docannexe/image/1572/img-20.jpg
Fichier	image/jpeg, 164k
Titre	Fig. 19 : Imitation par Trân Quang Hai du style *khoomei* tuva de la fig. 18.
Légen de	Technique à deux cavités. Voix peu nasalisée. Contraction pharyngienne modérée. Bouche moins ouverte que pour le *sigit*. Mouvements rythmiques de la lèvre inférieure vers la lèvre supérieure : pulsation rythmique visible sous forme de traits verticaux alternativement au-dessus et au-dessous de la ligne horizontale.
URL	http://journals.openedition.org/ethnomusicolo gie/docannexe/image/1572/img-21.jpg
Fichier	image/jpeg, 128k
Titre	Fig. 20 : Imitation par Trân Quang Hai du style *borbannadir* tuva de la fig. 15.
Légen de	Technique à deux cavités. Voix nasalisée. Contraction pharyngienne modérée comme pour la fig. 18a, mais la bouche encore moins ouverte, arrondie. Coups de langue rythmiques contre le palais, bien marqués sur H3 du bourdon et sur les harmoniques supérieurs. H1 (175 Hz), 2 et 3 très marqués ; mélodie d'harmoniques H10 (1750 Hz) et H 12 (2050 Hz).
URL	http://journals.openedition.org/ethnomusicolo gie/docannexe/image/1572/img-22.jpg
Fichier	image/jpeg, 132k

300

Fig. 21 : Tuva (URSS). CD

Titre Smithsonian/Folkways, n° 15. Style *ezengileer*, par Marzhimal Ondar.

Légende H1 (120 Hz), 2, 3, 4 du bourdon très marqués. Mélodie d'harmoniques H6 (720 Hz), 7, 8, 9, 10, 12 (1440 Hz). Le tracé est caractérisé par des accents rythmiques « en zigzag » sur 2 ou 3 harmoniques (l'extrait choisi ne comporte pas le frappement de doigts sur un bol de thé, indiqué sur la notice du CD). Dans l'aigu, une deuxième zone d'harmoniques entre H22 et H24 (2880 Hz).

URL http://journals.openedition.org/ethnomusicolo gie/docannexe/image/1572/img-23.jpg

Fichier image/jpeg, 180k

Fig. 22 : Tuva (URSS). CD

Titre Smithsonian/Folkways, n° 13. Pièce intitulée « *Borbannadir* with finger strokes », par Tumat Kara-ool.

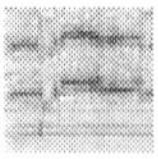

Légende H1 (180 Hz) faible. « Hachures » irrégulieres sur H2, rythmiquement différentes du vibrato en forme d'ondulations marqué sur les harmoniques supérieurs. Mélodie d'harmoniques H6 (1080), 8, 9, 10 (1800 Hz). Deuxième zone de mélodie d'harmoniques à l'octave, sauf H10 — H18.

URL http://journals.openedition.org/ethnomusicolo gie/docannexe/image/1572/img-24.jpg

Fichier image/jpeg, 156k

Fig. 23 : Touva (URSS). CD

Titre Smithsonian/Folkways, n° 3. Style *sigit*, pièce « *Alash* » par Mergen Mongush.

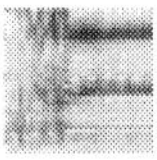

Début chanté avec des paroles en voix naturelle. Abaissement momentané du fondamental à une tierce mineure. H1 (190 Hz), 2 et 3 du bourdon marqués. Mélodie d'harmoniques H8 (1520 Hz), 9, 10 et 12 ;

Légend e ornements rythmiques sur H10 et 13. Dans l'aigu, « bourdon harmonique » à l'octave de la mélodie d'harmoniques (H9 — H18) et à la quinte (H12 — H18). Zone de rejection d'harmoniques entre le bourdon (H1 à H3) et la mélodie d'harmoniques, et entre celle-ci et le bourdon aigu (H18).

URL http://journals.openedition.org/ethnomusicolo gie/docannexe/image/1572/img-25.jpg

Fichier image/jpeg, 152k

Fig. 24 : Touva (URSS). Disque Melodia,

Titre face A, plage 1. Style *sigit*, pièce « *Reka Alas* » (même pièce que fig. 23).

Début chanté avec des paroles en voix naturelle. Abaissement momentané du fondamental d'une tierce mineure. H1 (170

Légen de Hz) et 2 marqués. Mélodie d'harmoniques H9 (1530 Hz), 10, 12 (2030 Hz) ; ornements rythmques sur H10 et 11. Absence de deuxième zone dans l'aigu.

URL http://journals.openedition.org/ethnomusicolo gie/docannexe/image/1572/img-26.jpg

Fichier image/jpeg, 148k

302

Titre Fig. 25 : Mongolie. Disque Tangent, face B, plage 1. Pièce intitulé « *Mouth music* », par Sundui (cf. aussi le film *Le chant des harmoniques*). Style non nommé sur la notice du disque, mais sans doute « *khöömi* de ventre », le style préféré de Sundui.

Légende H1 (210 Hz) et 2 marqués, sauf quand la mélodie d'harmoniques est sur H12. Mélodie d'harmoniques à bande large H5 (1050 Hz), 6, 7, 8, 9, 10 et 12 (2510 Hz). Vibrato en forme d'ondulations.

URL http://journals.openedition.org/ethnomusicolo gie/docannexe/image/1572/img-27.jpg

Fichier image/jpeg, 156k

Titre Fig. 26 : Imitation par Trân Quang Hai du style *sigit* touvain de la fig. 23.

Légende Technique à deux cavités. Forte nasalisation. Contraction abdominale et pharyngienne. Rétrécissement de la colonne d'air. Pour obtenir les ornements rythmiques (H10 à partir de la ligne mélodique H9, et H13 à partir de la ligne mélodique H12), la pointe de la langue est légèrement aplatie contre le palais. H1 (145 Hz) et H2 très marqués. Même mélodie d'harmoniques que fig. 23 et 24. Absence de deuxième zone dans l'aigu, comme fig. 24.

URL http://journals.openedition.org/ethnomusicolo gie/docannexe/image/1572/img-28.jpg

Fichier image/jpeg, 140k

303

Titre	Fig. 27 : Rajasthan. Enregistrement J. Levy. Phonothèque du Musée de l'Homme BM78.2.1.
Légende	H1 (170 Hz) et 2 très marqués. Mélodie d'harmoniques H5 (850 Hz), 6, 8, 9,10, 11, 12, 13, 16 (2720 Hz), à large bande. Accents rythmiques, sans doute pour imiter le jeu de la guimbarde. Plus grand ambitus de toutes les pièces analysées dans cet article.
URL	http://journals.openedition.org/ethnomusicolo gie/docannexe/image/1572/img-29.jpg
Fichier	image/jpeg, 152k
Titre	Fig. 28 : Imitation par Trân Quang Hai du chant du Rajasthan de la fig. 27.
Légende	Technique à deux cavités. Voix fortement nasalisée. Forte contraction pharyngienne et abdominale (comme pour le *sigit*). Coups de langue rythmiques contre le palais, ce qui donne sur le tracé des lignes verticales comme sur la fig. 27. H1 (150 Hz), H5 (750 Hz) à H 16 (2400 Hz).
URL	http://journals.openedition.org/ethnomusicolo gie/docannexe/image/1572/img-30.jpg
Fichier	image/jpeg, 144k
Titre	Fig. 29 : Mongolie. Probablement style *tzeedznii khöömii* (« *khöömii* de poitrine »), appelé dans le film Le chant des harmoniques par erreur *bagalzuuriin khöömi*, (« *khöömi* de gorge »). Démonstration pour l'interview, par T. Ganbold.

H1 (180 Hz) marqué, H2 très marqué.

Légende Mélodie d'harmoniques H8 (1440 Hz), 9, 10 (1800 Hz). Dans l'aigu, 2ᵉ zone à l'octave (H18 à 3240 Hz).

URL http://journals.openedition.org/ethnomusicolo gie/docannexe/image/1572/img-31.jpg

Fichier image/jpeg, 136k

Titre Fig. 30 : Même chanteur. Style *khamryn khöömii* (« *khöömii* de nez »).

Légende H1 (170 Hz), 2 et 3 marqués. Mélodie d'harmoniques très faible H8, 9 et 10, « noyée » dans les harmoniques couvrant toute l'étendue du spectre.

URL http://journals.openedition.org/ethnomusicolo gie/docannexe/image/1572/img-32.jpg

Fichier image/jpeg, 120k

Titre Fig. 31 : Même signal que fig. 29.

Légende Analyse à 8 KHz, montrant une troisième zone à large bande au dessus de 4000 Hz.

URL http://journals.openedition.org/ethnomusicolo gie/docannexe/image/1572/img-33.jpg

Fichier image/jpeg, 144k

Titre Fig. 32 : Même signal que fig. 30.

Légende Analyse à 8 KHz, montrant une troisième zone à large bande au dessus de 4000 Hz.

URL http://journals.openedition.org/ethnomusicolo gie/docannexe/image/1572/img-34.jpg

Fichier image/jpeg, 136k

Titre Fig. 33 : Mongolie. Probablement style *bagalzuuliin khöömii*, (« *khöömii* de gorge »),

305

appelé dans le film *Le chant des harmoniques* par erreur *tseedznii khöömi* (« *khöömi* de poitrine »). Démonstration pour l'interview, par T. Ganbold.

Légende	Bouche grande ouverte. H1 (170 Hz), 2, 3, 5, 6 du bourdon très marqués. Mélodie d'harmoniques H8 (1360 Hz), 9, 10 (1700 Hz). Dans l'aigu, une deuxième zone d'harmoniques à bande large H16 à 20 (2720 à 3400 Hz). Une analyse à 8000 Hz (non reproduite ici) montre une troisième zone très marquée au-dessus de 4000 Hz.
URL	http://journals.openedition.org/ethnomusicologie/docannexe/image/1572/img-35.jpg
Fichier	image/jpeg, 164k
Titre	Fig. 34 : Imitation par Trân Quang Hai du style de la fig. 33.
Légende	Technique à deux cavités avec l'arrière de la langue mordue par les molaires. Contraction pharyngienne avec une rétrécissement de la colonne d'air, musculature du cou « remontée ». Bouche grande ouverte, lèvres légèrement étirées comme pour prononcer la voyelle i. H1 (170 Hz), 2, 3, 4, 5, 6 du bourdon très marqués. Mélodie d'harmoniques H8 (1360 Hz), 9, 10 (1700 Hz).
URL	http://journals.openedition.org/ethnomusicologie/docannexe/image/1572/img-36.jpg
Fichier	image/jpeg, 176k
Titre	Fig. 35 : Essai par Trân Quang Hai.

H1 (220 Hz) ; mélodie d'harmoniques H8. Forte contraction abdominale et **Légende** pharyngienne. Conduit d'air très reserré. La vibration est ressentie plus fortement au-dessus de la pomme d'Adam.

URL http://journals.openedition.org/ethnomusicolo gie/docannexe/image/1572/img-37.jpg

Fichier image/jpeg, 128k

Titre Fig. 36 : Essai par Trân Quang Hai.

H1 (220 Hz) ; mélodie d'harmoniques H8. Forte contraction abdominale et **Légende** pharyngienne. Conduit d'air plus large. La vibration est ressentie plus fortement au-dessous de la pomme d'Adam.

URL http://journals.openedition.org/ethnomusicolo gie/docannexe/image/1572/img-38.jpg

Fichier image/jpeg, 140k

Titre Fig. 37 : Essai par Trân Quang Hai.

H1 (220 Hz) ; mélodie d'harmoniques H8. Relaxation abdominale et pharyngienne. **Légende** Intensité faible ; pour obtenir un tracé noir, il fallait compenser en augmentant le niveau d'entrée du Sona-Graph.

URL http://journals.openedition.org/ethnomusicolo gie/docannexe/image/1572/img-39.jpg

Fichier image/jpeg, 120k

Titre Fig. 38 : Essai par Trân Quang Hai.

H1 (220 Hz) ; mélodie d'harmoniques **Légende** H8.Bouche fermée. Contractions comme pour la fig. 36. Intensité faible ; pour obtenir un

tracé noir, il fallait compenser en augmentant
le niveau d'entrée du Sona-Graph.

URL	http://journals.openedition.org/ethnomusicolo gie/docannexe/image/1572/img-40.jpg
Fichier	image/jpeg, 128k

Fig. 39 : *Sigit* touvain (cf. fig. 23). Ornements
rythmiques « en ponctuations » sur H10,
combinés avec du vibrato.

Titre	(see above)
URL	http://journals.openedition.org/ethnomusicolo gie/docannexe/image/1572/img-41.jpg
Fichier	image/jpeg, 108k

Fig. 40 : Chant du Rajasthan (cf. fig. 27).
Accents rythmiques marqués par des lignes
verticales sur toute l'étendue du spectre.

Titre	(see above)
URL	http://journals.openedition.org/ethnomusicolo gie/docannexe/image/1572/img-42.jpg
Fichier	image/jpeg, 116k

Fig. 41 : « *Khöömii* de ventre » mongol (cf.
fig. 25). Vibrato « en ondulations ».

Titre	(see above)
URL	http://journals.openedition.org/ethnomusicolo gie/docannexe/image/1572/img-43.jpg
Fichier	image/jpeg, 124k

Fig. 42 : *Kargiraa* touvain (cf. fig. 5). Vibrato
« en ondulations ».

Titre	(see above)
URL	http://journals.openedition.org/ethnomusicolo gie/docannexe/image/1572/img-44.jpg
Fichier	image/jpeg, 128k

Titre Fig. 43 : *Borbannadir* touvain à fondamental grave (cf. fig. 13). Pulsation « en zigzag » sur la mélodie d'harmoniques à bande large.

URL http://journals.openedition.org/ethnomusicolo gie/docannexe/image/1572/img-45.jpg

Fichier image/jpeg, 120k

Titre Fig. 44 : *Borbannadir* touvain à fondamental aigu (cf. fig. 22). Accents rythmiques « en hachures » sur H2 par frappement de doigt(s) sur les lèvres.

URL http://journals.openedition.org/ethnomusicolo gie/docannexe/image/1572/img-46.jpg

Fichier image/jpeg, 116k

Titre Fig. 45 : Khomei touvain (cf. fig. 18). Pulsation rythmique marquée par des traits verticaux alternativement au-dessus et au-dessous de la ligne horizontale.

URL http://journals.openedition.org/ethnomusicolo gie/docannexe/image/1572/img-47.jpg

Fichier image/jpeg, 120k

Titre Fig. 46 : Ezengileer touvain (cf. fig. 21). Accents rythmiques marqués par des traits verticaux alternativement au-dessus et au-dessous de la ligne horizontale.

URL http://journals.openedition.org/ethnomusicolo gie/docannexe/image/1572/img-48.jpg

Fichier image/jpeg, 124k

Titre Fig. 47 : Expérimentation d'un « bourdon harmonique » dans l'aigu, avec variation du fondamental, par Trân Quang Hai.

309

Légende	Technique à deux cavités. Voix fortement nasalisée. Contraction pharyngienne et abdominale. Échelle montante des fondamentaux La1 (135 Hz), Re2, Mi2, La2 (270 Hz), et redescendante au La1. « Bourdon harmonique » de 1380 Hz réalisé successivement par H12, 9, 8, 6, 8, 9, 12.
URL	http://journals.openedition.org/ethnomusicolo gie/docannexe/image/1572/img-49.jpg
Fichier	image/jpeg, 140k
Titre	Fig. 48 : Expérimentation d'un mouvement contraire entre bourdon et mélodie d'harmoniques, par Trân Quang Hai.
Légende	Technique à deux cavités. Voix fortement nasalisée. Contraction pharyngienne et abdominale. Échelle diatonique ascendante des fondamentaux du La1 (110 Hz) au La2 (220 Hz) et redescendante. Échelles d'harmoniques en mouvement contraire, descendante de H19 au H4 et remontant à H19.
URL	http://journals.openedition.org/ethnomusicologie/docannexe/image/1 572/img-50.jpg
Fichier	image/jpeg, 134k

Pour citer cet article

Référence papier

Hugo Zemp et Trân Quang Hai, « Recherches expérimentales sur le chant diphonique », *Cahiers d'ethnomusicologie*, 4 | 1991, 27-68.

Référence électronique

Hugo Zemp et Trân Quang Hai, « Recherches expérimentales sur le chant diphonique », *Cahiers d'ethnomusicologie* [En ligne], 4 | 1991, mis en ligne le 01 janvier 2012, consulté le 31 mars 2018. URL : http://journals.openedition.org/ethnomusicologie/1572

Haut de page

Auteurs

Hugo Zemp

Hugo Zemp est directeur de recherche au CNRS (UPR 165, Musée de l'Homme, Paris). Il a effectué des recherches en Afrique occidentale (Côte d'Ivoire), en Océanie (Iles Salomon) et en Suisse. Directeur des éditions de disques « Collection CNRS – Musée de l'Homme », il enseigne l'utilisation de l'outil audiovisuel à l'Université de Paris X-Nanterre.

Articles du même auteur

Composer et interpréter des rythmes [Texte intégral]

Musique et langage tambouriné chez les 'Aré'aré

Paru dans *Cahiers d'ethnomusicologie*, 10 | 1997

Trân Quang Hai

TRÂN Quang Hai, ingénieur d'études au CNRS (UPR 165, Musée de l'Homme, Paris), s'est spécialisé dans les recherches musicales d'Asie du Sud-Est. Issu d'une famille vietnamienne de cinq générations de musiciens, il pratique plusieurs instruments de musique vietnamiens et asiatiques, et donne de nombreux concerts dans le monde. Il est l'auteur de nombreux articles et l'auteur-interprète de quinze disques.

311

Articles du même auteur

<u>Rollin RACHELE</u>: *Overtone Singing Study Guide* [Texte intégral]

Amsterdam: Cryptic Voices Productions, 1996. 127 p.

Paru dans *Cahiers d'ethnomusicologie*, <u>11 | 1998</u>

Droits d'auteur

http://journals.openedition.org/ethnomusicologie/1572

Numbers in Asian Music

Trần Quang Hải

National Center for Scientific Research, France.

The ancients saw music as an application of cosmic algebra. The Chinese, in their science, considered only the qualitative aspect of the Numbers that they manipulated as signs and symbols. Among the three functions of numbers, the distinction between cardinal and ordinal use is less essential than the distributive function. Thanks to this quality, numbers provide the function of uniting a set, of grouping.

The ratios expressing relationships among musical sounds have a correspondence in all other aspects of an event. The governance of

313

these relations allows comparisons between musical harmony and all other harmonic classifications: colours, shapes or planets.

Theory

The number 5 represents the 5 elements, the 5 movements. "Five" evokes the 5 senses, the 5 organs that are a coagulation of breaths (as wind instruments).

Element	EARTH	METAL	WOOD	FIRE	WATER
Notes	Gong	Shang	Jiao	Zhi	Yi
European Notes	FA F	SOL G	LA A	DO C	RE D
Organ	Spleen Stomach	Lungs Small Intestine Large Intestine	Liver Gall bladder	Heart Intestine	Kidneys Bladder
Colour	Yellow	White	Blue-Green	Red	Black

Planet	Saturn	Venus	Jupiter	Mars	Mercury
Emblem	Phoenix	Tiger	Dragon	Bird	Turtle
Function	Emperor	Minister	People	Public Services (Military / Religious)	Products (objects)
Number	5–10	4–9	3–8	2–7	1–6

The pentatonic range has a centre (GONG) surrounded by four notes assimilated to the four directions in space (SHANG-West, JIAO-East, ZHI-South, YI-North).

It is therefore the law of numbers that governs the proportions of the musical edifice. Sounds, just like numbers, obey the stimuli of attraction and repulsion. Their successive or simultaneous order – i.e. melodic and harmonic movements of the chords respectively – allows for an apparent structure of musical form. Sounds are ordered, paired up and make up structures that evoke real and imaginary worlds.

The root note (also known as tonic or keynote) constitutes the basis and the centre: it is the reference point that allows the construction of the musical edifice.

In the example where the tonic is the FA, the DO note will maintain a fifth interval with its tonic. The very note DO will play a role of fourth in a range of SOL. Our usual DO (Ut) is a tonic in the construction of the classical scale model.

The first and basic tube (Huang Zhong) reproduces the FA (Gong tonic). This FA is close to the FA sharp of the physics scale with its 708.76 vibrations per second. This generator tube represents the Central Palace around which the other elements gather. Yellow is the emblematic colour of the centre: it evokes the Sun, centre of the Sky or heart of the flower. It is reserved to the Emperor, central individual on Earth.

The 12 LÜ or Musical Tubes

We will not insist on the well-known legend of the discovery of the LÜ scale at the hands of Ling Lu (Linh Luân), a music master at the time of the famous Emperor Huangdi (Hùynh Dê, 2697-2597 before our era). In the solitary valley of the mount Kouen Louen (Côn Lôn), at the western borders of the empire, he found bamboos of the same thickness and obtained the fundamental sound, the HUANGZHONG (Hoàng Chung, the Yellow Bell) by blowing in one of the canes after cutting it in between two knots. He obtained the complete LÜ scale thanks to the sound made by a male and a female phoenix.

The LÜ scale would basically correspond to the modern chromatic scale. The absolute pitch of the fundamental sound, the HUANGZHONG, changes according to the dynasty. We will choose the FA, just like Louis Laloy, a French missionary specialist in Chinese music at the beginning of the nineteenth century.

The LÜ scale will then be:

HUANGZHONG (Hoàng Chung, the Yellow Bell): FA

TALÜ (Dai Lu, The Great Lyu): FA#

TAIZU (Thai Thô'c, The Great Iron of Arrow): SOL

JIAZHONG (Gia'p Chung: The Narrow or Still Bell?): SOL#

GUXIAN (Cô Tây, Ancient Purification): LA

ZHONGLÜ (Trong Lu, cadet Lyu) : LA#

RUIBIN (Nhuy Tân, Beneficial Fertility) SI

LINZHONG (Lâm Chung, The Bell of the Woods): DO

YIZE (Di Tac, The Same Rule): DO#

NANLÜ (Nam Lu, The Lyu of the South): RE

WUHI (Vô Xa, the Imperfect): RE#

YINGZHONG (Ung Chung, The Bell of the Eco): MI

But, when composing their melodies, the Chinese did not use the scale of the 12 sounds thus obtained – starting from the tonic note, the HUANGZHONG, through a succession of fifths. Instead, they were content with the five degrees that form the pentatonic scale GONG, SHANG, JIAO, ZHI, YI (Cung, Thuong, Giôc, Chuy, Vu). In the SHI JI (Su Ky: Historical Memoirs), Xi Ma Tian (Tu Ma Thiên), has given the dimensions of the tubes that create the notes of the Chinese pentatonic scale:

9 x 9 = 81 (placing 81 millet grains one next to the other gives a length corresponding to that of a bamboo cane giving the fundamental sound of the Yellow Bell HUANGZHONG).

In their cosmogonic system, the Chinese determined relations based on the law of numbers. These relations are also valid in the music world. The 12 musical tubes, or LÜLÜ, are the basis of this music theory. They generate in turn, in a rhythmic proportion, both by diminishing by a third and by increasing by a third: generation therefore happens through the action of the Three.

According to the type of operation carried out, two generations of tubes are created. The inferior generation provides a shorter tube, whose sound is more acute than the other one and length is reduced by a third. The superior generation provides a longer and deeper sound than the previous one, with respect to which it has been increased by a third.

The inferior generation is the result of a multiplication by two thirds, that is the inverse of a fifth. So, the first tube measuring 81 produces the second shortest tube: $81 \times 2/3 = 54$. Therefore, from FA (81) and DO (54) there exists a fifth.

The superior generation is the result of a fourth, since a 4/3 ratio is what characterises it. Therefore, the second tube (54) produces the third tube: $54 \times 4/3 = 72$. From DO (54) to SOL (72, longer and therefore deeper), there exists a fourth.

FA first tube 81

DO second tube 54 81 x 2/3

SOL third tube 72 54 x 4/3

RE fourth tube 48 72 x 2/3

LA fifth tube 64 48 x 4/3

MI sixth tube 42 64 x 2/3

SI seventh tube 57 42 x 4/3

FA# eighth tube 76 57 x 4/3 inversion

DO# ninth tube 51 76 x 2/3 inversion

SOL# tenth tube 68 51 x 4/3 inversion

RE# eleventh tube 45 68 x 2/3 inversion

LA# twelfth tube 60 45 x 4/3 inversion

The GONG (Cung) note = FA.

2/3 of 81 give 81 x 2/3 = 54; this note is known as ZHI (Chùy): DO

4/3 of 54 give 54 x 4/3 = 72; this is the note known as SHANG (Thuong): SOL

2/3 of 72 give 72 x 2/3 = 48; this note is known as YI (Vu): RE

4/3 of 48 give 48 x 4/3 = 64; note known as JIAO (Giôc): LA

Edouard Chavannes quoted and commented Lyus's passage in appendix II, p. 636, of the third volume of his Historical Memoirs: the HUANGZHONG produces the LINZHONG; the LINGZHONG produces the TAIZU; the TAIZU produces the NANLÜ; the NANLÜ produces the GUXIAN and so on. Another part is added to the three parts of the generator to create a superior generation; one part is taken from the three parts of the generator to create an inferior generation. The HUANGZHONG, the TAIZU; the JIAZHONG, the

GUXIAN, the ZHONGLÜ, the RUIBIN belong to the superior generation; the LINZHONG, the YIZE, the NANLÜ, the WUYI, the YINGZHONG belong to the inferior generation.

According to LIU PUWEI, the tube whose length is 4/3 of the generator tube belong to the superior generation and provides the fourth inferior, that is the low octave of the fifth of the sound of the generator tube. The tube whose length is 2/3 of the generator tube belongs to the inferior generation and provides the fifth of the sound of the generator tube.

These five notes correspond – according to SIMA QIAN, quoted by Maurice Courant – to "the 5 LÜ" HUANGZHONG, TAIZU, GUXIAN, LINZHONG and NANLÜ, the only ones whose measure is expressed in whole numbers starting from the basic 81:

GONG (81): Huangzhong: FA

SHANG (72): Taizu: SOL

JIAO (64): Guxian: LA

ZHI (54): Linzhong: DO

YI (48): Nanlü RE

This scale would have been used under the Yin dynasty (1776-1154 B.C.). According to Maurice Courant, the heptatonic scale – obtained by adding the two complementary or auxiliary notes BIEN GONG (Biên Cung) and BIEN ZHI (Biên Chùy) to the pentatonic scale – "existed at least a dozen centuries before the Christian era". These auxiliary degrees are obtained by pushing the succession of fifths up to the seventh, starting from the fundamental sound. If we give the GONG (Hoàng Chung) degree the pitch of the FA, the

BIEN GONG will have the pitch of a MI and the BIEN ZHI that of a TI.

Therefore, the cycles obtained starting from the fifths present analogies with the movements of the sun (seasons), of the moon (moon months), but also with planets mirroring in the organs. The Chinese associate them with a symbolic colour that has a therapeutic value.

Symbolism in Musical Instruments

In Chinese mythology, there are eight instruments destined to let resound the eight forces of the compass rose. Each instrument has a sonorous body made of a different material, which determines its peculiar character.

1. The sound of SKIN corresponds to the North

2. The sound of CALABASH-GOURD corresponds to the N-E

3. The sound of BAMBOO corresponds to the East

4. The sound of WOOD corresponds to the S-E

5. The sound of SILK corresponds to the South

6. The sound of EARTH corresponds to the S-W

7. The sound of METAL corresponds to the West

8. The sound of STONE corresponds to the N-W

In the North, and at the SKIN, the drums are eight. The GOURD (or CALABASH), in the North-East, has the peculiarity of consisting of a series of 12 Liu, some YIN, some YANG. The instrument allowed making four different sounds at the same time.

The sound of BAMBOO, in the East, was produced by sonorous tubes (Koan Tse). There were three types of these, all of which had 12 tubes: deep, medium and acute sounds, corresponding to the Earth-Man-Sky triad). Later, they evolved towards a separation between yin and yang tubes that constituted two distinct and complementary instruments.

The sound of WOOD was represented by various instruments of which the Tchou – shaped like a bushel and named after Ursa Major – would initiate the concert in the same way as the Ursa indicates the beginning of the day or of the year with its position.

The sound of SILK was produced by stringed instruments known as Qin. These were five-string zithers that originally had a rounded top part representing the Sky and a flat front part representing the Earth. They had five strings to represent the five planets or the five elements.

The sound of EARTH was produced by instruments made of clay that gave a GONG – that is the tonic FA – as deep sound as well as four more tones (SHANG; JIAO; ZHI; Yi). In the West, the sound of METAL was rendered by twelve copper and tin bells that gave the twelve semitones of the LÜ. The sonorous STONES situated in the North-West were assigned to ceremonies that evoked the Sky, establishing a spiritual link thanks to the pure quality of their sounds.

Yoga

In Yoga, there exist 7 chakras corresponding to 7 vowels, 7 sounds or pitches, 7 overtones and 7 points of the human body. The author has carried out experimental research in the presence of overtones in Yoga. The result of his three-year study was presented at the International Congress of Yoga in France in 2002.

According to his research, the fundamental of voice should be at 150Hz.

Number Name of Chakras Location Overtones Vowels Number of Hz

1 Mulâdhâra coccyx H n° 4 U 600Hz

2 Svâdhishthâna genitals H n° 5 O 750Hz

3 Manipûra navel H n° 6 Ö 900Hz

4 Anâhata heart H n° 8 A 1200Hz

5 Vishuddha throat H n° 9 E 1350Hz

6 Ajnâ between H n°10 AE 1500Hz

eyebrows

7 Sahasrâra top of head H n°12 I 1800Hz

Instruments

The lute in the shape of a Vietnamese moon – DAN NGUYET or DAN KIM – was conceived in a harmonious style and in a totally empirical way. Every part of this instrument can be divided into three parts: the two deep strings (0.96 mm) and the high string (0.72 mm) have a vibrating length of 72 cm.

The instrument measures 108 cm overall; the sound board 36 cm; the thickness of the resonance chamber is 6 cm. The bridge is 9 cm

323

long and 3 cm high. The decorative part of the instrument, located opposite the bridge, measures 12 cm in length. The wooden pins measure 12 cm and there are 9 ring nuts measuring 3cm in width.

The Vietnamese monochord DAN DOC HUYEN (unique stringed instrument) or DAN BAU (gourd instrument) is the only musical instrument in the world using Pythagorean theory to create overtones by the division on harmonic knots of the unique steel string of the instrument into 2, 3, 4, 5, 6, 7, 8 equal parts corresponding to the series of overtones. (In fact, if the open string is tuned in C, the overtone 2 will be C an octave higher than the pitch of open string, 3 = G, 4=C 2nd octave higher, 5= E, 6=G, 7=Bb, 8= C 3rd octave higher.)

Chinese tradition has it that – over 5000 years ago – Emperor DU XI asked his lute maker to produce a zither. This imperial instrument was to be based on the relationship between the Sky and the Earth. It therefore had the length of three thuocs, six tâcs and one phân, so as to match the number 361 representing the 360 degrees of the circle plus the centre, that is unity and multitude. The height of the zither was eight tâcs and its bottom four tâcs, to match the eight half seasons and the four cardinal points or four seasons, that is space and time. Its thickness, two tâcs, bore the emblem of Sky-Earth. The twelve strings vibrated similarly to the twelve months of the year, while a thirteenth string represented the centre.

This story shows the domination of the Number and its application in Chinese thought.

Musical Notations

Around 1911, a musician playing the Chinese fiddle, called LIU Thien Hoa, adopted the cipher notation for writing musical scores proposed by Jean Jacques Rousseau in 1746, perfected by Pierre

324

Galin (1786-1821) and later made popular by Aimé Paris and Emile Chevé (1804-1864). The number 1 corresponds to the root note – whatever the tonic (DO, RE, FA, SOL, LA) – and the five main degrees correspond to the five number (1,2,3,4,5). The 6 and 7 represent intervals.

The cipher notation also appears in Indonesian music: it is found in the musical scores used in the GAMELAN.

Numbers are found in the notation used for Tuvan and Mongolian throat singing. The harmonics are numbered according to frequencies starting from the root note. A cipher notation was proposed to write musical scores for split-tone singing. Ted Levin and the author have used cipher notation to transcribe Tuvin and Mongolian folksongs.

Frequency Analysis Using a Sonagraph

The sonagraph, an instrument for measuring spectra, allows pushing split-tone singing beyond basic and experimental research. Since 1970, many people – including Emile Leipp, Gilles Léothaud, Trân Quang Hai, Hugo Zemp in France, Gunji Sumi in Japan, Ronald Walcott in the United States, Johan Sundberg in Sweden, Graziano Tisato in Italy, Werner Deutsch and Franz Födermayer in Austria – have utilised the sonagraph or similar types of instruments to increase the precision of the harmonics produced by split-tone singing thanks to hertzian spectroscopy.

An examination of sonagrams shows the diversity of styles in the split-tone singing of Tuvans, Mongolians, Tibetans and of the Xhosans in South Africa. It allows to establish a classification of styles, to identify the number of harmonics and better understand the how and why of vocal techniques – something that has so far been impossible. The sonagraph allowed Trân Quang Hai to carry out

325

introspective experimental research in overtone singing (with one tonic and two independent partials or harmonics) as well as in "harmonic drone" with variation of the tonic – DO (harmonic 12), FA (harmonic 9), SOL (harmonic 8) and DO octave (harmonic 6 to create the same harmonic pitch). Other experiments by Trân Quang Hai that have produced interesting results are those on the realisation of different spectra starting from ascending and descending singing scale (normal voice, overtone voice with parallel harmonics, overtone singing with opposite moving harmonics between drone and harmonic melody). Basing himself on self-analysis, his research, whose originality lies in its experimental character, has led him to highlight the link between the harmonic drone and the tonic melody, which is the opposite of the initial principle of traditional overtone singing. Moreover, he has interwoven the two melodies (tonic and harmonic); explored overtone singing with one tonic and two independent partials or harmonics and highlighted the three harmonic zones on the basis of the same tonic sound.

Using the sonagraph and other medical systems of analysis (laryngoscopy, fibroscopy, stroboscopy, scanner), the author has been able to propose a new dimension of undertone study with which to develop undertones or sub-fundamentals by creating F-2 (an octave lower than the sung fundamental), F-3 (an octave + a fifth lower than the fundamental) or F-4 (2 octaves below the sung fundamental). This new aspect of research on undertones has attracted a number of researchers, namely Leonardo Fuks (Brazil), Johan Sunberg (Sweden), Masashi Yamada (Japan), Tran Quang Hai (France), Mark Van Tongeren (The Netherlands), and a few overtone singers from the Western world (Steve Sklar from the USA, Bernard Dubreuil from Canada).

This article is a brief introduction to the use of numbers in various areas of Asian music. It represents merely the beginning of a study that will continue in the future.

Recommended Reading

Amiot J M (1780*) Mémoires sur la Musique des Chinois Tant Anciens Que Modernes*, vol. VI de la collection, Mémoires Concernant les Chinois, Paris, 185pp.

Deutsch W A, Födermayer F (1992) Zum Problem des zweistimmigen Sologesanges Mongolischer une Turk Völker, Von der Vielfalt Musikalischer Kultur, Festschrift für Josef Kuckerts (Wort und Musick 12), Verlag Ursula Müller-Speiser, Anif/Salzburg, Salzburg, pp 133–145.

Gunji (1980) An Acoustical Consideration of Xöömij, *Musical Voices of Asia*, The Japan Foundation, Heibonsha Ltd, Tokyo, pp 135–141.

Kunst J (1949) *Music in Java, Its History, Its Theory and Its Technique*, Second Edition, Translated from the Danish Original by Emil Van Loo, vol 1, 265 pp, vol 2, 175 pp, Amsterdam.

Laloy L (1910) *La Musique Chinoise*, Editions Henri Laurens, Paris, 128 pp.

Leipp E (1971) Considération Acoustique sur le Chant Diphonique, *Bulletin du Groupe d'Acoustique Musicale*, 58, Paris, pp 1–10.

Leothaud G (1989) Considérations Acoustiques et Musicales Sur le Chant Diphonique, *Le Chant Diphonique*, Dossier, Institut de la Voix, Limoges, 1:17–43.

Picard E (1991) *La Musique Chinoise*, Editions Minerve, Paris, 215 pp.

Rousseau JJ (1979) Dissertation Sur la Musique, *Ecrits Sur la Musique*, Editions Stock, Paris.

Sunberg J (1977) The Acoustics of the Singing Voice, in *Scientific American* 236, USA, pp.82–91.

Tisato G (1990) Il Canto degli Armonici, Nuove Tecnologie e Documentazione Etnomusicologica, *Culture Musicali*, 15, 16, Rome.

Tongeren M Van (2002) *Overtone Singing / Physics and Metaphysics of Harmonics in East and West*, 1st edition, Fusica Publishers, 1 accompanying CD, Amsterdam, 271 pp.

Trân Quang Hai, Guilou D (1980) Original Research and Acoustical Analysis in Connection with the Xöömi Style of Biphonic Singing, *Musical Voices of Asia*, The Japan Foundation, Heibonsha Ltd, Tokio, pp 162–173.

Trân Quang Hai, Zemp H (1991) Recherches Expérimentales Sur le Chant Diphonique, *Cahiers de Musiques Traditionnelles* : VOIX, Ateliers d'Ethnomusicologie/AIMP, Genève, 4:27–68.

Trân Quang Hai (1995) Le Chant Diphonique: Description Historique, Styles, Aspect Acoustique et Spectral, EM, *Annuario degli Archivi di Etnomusicologia dell'Accademia Nazionale di Santa Cecilia*, Roma, 2:123–150.

Trân Quang Hai (1995) Survey of Overtone Singing Style, *EVTA* (European Voice Teachers Association, Documentation 1994 (Atti di Congresso) Detmold, pp 49–62.

Trân Quang Hai (2002) A la decouverte du chant diphonique, in G.Cornut (editor), *Moyens d'investigation et pedagogie de la voix chantee,* Symetrie (publishers), 1 accompanying CD-Rom, Lyon, pp 117–132.

Walcott R (1974) The Chöömij of Mongolia – A Spectral Analysis of Overtone Singing, *Selected Reports in Ethnomusicology* 2 (1), UCLA, Los Angeles, pp 55–59.

Zemp H, Trân Quang Hai (1991) *Recherches Expérimentales Sur le Chant Diphonique* (voir Trân Quang Hai, Zemp H).

Discography

This selected discography considers only cd.

Tuva

Shu-De. Voices from the Distant Steppe, Realworld CDRW 41, London, U.K., 1994.

Tuva / Tuvinian Singers and Musicians, World Network 55.838, Frankfurt, Germany, 1993.

Tuva - Echoes from the Spirit World, Pan Records PAN 2013 CD, Leiden, the Netherlands, 1992

Tuva: Voices From the Center of Asia, Smithsonian Folkways CD SF 40017, Washington, USA, 1990.

Mongolia

Jargalant Altai/Xöömi and Other Vocal Instrumental Music From Mongolia, Pan Records PAN 2050CD, Ethnic Series, Leiden, Hollande, 1996.

White Moon / Tsagaan Sar/ Traditional and Popular Music from Mongolia, Pan Records PAN 2010 CD, Leiden, The Netherlands, 1992.

Mongolian Music, Hungaroton HCD 18013–14, collection UNESCO, Budapest, Hungary, 1990.

Mongolie: Musique et Chants de Tradition Populaire, GREM G 7511, Paris, France, 1986.

Siberia

Chant Epiques et Diphoniques: Asie Centrale, Sibérie, vol. 1, Maison des Cultures du Monde, W 260067, Paris, France, 1996.

Uzlyau: Guttural Singing of the Peoples of the Sayan, Altai and Ural Mountains, Pan Records PAN 2019CD, Leiden, Hollande, 1993.

Vietnam

Tieng Dan Bâu / Thanh Tâm, (The Sound of the Monochord / Thanh Tâm), Dihavina, Hanoi, Vietnam, 1999.

Vietnam: Dreams and Reality / Trân Quang Hai & Bach Yên, Playasound PS 65020, Paris, France, 1988.

Filmography

Le Chant des Harmoniques (English Version: The Song of Harmonics, 16 mm, 38 minutes. Authors: Trân Quang Hai and Hugo Zemp. Realisation: Hugo Zemp. Co-production CNRS Audiovisuel et Societé Française d'Ethnomusicologie, 1989. Distribution : CNRS Audiovisuel, 1 Place Aristide Briand, F–92195 Meudon, France.

Caratteristiche fisiologiche e acustiche del Canto Difonico

Graziano G. Tisato, Andrea Ricci Maccarini, and

Tran Quang Hai

Introduzione

Il Canto Difonico (Overtone Singing o Canto delle Armoniche) è una tecnica di canto affascinante dal punto di vista musicale, ma particolarmente interessante anche dal punto di vista scientifico. In effetti con questa tecnica si ottiene lo sdoppiamento del suono vocale in due suoni distinti: il più basso corrisponde alla voce normale, nel consueto registro del cantante, mentre il più alto è un suono flautato, corrispondente ad una delle parziali armoniche, in un registro acuto (o molto acuto). A seconda dell'altezza della

331

fondamentale, dello stile e della bravura, l'armonica percepita può andare dalla seconda alla 18° (e anche oltre).

Per quanto riguarda la letteratura scientifica, il Canto Difonico compare per la prima volta in una memoria presentata da Manuel Garcia di fronte all'Accademia delle Scienze a Parigi il 16 novembre 1840, relativa alla difonia ascoltata da cantanti Bashiri negli Urali (Garcia, 1847). In un trattato di acustica pubblicato qualche decennio più tardi (Radau, 1880), la realtà di questo tipo di canto è messa in discussione: *"...Si deve classificare fra i miracoli ciò che Garcia racconta dei contadini russi da cui avrebbe sentito cantare contemporaneamente una melodia con voce di petto e un'altra con voce di testa".*

Deve trascorrere quasi un secolo dal 1840 prima che si ottenga un riscontro obbiettivo della verità del rapporto di Garcia, con le registrazioni fatte nel 1934, fra i Tuva, da etnologi russi. Di fronte all'evidenza della analisi compiuta nel 1964 da Aksenov su quelle registrazioni, i ricercatori cominciarono a prendere in considerazione il problema del Canto Difonico (Aksenov, 1964, 1967, 1973). Aksenov è il primo ad attribuire la spiegazione del fenomeno al filtraggio selettivo dell'inviluppo formantico del tratto vocale sul suono glottico, e a paragonarlo allo scacciapensieri (con la differenza che la lamina di questo strumento può ovviamente produrre solo una fondamentale fissa). In quel periodo compare anche un articolo sul Journal of Acoustical Society of America (JASA) sulla difonia nel canto di alcune sette buddiste tibetane, in cui gli autori interpretano correttamente l'azione delle formanti sulla sorgente glottica, senza tuttavia riuscire a spiegare come i monaci possano produrre fondamentali così basse (Smith *et al.,* 1967).

A partire dal 1969, Leipp con il Gruppo di Acustica Musicale (GAM) dell'Università Paris VI s'interessa al fenomeno dal punto di vista acustico (Leipp, 1971). Tran Quang Hai, del Musée de l'Homme di Parigi, intraprende in quel periodo una serie di ricerche sistematiche, che portano alla scoperta della presenza del Canto Difonico in un numero insospettato di tradizioni culturali diverse (Tran Quang,1975, 1980, 1989, 1991a, 1991b, 1995, 1998, 1999, 2000, e il sito Web www.baotram.ovh.org). L'aspetto distintivo della ricerca di Tran Quang Hai è la sperimentazione e verifica sulla propria voce delle diverse tecniche e stili di canto, che gli ha permesso la messa a punto di metodi facili di apprendimento (Tran Quang, 1989). Nel 1989 Tisato analizza e sintetizza il Canto Difonico con un modello LPC, dimostrando per questa via che la percezione degli armonici dipende esclusivamente dalle risonanze del tratto vocale (Tisato, 1989a, 1991). Nello stesso anno anche il rilevamento endoscopico delle corde vocali di Tran Quang Hai confermava la normalità della vibrazione laringea (Sauvage, 1989, Pailler, 1989). Nel 1992 compare uno studio più approfondito dal punto di vista fonetico e percettivo, che mette in risalto la funzione della nasalizzazione nella percezione della difonia, la presenza di un' adduzione molto forte delle corde vocali e una loro chiusura prolungata (Bloothooft *et al.,* 1992). Gli autori contestano l'ipotesi fatta da Dmitriev che il Canto Difonico sia una diplofonia, con due sorgenti sonore prodotte dalle vere e dalle false corde vocali (Dmitriev *et al.,* 1983). Nel 1999 Levin pubblica sul sito Web di Scientific American un articolo particolarmente interessante per gli esempi musicali che si possono ascoltare, le radiografie filmate della posizione degli articolatori e della lingua, e la spiegazione delle tecniche di produzione dei vari stili del Canto Difonico (Levin *et al.*, 1999, http://www.sciam.com/1999/0999issue/0999levin.html).

Il lavoro che presentiamo qui è il risultato di una recente sessione di lavoro con Tran Quang Hai (ottobre 2001), in cui abbiamo esaminato i meccanismi di produzione del canto difonico con fibroendoscopia. La strumentazione utilizzata era costituita da un fibroendoscopio flessibile collegato ad una fonte di luce stroboscopica, per valutare quello che succedeva a livello della faringe e della laringe, e un'ottica rigida 0°, collegata ad una fonte di luce alogena, per esaminare il cavo orale.

Fig. 1 Azione dell'articolazione sulla posizione di F1 e F2: l'apertura della bocca sposta F1 e F2 nella stessa direzione, mentre il movimento antero-posteriore della lingua determina il movimento contrario di F1 e F2. (ad. da Cosi et al., 1995)

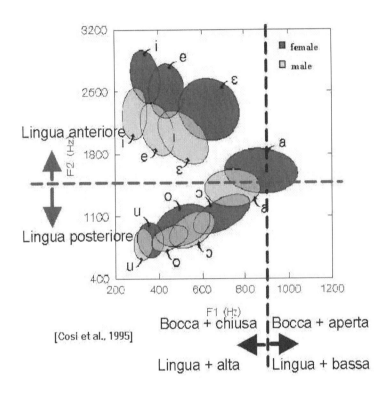

La tradizione del Canto Difonico

Il Canto Difonico, ignorato per centinaia di anni dall'Occidente, si è rivelato molto più diffuso di quello che si potesse immaginare nei primi anni della scoperta: lo troviamo praticato in tutta l'Asia centrale dalla Bashiria (parte europea della Russia vicino agli Urali meridionali), alla Mongolia, passando dalle popolazioni dell'Altai, della Repubblica Tuva (confinante con la Mongolia) fino ai Khakash (situati a nord di Tuva).

I Tuva hanno sviluppato una molteplicità di stili sostanzialmente riconducibili a 5: *Kargiraa* (canto con fondamentali molto basse), *Khomei* (che significa gola o faringe e che è il termine generalmente usato per indicare il Canto Difonico), *Borbannadir* (simile al *Kargiraa*, con fondamentali un po' più elevate), *Ezengileer* (caratterizzato da passaggi ritmici veloci fra le armoniche difoniche), *Sigit* (simile ad un fischio, in cui la fondamentale e le armoniche basse sono molto deboli).

In Mongolia la maggior parte degli stili prende il nome dalla zona di risonanza del canto: *Xamryn Xöömi* (*Xöömi* nasale), *Bagalzuuryn Xöömi* (*Xöömi* di gola), *Tseedznii Xöömi* (*Xöömi* di petto), *Kevliin Xöömi* (*Xöömi* di ventre) , *Xarkiraa Xöömi* (corrispondente al *Kargiraa* Tuva, è uno *Xöömi* narrativo con fondamentali molto basse), *Isgerex* (voce di flauto dentale, stile usato raramente). Si verifica fra gli stessi cantanti mongoli qualche confusione sulla esatta denominazione del loro canto (Tran Quang, 1991a). Caratteristica, anche se non usata in generale, è la presenza in alcuni cantanti mongoli di un vibrato piuttosto marcato (ad esempio, in Sundui e Ganbold).

Le popolazioni Khakash praticano tre tipi di canto difonico (*Kargirar, Kuveder* o *Kilenge* e *Sigirtip*), corrispondenti a quelli Tuva (*Kargiraa, Ezengileer, Sigit*). Anche presso gli abitanti delle montagne dell'Altai si ritrovano questi tre stili, rispettivamente *Karkira, Kiomioi* e *Sibiski*. Le popolazioni della Bashiria, infine, usano la difonia secondo lo stile *Uzlau* (simile all'*Ezengileer* dei Tuva) per accompagnare i canti epici. Una tradizione di canto popolare epico in cui si introduce la difonia esiste anche in Uzbekistan e Kazakistan (Levin *et al.*, 1999).

John Levy ha scoperto nel 1967 un cantante del Rajastan che praticava il Canto Difonico e che se ne serviva per imitare lo scacciapensieri (Tran Quang, 1991a). Si deve comunque dire che questo è rimasto l'unico esempio di Canto Difonico in territorio indiano. Nel 1983 l'etnomusicologo Dave Dargie ha scoperto un tipo di difonia praticata tradizionalmente presso le donne delle popolazioni Xhosa dell'Africa del Sud (Dargie, 1985).

Una tradizione completamente diversa è quella dei monaci tibetani delle scuole buddiste Gyuto e Gyume. Lo scopo del canto in questo caso è di tipo religioso: secondo la loro visione, il suono è una rappresentazione fedele della realtà vibratoria dell'universo, sintetizzata nel suono Om (o meglio Aum). Il cosmo, secondo i buddisti tibetani, è un aggregato di energie interagenti, nessuna delle quali esiste di per sé, che trovano una rappresentazione pittorica come divinità (pacifiche o irate). Esiste una simbologia che lega l'aspetto visivo (Yantra e Mandala) e l'aspetto sonoro (Mantra) di tutte le cose. La conoscenza dell'influsso mantrico del suono permette di agire sul mondo e sugli uomini.

Sembra che sia stato Tzong Khapa (1357-1419), il fondatore del Lamaismo in Tibet, a introdurre la pratica del Canto Difonico nei monasteri Gyuto. La tradizione dice che aveva ricevuto questo insegnamento dalla sua divinità protettrice, Maha Bhairava, incarnazione di Avalokiteshvara, il Signore della Compassione. Maha Bhairava è una delle divinità terrifiche (*bhairava*), simboleggiata come un bufalo infuriato (Tran Quang, 2000). Il canto dei monaci Gyuto, da loro paragonato al muggito di un toro, è simile allo stile Tuva *Borbannadir* con fondamentali basse. L'altezza della voce può scendere fino al La 55 Hz, una quinta sotto alla nota più bassa prevista per un cantante basso nella nostra tradizione. L'articolazione della vocale /o/ e l'arrotondamento delle labbra tende intenzionalmente a rinforzare l'armonico 5° e il 10°. Il suono difonico che si percepisce è dunque una terza maggiore rispetto alla seconda ottava (4° armonico) del bordone di base. Il canto è messo in relazione all'elemento fuoco. I monaci della scuola Gyume esaltano invece la 12° armonica, corrispondente ad una quinta sopra alla terza ottava (8° armonico) del bordone di base. In questa tradizione il canto simboleggia l'elemento acqua.

Il Canto Difonico in Occidente

Il Canto Difonico ha incontrato in Occidente un successo inaspettato. La diffusione è cominciata in campo musicale con il tentativo delle avanguardie di sfruttamento di tutte le possibilità espressive della voce e con l'influsso derivato dal contatto con tradizioni culturali diverse dalla nostra. Il primo in assoluto ad utilizzare una modalità difonica della voce in campo artistico è stato Karlheinz Stockhausen nell'opera Stimmung (Stockhausen, 1968). Seguito poi da un folto gruppo di artisti fra cui il gruppo EVTE (Extended Vocal Techniques Ensemble) dell'Università di California di San Diego nel 1972, Laneri e il gruppo Prima Materia nel 1973 (Laneri, 1981, 2002), Tran Quang Hai nel 1975, Demetrio Stratos nel 1977 (Stratos, 1978, Ferrero *et al.*, 1980), Meredith Monk nel 1980, David Hykes e l'Harmonic Choir nel 1983 (Hykes, 1983), Joan La Barbara nel 1985, Michael Vetter nel 1985, Christian Bollmann nel 1985, Noah Pikes nel 1985, Michael Reimann nel 1986, Tamia nel 1987, Bodjo Pinek nel 1987, Josephine Truman nel 1987, Quatuor Nomad nel 1989, Iegor Reznikoff nel 1989, Valentin Clastrier nel 1990, Rollin Rachele nel 1990 (Rachele, 1996),

337

Thomas Clements nel 1990, Sarah Hopkins nel 1990, Les Voix Diphoniques nel 1997.

Una menzione particolare deve andare al gruppo EVTE per il lavoro sistematico compiuto nell'ampliare il vocabolario espressivo e le modalità compositive relative alla voce, anche nel campo difonico. Il lessico codificato comprendeva un intero repertorio di effetti vocali: rinforzamento di armoniche, vari tipi di ululato, canto tibetano (anche con effetti difonici), schiocchi e sfrigolii di differente intensità e altezza, suoni multifonici, ecc. (Kavash, 1980).

La diffusione del Canto Difonico nel mondo occidentale si è caratterizzata per un alone di misticismo che non era presente nelle culture originali (escludendo, come si è detto, il Buddismo tibetano). Questo non è sorprendente, dal momento che questo tipo di canto sembra trascendere la dimensione sonora consueta. Quando poi si riesce personalmente nella "magia" di scomporre la propria voce in una melodia armonica, si sperimenta una sensazione di euforia. La stranezza del fenomeno da solo non basterebbe a giustificare un interesse così grande, se non fosse che, effettivamente, la realizzazione di questa tecnica di canto richiede uno sviluppo delle capacità di attenzione e percezione tali da facilitare gli stati di concentrazione e meditazione. Non sorprende neppure, sulla base delle considerazioni fatte, che si cominci ad utilizzare il Canto Difonico in musicoterapia (da parte, ad esempio, dello stesso Tran Quang Hai, di Dominique Bertrand in Francia e di Jill Purce in Inghilterra).

Le formazione delle immagini uditive

Ma perché il Canto Difonico si rivela essere una esperienza così strana? La risposta ovvia è che normalmente noi percepiamo una voce con una unica altezza e un timbro caratteristico.

Come è noto, l'onda di pressione che arriva al timpano dell'orecchio è la risultante dell'interazione di vari eventi sonori, ognuno dei quali è composto a sua volta da un aggregato di parziali sinusoidali. Questo flusso sonoro è separato a livello della membrana basilare in componenti frequenziali con un inviluppo di ampiezza e frequenza determinato. La scomposizione spettrale è condizionata da tre fenomeni principali:

1 – La sensibilità dell'orecchio che varia notevolmente con la frequenza (curve isofoniche di Fletcher e Munson, 1933).

2 – Il mascheramento operato dalle componenti in bassa frequenza rispetto a quelle di frequenza più elevata all'interno di una stessa banda critica (Zwicker, 1957).

3 – I fattori temporali che intervengono in questo processo, per cui l'individuazione delle componenti frequenziali basse è ritardata rispetto a quelle più acute (Whitfield, 1977).

A questo punto, i dati analitici del flusso sonoro sono organizzati (fusi, integrati) in separate immagini uditive, secondo fattori psicologici gestaltici (Bregman, 1990). Il processo avviene raggruppando assieme quelle parziali sonore che hanno un andamento omogeneo di ampiezza, durata e frequenza. In maniera sostanzialmente simile alla percezione visiva, che aggrega i quanti luminosi della retina in figure semplici (cerchio, rettangolo, poligono, ecc.), questo processo di fusione percettiva dei quanti sonori porta a rappresentazioni mentali unitarie che prendono il nome di voci, strumenti musicali di un certo tipo, rumori, ecc.

Nel caso sonoro, come in quello visivo, la percezione deve lavorare secondo una dimensione simultanea, che prende in considerazione tutti gli elementi contemporaneamente presenti sulla scena (uditiva o visiva), e una dimensione sequenziale, che tiene conto delle variazioni degli elementi nel tempo.

Lo scopo di questa organizzazione percettiva in categorie mentali è vitale per la sopravvivenza, dal momento che permette di individuare gli eventi (sonori o visivi) e di adottare una strategia comportamentale adeguata.

La separazione dell'immagine uditiva nel Canto Difonico

Come abbiamo visto, il nostro sistema uditivo è condizionato a percepire una sola fondamentale di un suono complesso, anche quando questo sia quasi-armonico o inarmonico (si pensi ad esempio ad una campana) (Plomp, 1967). Normalmente in un suono i meccanismi percettivi rendono difficoltoso l'ascolto delle componenti frequenziali separate. Nei bambini la sensibilità uditiva alle singole componenti e le possibilità articolatorie sono più sviluppate che negli adulti, per i processi di apprendimento che eliminano molte di queste potenzialità (Jakobson, 1968).

Con la tecnica del Canto Difonico si acquisisce un controllo dell'articolazione del tratto vocale tale da portare una delle risonanze (in genere la 1° o la 2°) in corrispondenza esatta di una delle armoniche. A questo punto l'energia di quella componente aumenta in modo considerevole, anche di una trentina di dB, e può essere udita come un suono puro distinto dalla voce. In effetti, in questo caso, la parziale in questione non è più mascherata dalle componenti basse ed inoltre, secondo i principi di fusione detti, non può più essere raggruppata con le altre armoniche, che sono accomunate da un "destino comune", data l'anomalia del suo andamento. Si verifica dunque un caso di separazione dell'immagine uditiva unitaria in due suoni distinti.

È necessario ovviamente un periodo di addestramento per riuscire in questo compito. Nella nostra tradizione musicale esiste qualcosa di paragonabile nella tecnica della cosiddetta "formante del cantante", che consiste nell'allargare la faringe e abbassare la laringe, creando un risuonatore che permette di esaltare un gruppo di parziali frequenziali fra i 2000 e 4000 Hz (Fig. 2-3). I cantanti hanno sviluppato questa capacità probabilmente per sfruttare al meglio la zona di massima sensibilità dell'orecchio, per cui riescono a far sentire la loro voce al di sopra dell'orchestra (caratterizzata da un profilo energetico complessivo quasi triangolare più spostato sulle basse frequenze) (Sundberg, 1987).

Fig. 2 Inviluppo spettrale per il tratto vocale uniforme. Nel caso ideale (tubo senza perdite, lungo 17 cm) le formanti si trovano a multipli dispari dei 500 Hz.

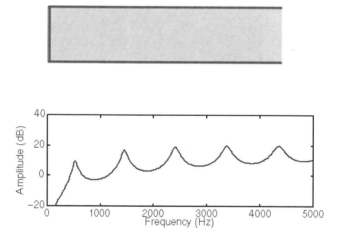

Fig. 3 Inviluppo spettrale per effetto di un restringimento del tubo: le prime 3 formanti si spostano verso l'acuto, mentre la 4° e la 5° si spostano verso le basse frequenze. Si crea così una zona di esaltazione delle parziali fra i 2000 e 4000 Hz, tipica della formante del cantante.

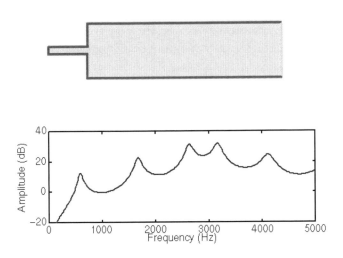

Tecnica del Canto Difonico ad una cavità

Questa modalità di produzione del Canto Difonico è la più semplice e consiste nel muovere semplicemente le labbra come se si pronunciasse la sequenza vocalica da /u/ a /i/ (oppure anche da /o/ ad /a/). La lingua rimane appiattita sul pavimento del cavo. La vibrazione glottica è normale sia per quanto riguarda le corde vocali che per le false corde. Se il movimento articolatorio è sufficientemente lento e preciso si avvertono chiaramente emergere gli armonici più bassi uno dopo l'altro. In effetti si sta agendo solo sull'apertura della bocca, allungando con la /u/ oppure riducendo con la /i/, la lunghezza complessiva del tratto vocale. L'effetto è quello di spostare concordemente la posizione delle prime tre risonanze verso il basso (/u/) oppure verso l'acuto (/i/) (Fig. 4). Come si può vedere dalla Fig. 1, la posizione della 1° formante per questo tipo di articolazione è limitata fra 250 e 1000 Hz, per cui

342

l'armonico più elevato che si può percepire può arrivare al 12°, a seconda dell'altezza della fondamentale di partenza. In effetti questa non è una tecnica che permetta di sentire chiaramente gli armonici molto acuti, per le perdite di energia sonora dovute alla radiazione dalla bocca spalancata. La percezione dell'armonico esaltato dalla risonanza migliora, se si crea una antirisonanza che attenui le armoniche più basse rispetto a quella che si vuole far ascoltare. Questo effetto si ottiene naturalmente nasalizzando il suono, con la comparsa di una antirisonanza che tuttavia non può scendere molto sotto ai 400 Hz (Stevens, 1998). La comparsa di questa antirisonanza può portare anche ad un'altra interpretazione della difonia, come azione della 2° formante (e non della 1°), dal momento che la 1° potrebbe essere attenuata dall'antirisonanza stessa. In ogni caso i 350-400 Hz costituiscono un limite inferiore per la difonia e spiega perché non ci possa essere una chiara percezione degli armonici più bassi (Bloothooft *et al.*, 1992). La nasalizzazione ha anche l'effetto di sopprimere la terza formante, il che può spiegare la debole energia nella zona delle alte frequenze con questa tecnica (Fant, 1960).

Il rango di frequenza per gli armonici creati con questa tecnica varia dunque fra 350 e 1000 Hz e la quantità di note difoniche possibili dipende dall'altezza della fondamentale. Ad esempio, partendo da una altezza di un Fa+ 90 Hz, le armoniche percepibili che può creare Tran Quang Hai vanno dalla 4° (Fa+ 360 Hz) alla 12° (Do#- 1080 Hz). La scala (trasposta in Do) a disposizione del cantante è dunque Do, Mi-, Sol, La#-, Do, Re, Mi-, Fa#-, Sol. Se invece l'altezza della fondamentale passa all'ottava Fa+ 180 Hz, le armoniche a disposizione si riducono alla 3°, 4°, 5°, e 6°, dando una scala con sole 4 note utilizzabili nella melodia (Sol, Do, Mi-, Sol). Ne segue che la voce femminile è penalizzata per quanto riguarda il Canto Difonico.

Tecnica del Canto Difonico a due cavità

La "ricetta" data da Tran Quang Hai per questa tecnica è la seguente:

1 – Cantare con la voce di gola (qualcosa come /ang/).

2 – Pronunciare la lettera /l/ o la sequenza /li/. Non appena la lingua tocca il centro della volta del palato, mantenere la posizione.

3 – Pronunciare la vocale /u/, continuando a tenere la lingua incollata contro il punto detto fra il palato duro e il palato molle.

4 – Contrarre i muscoli del collo e dell'addome, come se si cercasse di sollevare un oggetto molto pesante.

5 – Conferire al suono un timbro molto nasalizzato, amplificando le fosse nasali.

Fig. 4 Articolazione e posizione delle prime tre formanti per una variazione della sezione trasversale del tratto vocale. Un restringimento alle labbra sposta contemporaneamente le tre formanti verso il basso, scurendo il timbro sonoro come nelle vocali /u/ e /o/. Il restringimento alla glottide produce l'effetto contrario, portando le formanti e cioè l'energia verso le alte frequenze e rendendo il suono più brillante. (adattamento da Stevens, 1998).

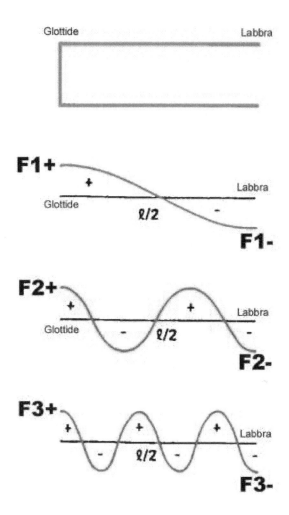

6 – Pronunciare la sequenza delle vocali /u/ e /i/ (oppure anche /o/ e /a/) legate fra di loro, ma alternate parecchie volte l'una con l'altra. Si ottengono così il bordone e le armoniche in sequenza ascendente o discendente, secondo la volontà del cantante.

7 – Si varia la posizione delle labbra o quella della lingua per modulare la melodia delle armoniche. Una concentrazione muscolare forte permette di far emergere la difonia con più chiarezza.

Fig.5 Tecnica a 2 cavità: la punta della lingua si muove lungo il palato, dividendo il tratto vocale in 2 risuonatori.

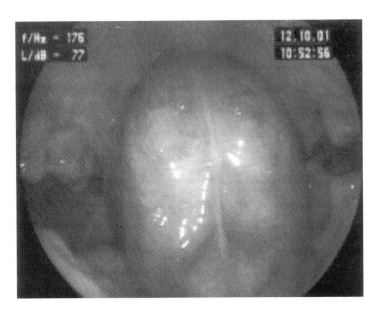

Con questa tecnica, si divide il tratto vocale in due risuonatori distinti, ognuno dei quali accordato sulla propria lunghezza d'onda: come si vede dalla Fig. 1 e 4, lo spostamento delle formanti non è più concorde, ma dipende dal punto in cui la lingua si posiziona. Se si suppone ad esempio che la strozzatura sia ad un terzo della lunghezza complessiva (più o meno 6 cm), si ottiene uno spostamento della 1° formante verso il basso (sempre relativamente alla posizione ideale di un tubo ideale uniforme, 500 Hz, vedi Fig. 2), mentre la 2° formante si sposta molto verso l'acuto. Questo è una situazione che si verifica in una /i/, ad esempio. In questo caso, rispetto alla tecnica con una cavità, l'armonico difonico è esaltato dalla 2° formante e dunque il rango di variazione potrà essere molto più esteso che nel caso precedente (Fig. 1). Teoricamente (ma lo si verifica anche sperimentalmente), l'armonico udibile può arrivare ai 2800 Hz, per cui l'armonico più elevato che si può percepire può arrivare al 18°-20°, a seconda dell'altezza della fondamentale di partenza. Con questa tecnica si evita il problema dell'irradiazione dell'energia sonora dalla bocca, per cui non c'è la medesima necessità di nasalizzare il suono vocale, se non per attenuare ulteriormente le parziali basse e migliorare la percezione di quelle elevate. Rimane comunque l'esigenza di disporre di componenti sonore (soprattutto quelle più elevate in frequenza) con energia sufficiente per essere udibili distintamente. Questo spiega la necessità delle contrazioni muscolari appena descritte. La laringe produce un suono pressato, con la ipercontrazione delle corde vocali e delle false corde (che arrivano a coprire le corde vere, anche per un avvicinamento delle aritenoidi al piede dell'epiglottide) (Fig. 15).

La selezione dell'armonico può avvenire in tre modi distinti:

1 – Si può spostare la punta della lingua avanti o indietro lungo il palato (come avviene nello stile *Khomei*), senza rigonfiarla. Lo spostamento verso i denti permette di selezionare le armoniche più acute e lo spostamento verso il velo le armoniche più gravi (Fig. 5).

2 – Si può tener fissa la posizione della punta della lingua dietro i denti e muovere il corpo e la base della lingua, gonfiandola verso il velo palatino o abbassandola fra i denti (stile *Sigit*).

3 – Una terza possibilità prevede di muovere la radice della lingua a livello della gola piuttosto che lungo il palato. Si muove la base della lingua in avanti fino a far comparire le vallecule glosso-epiglottiche (spazi fra la radice della lingua e l'epiglottide), facendo emergere gli armonici medio-alti. Per gli armonici più alti, l'epiglottide oscilla in avanti chiudendo le vallecule (Levin *et al.*, 1999).

In ogni caso leggeri movimenti delle labbra permettono di aggiustare in maniera più precisa la posizione della formante sull'armonico voluto.

Tran Quang Hai ha scoperto anche un altro metodo per produrre scale di armonici, che consiste nel tener la lingua fissa pressata con i molari superiori e di articolare ciclicamente il solito passaggio vocalico /u/ e /i/. Gli armonici prodotti sono molto acuti e coprono un rango che può andare da 2000 a 3500 Hz. Questo metodo ha un interesse puramente dimostrativo delle possibilità di difonia, visto che non permette la selezione della nota voluta (Tran Quang, 1991a).

Fig. 6 Nel canto Kargiraa (sinistra) le aritenoidi entrano in vibrazione, a differenza del canto tibetano (destra).

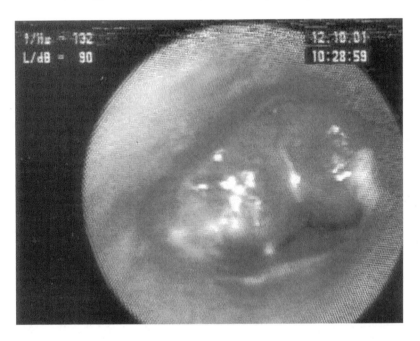

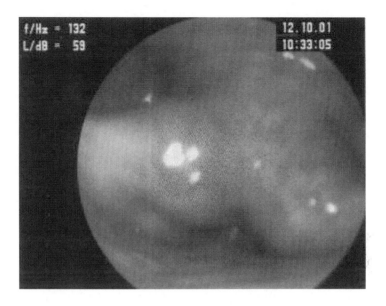

Stile *Kargiraa*

In questo stile di canto le fondamentali sono in un registro estremamente basso (fino al La 55 Hz, ma anche sotto). Il suono prodotto è molto intenso e ricco di componenti armoniche (Fig. 7). Il canto utilizza la 6°, 7°, 8°, 9°, 10° e 12° parziale, corrispondenti a Sol4 392 Hz, La#4- 457 Hz, Do5 523 Hz, Re5 588 Hz, Mi5- 654 Hz, Sol5 784 Hz, quando la fondamentale sia un Do 65.4 Hz. La selezione dell'armonico è fatta mediante l'articolazione di una particolare vocale (/u/, /o/, /❷/, /a/, ecc.), che il cantante ha imparato ad associare con la nota voluta. In questo canto possono entrare in vibrazione anche le strutture sopraglottiche (le cartilagini aritenoidi, le false corde vocali, le pliche ariepiglottiche che connettono le aritenoidi all'epiglottide, e il piede dell'epiglottide) (Levin *et al.*, 1999), con una fondamentale che è una ottava sotto il registro della voce normale, ma che può arrivare ad una ottava ed una quinta sotto al normale (Fuks *et al.*, 1998). Nel caso degli esempi di *Kargiraa* cantati daTran Quang Hai, abbiamo riscontrato con la fibroendoscopia che le aritenoidi entrano in vibrazione, pressate tra loro e contro il piede dell'epiglottide, nascondendo completamente

349

le corde vocali (Fig. 6). L'onda mucosa della "nuova glottide" viene prodotta nella fessura tra le due aritenoidi (Fig. 6). Una situazione analoga si viene a realizzare negli operati di laringectomia subtotale, in cui vengono asportate le corde vocali e parte dell'epiglottide, lasciando intatte solo le aritenoidi. In effetti il timbro della voce nel *Kargiraa* ricorda quello dei laringectomizzati.

Fig. 7 Tuva: Vasili Chazir canta "Artii-sayir" nello stile Kargiraa (Smithsonian/Folkways 18)
La fondamentale è un Si1 61.2 Hz. Gli armonici difonici sono 6° (Fa#4- 367 HZ), 8° (Si4 490 Hz), 9° (Do#5 550 Hz), 10° (Re#5- 612 Hz) e 12° (Fa#5- 734 Hz). Chiaramente visibili fra 950 e 1600 Hz gli armonici in ottava con quelli difonici. Attorno ai 2600-2700 Hz si nota una ulteriore zona formantica che amplifica la 43° e 44° armonica

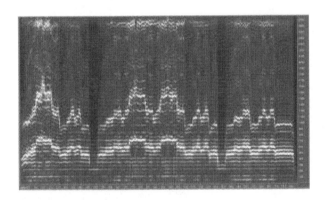

Ci sono varianti di *Kargiraa* nella tradizione Tuva: il *Kargiraa* della Montagna (*Dag Kargiraa*), praticato sulle montagne producendo un eco e cantando con esso, e il *Kargiraa* della Steppa (*Xovu Kargiraa*), usato quando si cavalca con il vento che entra nell'angolo della bocca e amplifica gli armonici. Il *Kargiraa* della Montagna utilizza il registro più grave e aggiunge la nasalizzazione del suono. Si caratterizza per una risonanza di petto e una tensione

350

sulla gola più moderata. il *Kargiraa* della Steppa si differenzia per le fondamentali più elevate, una contrazione maggiore della gola, e una risonanza di petto minima. Un terzo tipo di *Kargiraa* è quello detto del "ventaglio" (*Chelbig Kargiraa*), che prende in nome dall'uso di un ventaglio usato per produrre un flusso d'aria davanti alla bocca e generare vari effetti di *Kargiraa*.

Si deve distinguere il *Kargiraa* dei Tuva o dei Mongoli dal canto dei monaci tibetani, in cui la frequenza fondamentale bassa (circa 60 Hz) è invece ottenuta con il massimo rilassamento o allentamento possibile delle corde vocali, e in cui non si verifica la vibrazione delle strutture sopraglottiche, che risultano anzi contratte (Fig. 6). Il canto tibetano può invece rientrare nella categoria stilistica del *Borbannadir* con fondamentali basse.

Una ulteriore distinzione va fatta con l'effetto di friggio o crepitio (*vocal fry* o *creaky voice*), caratterizzato da un timbro metallico, che si può ottenere con pulsazioni glottiche di varia frequenza (anche molto bassa) e che però non presenta difonia (vedere un repertorio completo in Kavash, 1980).

Stile Borbannadir

Questo stile è caratterizzato da fondamentali nel registro basso o baritonale. Si distingue dal *Kargiraa* per fondamentali un po' più elevate (Fig. 8), per la risonanza più nasale, e per una pulsazione ritmica, con cui i cantanti imitano il mormorio dell'acqua nei ruscelli (Fig. 9), il cinguettio degli uccelli, ecc. Il termine *Borbannadir* significa in effetti "rotolare" e indica tanto l'effetto di trillo delle armoniche, come il suono più grave nei testi antichi. Il cantante riesce a creare un effetto di trifonia fra la fondamentale, un primo livello di armoniche a quinte parallele (rinforzando il 3° armonico) e un secondo livello con il tremolo delle armoniche superiori (Fig. 9). Per quanto riguarda il suono glottico, non c'è l'intervento delle strutture sopra-laringee.

Proprio per la parentela con il *Kargiraa*, il cantante può passare da uno stile all'altro nello stesso brano musicale.

Fig. 8 - Tuva, Stile Borbannadir: la fondamentale è un Fa#2 92 Hz molto attenuato. La pulsazione di circa 6 Hz è evidente soprattutto sulla 8°,9° e 11° armonica.

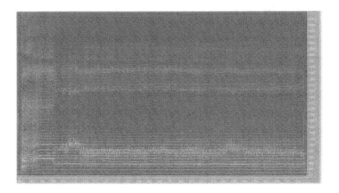

Stile Khomei

Khomei (che significa gola o faringe) è il termine usato per indicare il Canto Difonico in generale, ma anche una modalità distinta dalle altre. È considerato lo stile più antico da molti cantanti Tuva ed è quello che si è imposto per la sua facilità e dolcezza tecnica in tutto l'Occidente. Il canto *Khomei* è caratterizzato da una vibrazione glottica normale e rilassata, senza ipercontrazione delle aritenoidi (come ad esempio nello stile *Sigit*, vedi Fig. 11), e dal rilassamento dei muscoli addominali. Alcuni cantanti utilizzano anche abbellimenti come il vibrato.

Fig. 9 - Tuva: Anatoli Kuular - stile Borbannadir con fondamentale acuta (Mi3+ 169 Hz). Si tratta di una trifonia, data dalla fondamentale, il 3° armonico molto forte (Si4+ 507 Hz) in intervallo

352

di 5° con il Mi3) e il tremolo evidente soprattutto sulla 6° armonica (Si5+ 1014 Hz).

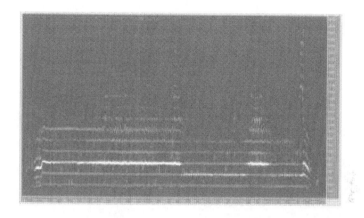

Fig. 10 - Tuva: stile Khomei. La fondamentale è un Fa#3+ 189 Hz piuttosto debole. Gli armonici usati qui sono 6°, 7°, 8°, 9°, 10° e 12°, corrispondenti a Do#6+ 1134, Mi6 1323 Hz, Fa#6+ 1512 Hz, Sol#6+ 1701 Hz, La#6+ 1890 Hz, Do#7+ 2268 Hz.

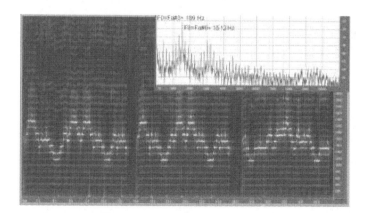

Fig. 11 Le aritenoidi nel canto difonico con tecnica Khomei sono in una posizione più arretrata rispetto allo stile Sigit (fig. 15). Il piano glottico è visibile e mostra le corde vocali nella fase di chiusura del ciclo vibratorio.

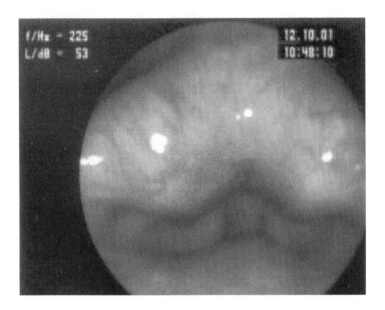

Stile Ezengileer

La parola *Ezengileer* significa "staffa" e vuole indicare che questo stile è caratterizzato da variazioni ritmiche simili al suono che le staffe metalliche producono sotto l'appoggio periodico dei piedi quando si sta galoppando (Fig. 12). L'*Ezengileer* è una variante dello stile *Sigit*, caratterizzato da oscillazioni ritmiche veloci fra le armoniche difoniche. C'è una grande varietà di timbro da un cantante all'altro, uniti da questo elemento comune che è il ritmo "del cavallo". Attualmente è raro sentirlo eseguire ed è giudicato uno stile piuttosto difficile

Fig. 12 - Tuva, Stile Ezengileer. La fondamentale è un La#2 117 Hz

354

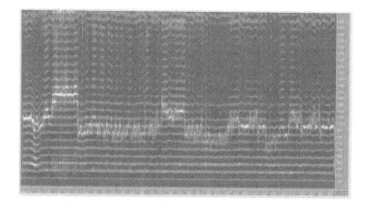

Fig. 13 Tuva: stile Sigit.La fondamentale è un Mi3+ 167 Hz di intensità molto debole. Gli armonici usati qui sono 8°, 9°, 10° e 12°, corrispondenti a Mi6+ 1336 Hz, Fa#6+ 1503 Hz, Sol#6+ 1670 Hz, Si6+ 2004 Hz. Si nota la scansione ritmica dovuta al passaggio veloce verticale fra le armoniche, con una periodicità variabile di circa 900 ms. È presente una seconda zona di risonanza in alta frequenza attorno ai 3000-3200 Hz

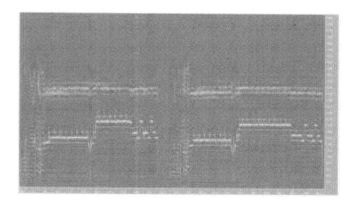

Fig. 14 Mongolia: Ganbold canta un Kevliin Xöömi (Xöömi di ventre, simile allo stile Sigit Tuva). La fondamentale è un Sol# 208 Hz piuttosto debole. Gli armonici usati qui sono 6°, 7°, 8°, 9°, 10° e 12°, corrispondenti a Re#6 1248 Hz, Fa#6- 1456 Hz, Sol#6 1664 Hz, La#6+ 1872 Hz, Do7- 2080 Hz, Re#7 2496 Hz. Presenza di un

vibrato molto ampio con una modulazione di frequenza di circa 6 Hz

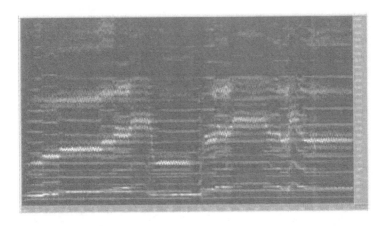

Stile Sigit

Sigit significa "fischio" ed in effetti questo stile è caratterizzato da una difonia, in cui la fondamentale e le armoniche basse sono molto indebolite e poco percepibili. L'armonico esaltato dalla risonanza sovrasta il bordone con un suono flautato (Fig. 13-14). In genere il brano comincia con un testo cantato, senza armonici percepibili. Alla fine della frase, il cantante intona il bordone su una fondamentale media (da Mi3 165 Hz a La3 220 Hz), su cui costruisce la linea melodica delle armoniche. In genere gli intervalli cantati corrispondono alla 9°, 10°, 12° armonica, ma si ascoltano anche melodie sulla 8°, 9°, 10°, 12° e 13° parziale.

Questo stile richiede una pressione notevole sul diaframma e una ipercontrazione della glottide. Il posizionamento della lingua è particolarmente critico dovendo selezionare armonici in alta frequenza (fino a 2800 Hz circa) e dunque molto vicini fra di loro. La fibroendoscopia sulla laringe di Tran ha mostrato una posizione delle aritenoidi molto avanzato a coprire quasi le corde vocali (fig. 15). L'effetto della costrizione del tratto vocale alla glottide è stato

356

illustrato in fig. 3: l'energia spettrale è spostata sulle alte frequenze, attenuando la fondamentale e le armoniche basse.

Fig. 15 Stile Sigit. Le aritenoidi si spostano marcatamente in avanti fino a nascondere il piano glottico. L'energia spettrale si distribuisce sulle alte frequenze attenuando la fondamentale e le componenti basse.

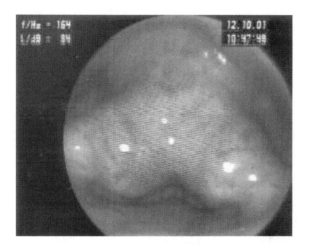

Bibliografia

Aksenov, A.N. (1964). "Tuvinskaja narodnaja muzyka", Mosca.

Aksenov, A.N. (1967). "Die stile der Tuvinischen zweistimmigen sologesanges", Sowjetische Volkslied- und Volksmusikforschung, pp. 293-308, Berlin.

Aksenov, A.N. (1973). "Tuvin folk music", Journal of the Society for Asian Music, Vol. 4, n. 2, pp. 7-18, New York.

Bregman, A. (1990). *Auditory scene analysis: the perceptual organization of sound*, MIT Press, Cambridge.

Dargie, D. (1985). "Some Recent Discoveries and Recordings in Xhosa Music", 5th Symposium on Ethnomusicology, University of Cape Town, International Library of African Music (ed), pp. 29-35, Grahamtown.

Desjacques, A. (1985). "Une considération phonétique sur quelques techniques vocales diphoniques mongoles", Bulletin du Centre d'Etudes de Musique Orientale, 31, pp. 46-55, Paris.

Dmitriev, L. - Chernov, B. - Maslow, V. (1983). "Functioning of the voice mechanism in double voice Touvinian singing", Folia Phoniatrica, Vol. 35, pp. 193-197.

Fant, G. (1960). *Acoustic theory of speech production*, Mouton, The Hague.

Ferrero F. - Croatto L. - Accordi M. (1980). "Descrizione elettroacustica di alcuni tipi di vocalizzo di Demetrio Stratos", Rivista Italiana di Acustica, Vol. IV, n. 3, pp. 229-258.

Ferrero, F., Ricci Maccarini, A., Tisato, G. (1991). "I suoni multifonici nella voce umana", Proc. XIX Convegno AIA, Napoli, pp. 415-422.

Fletcher, H., Munson, W.A. (1933). "Loudness, Its Definition, Measurement and Calculation", Vol. 5, 2, pp. 82-108.

Fuks L., Hammarberg B.,Sundberg J. (1998): "A self-sustained vocal-ventricular phonation mode: acoustical, aerodynamic and glottographic evidences", *KTH TMH-QPSR* 3/1998, pp. 49-59, Stockholm

Garcia, M. (1847). *Traitè complet de l'art du chant*, Paris.

Gunji, S. (1980): "An acoustical consideration of Xöömij", Musical Voices of Asia, pp. 135-141, The Japan Foundation (ed), Heibonsha Ltd, Tokyo.

Hamayon, R. 1980: "Mongol Music", New Grove's Dictionary of Music and Musicians 12, pp. 482-485, Stanley Sadie (ed), MacMillan Publishers, Londres.

Harvilahti, L. (1983). "A Two Voiced Song With No Word", Suomalais-ugrilaisen seuran aikakauskirja 78, pp. 43-56, Helsinki.

Kavasch D. (1980). "An introduction to extended vocal techniques", Report of CME, Univ. of California, San Diego, Vol. 1, n. 2, pp. 1-20, con cassetta di esempi sonori.

Jakobson, R. (1968). *Child language, aphasia and phonological universe*, La Hayes, Mouton.

Laneri, R. (1983). "Vocal techniques of overtone production", NPCA Quarterly Journal, Vol XII, n. 2-3, pp. 26-30.

Laneri, R. (2002). *La voce dell'arcobaleno*, Ed. Il Punto d'Incontro, Vicenza.

Leotar, F. (1998). *"Etudes sur la musique Touva"*, maîtrise de l'Université de Nanterre - Paris X, 128 pages, 2 cassettes.

Leothaud, G. (1989). "Considérations acoustiques et musicales sur le chant diphonique", dossier n° 1, Le chant diphonique, pp. 17-43, Institut de la Voix, Limoges.

Levin, Th. - Edgerton, M. (1999). "The Throat Singers of Tuva", http://www.sciam.com/1999/0999issue/0999levin.html

Pailler, J.P. (1989). "Examen video du larynx et de la cavité buccale de Monsieur Trân Quang Hai", dossier n°1, Le Chant Diphonique, pp. 11-13, Institut de la Voix, Limoges.

Pegg, C. (1992). "Mongolian conceptualizations of Overtone Singing (Xöömii)", The British Journal of Ethnomusicology (1), pp. 31-53, Londres.

Plomp, R. (1967). "Pitch of complex tones", JASA, Vol 41 (6), pp. 1526-1533.

Rachele, R. (1996). "Overtone Singing Study Guide", Cryptic Voices Productions (ed), pp. 1-127, Amsterdam .

Sauvage, J.P. (1989). " Observation clinique de Monsieur Trân Quang Hai", dossier n° 1, Le Chant diphonique, pp. 3-10, Institut de la Voix, Limoges.

Smith, H., Stevens, K.N., Tomlinson, R.S. (1967). "On an unusual mode of singing of certain Tibetan Lamas", JASA. 41 (5), pp. 1262-4, USA.

Stevens K. (1998), *Acoustic Phonetics*, MIT Press, Cambridge.

Sundberg, J. (1987). *The science of the singing voice*, Northern Illinois University Press, De Kalb, Illinois.

Tisato, G. (1989a), "Analisi e sintesi del Canto Difonico", Proc. VII Colloquio di Informatica Musicale (CIM), Cagliari, pp. 33-51, 1989.

Tisato, G. (1989b), "Il canto degli armonici", in *Culture Musicali, Quaderni di Etnomusicologia,* Ed. La Casa Usher, Vol. 15-16, pp. 44-68.

Tisato, G. - Ricci Maccarini, A.R. (1991). "Analysis and synthesis of Diphonic Singing", Bulletin d'Audiophonologie, Vol. 7, n. 5&6, pp. 619-648, Besançon.

Tongeren, M. Van (1994). *"Xöömij in Tuva: new developments, new dimensions"*, Thèse de maîtrise, Ethnomusicologisch Centrum "Jaap Kunst", Universiteit van Amsterdam.

Tongeren, M. Van (1995). "A Tuvan perspective on Throat Singing", Oideion, The Performing Arts Worldwide, 2, pp. 293-312, Université de Leiden.

Tran Quang Hai (1975). "Technique de la voix chantée mongole: Xöömij", Bulletin du CEMO, n. 14 & 15, pp. 32-36, Paris.

Tran Quang Hai - Guilou, D. (1980). "Original research and acoustical analysis in connection with the xöömij style of biphonic singing", Musical Voices of Asia, pp. 162-173, The Japan Foundation (ed), Heibonsha Ltd, Tokyo.

Tran Quang Hai (1989). "Réalisation du chant diphonique", dossier n°1, Le Chant diphonique, pp. 15-16, Institut de la Voix, Limoges.

Tran Quang Hai - Zemp, H. (1991a). "Recherches expérimentales sur le chant diphonique", Cahiers de Musiques traditionnelles, Vol. 4, pp. 27-68, Genève.

Tran Quang Hai (1991b). "New experimental about the Overtone Singing style", Bulletin d'Audiophonologie, Vol. 7, n. 5&6, pp. 607-618, Besançon.

Tran Quang Hai (1995). " Le chant diphonique: description, historique, styles, aspect acoustique et spectral", EM, Annuario degli Archivi di Etnomusicologia dell'Accademia Nazionale di Santa Cecilia, n. 2, pp. 123-150, Roma.

Tran Quang Hai (1997a). "Recherches introspectives sur le chant diphonique et leurs applications", Penser La Voix, (ed) La Licorne, pp. 195-210, Poitiers.

Tran Quang Hai (1997b). " Overtones in Central Asia and in South Africa (Xhosa Vocal Styles), Proceedings of the First South African Music and Dance Conference and 15th Symposium on Ethnomusicology, pp. 422-432, Univ. de Cape Town, Afrique du Sud.

Tran Quang Hai (1998). " Survey of overtone singing style", Die Ausdruckswelt der Stimme, 1-Stuttgarter Stimmtage/ Horst Gunderman, (ed) Hüthig, pp. 77-83, Allemagne.

Tran Quang Hai (1999). "Overtones used in Tibetan Buddhist Chanting and in Tuvin Shamanism", Ritual and Music, Lithuanian Academy of Music, Department of Ethnomusicology, pp. 129-136, Vilnius.

Tran Quang Hai (2000). "Musique Touva", www.baotram.ovh.org\tuva.html

Vlachou, E. (1985). *"Recherches vocales contemporaines: chant diphonique"*, Thèse de maîtrise, Université de Paris VIII-Saint Denis, direction de D. Charles, 90 pages, Paris.

Walcott, R. (1974). "The Chöömij of Mongolia - A spectral analysis of overtone singing", Selected Reports in Ethnomusicology 2 (1), pp. 55-59, UCLA, Los Angeles.

Whitfield, I. C. (1978). "The neural code". In *Handbook of perception*, (ed) Carterette & Friedman, Academic, Vol IV, 5, New York.

Zue, V. (1989). *"Acoustic theory of speech production"*, preliminary draft, Dep. Electrical Eng. & Computer Science, MIT, Cambridge.

Zwicker, E., Flottorp, G., Stevens, S. S. (1957). "Critical bandwidth in loudness summation". JASA, Vol. 29 (5), pp. 548-557.

Discografia

TUVA

"Tuva: Voices from the Center of Asia", Smithsonian Folkways CD SF 40017, Washington, USA, 1990.

"Tuva: Voices from the Land of the Eagles", Pan Records, PAN 2005 CD, Leiden, Netherlands, 1991.

"Tuva: Echoes from the Spirit World", Pan Records, PAN 2013 CD, Leiden, Netherlands, 1992.

"Tuvinian Singers and Musicians - Ch'oomej: Throat-Singing from the Center of Asia", World Network, Vol. 21, USA, 1993.

"Huun-Huur-Tu: Old Songs and Tunes of Tuva", Shanachie Records 64050, Newton, USA, 1993.

"Huun-Huur-Tu: The Orphan's Lament", Shanachie Records 64058, Newton, USA, 1994.

"Huun-Huur-Tu: If I'd Been Born an Eagle", Shanachie Records, Newton, USA, 1997.

"Shu-De, Voices from the Distant Steppe", Real World Records, CD RW 41, UK, 1994.

"Musiques traditionnelles d'Asie centrale: Chants Harmoniques Touvas", Silex Y 225222, Paris, France, 1995.

"Shu-de / Kongurei: Voices from Tuva", New Tone NT6745, Robi Droli, San Germano, Italia, 1996.

"Chirgilchin: The Wolf and the Kid", Shanachie Records, Newton, USA, 1996.

"Deep in the Heart of Tuva", Ellipsis Arts, USA, 1996.

MONGOLIA

"Mongolie: Musique et Chants de tradition populaire", GREM G 7511, Paris, France, 1986.

"Mongolie: Musique vocale et instrumentale", Maison des Cultures du Monde, W 260009, collection INEDIT, Paris, France, 1989.

"Mongolian Folk Music", Hungaroton, HCD 18013-14, UNESCO, Budapest, Hongrie, 1990.

"White Moon", Pan Records, PAN 2010CD, Leiden, Netherlands, 1992.

"Folk Music from Mongolia-Karakorum", Hamburgisches Museum für Völkerkunde, Hambourg, Allemagne, 1993.

"Vocal & Instrumental Music of Mongolia", Topic Records TSCD909, London, UK., 1994.

"Jargalant Altai: Xöömii and Other Vocal and Instrumental Music from Mongolia", Pan Records PAN 2050CD, Ethnic Series, Leiden, Netherlands, 1996.

RUSSIA

"Uzlyau: Guttural Singing of the Peoples of the Sayan, Altai and Ural Mountains", Pan Records PAN 2019CD, Leiden, Netherlands, 1993.

"Chant Épiques et Diphoniques: Asie Centrale, Sibérie, Vol 1", Maison des Cultures du Monde, W 260067, Paris, France, 1996.

TIBET

"The Gyuto Monks: Tibetan Tantric Choir", Windham Hill Records WD-2001, Stanford, California, USA, 1987.

"The Gyuto Monks: Freedom Chants from the Roof of the World", Rykodisc RCD 20113, Salem, Maryland, USA, 1989.

"Tibet: The heart of Dharma. Buddha's teachings and the music they inspired", Ellipsis Arts 4050, New York, USA, 1996.

SUD AFRICA

"Le chant des femmes Xhosa", The Ngqoko Women's Ensemble, VDE CD 879, 1996.

TRAN QUANG HAI HAVE MET THESE ETHNOMUSICOLOGISTS DURING HIS TIME WORKING AS AN EXECUTIVE BOARD MEMBER OF THE ICTM (2005 -2017)

Executive Board Members of The Ictm In 2017, Limerick, Ireland

Executive Board Members Of The Ictm In Astana, Kazakhstan, 2015
Members Of The Executive Board Committee Of The Ictm

367

Salwa El Shawan Castello Bianco (Portugal) & Tran Quang Hai

Svanibor Pettan (Slovenia) & Tran Quang Hai

Razia Sultanova (Uk) & Tran Quang Hai

Don Niles (Papua New Guinea) & Tran Quang Hai

Stephen Wild (Australia) & Tran Quang Hai

Mohid Anis Md Nor (Malaysia) & Tran Quang Hai

Tan Sooi Beng (Malaysia) & Tran Quang Hai

Samuel Araujo (Brazil) & Tran Quang Hai

Terada Yoshitaka (Japan) & Tran Quang Hai

Catherine Foley (Ireland) & Tran Quang Hai

Jean Kidula (Usa) & Tran Quang Hai

Jonathan Stock (Uk) & Tran Quang Hai

Lawrence Witzleben (Usa) & Tran Quang Hai

Naila Ceribasic (Croatia) & Tran Quang Hai

Xiao Mei (China) & Tran Quang Hai

Tim Rice (Usa) & Tran Quang Hai

Carlos Yoder (Argentina) & Tran Quang Hai

Aiman Mussakajayeva, Rector Of The Kazakh National University
Of Arts, Astana, Kazakhstan, & Tran Quang Hai

Ursula Hemetek (Austria) & Tran Quang Hai

Beverley Diamond (Canada) & Tran Quang Hai

Wim Van Zanten (The Netherlands) & Tran Quang Hai

OTHER ETHNOMUSICOLOGISTS I HAVE MET AT DIFFERENT ICTM WORLD CONFERENCES

William Malm (Usa) & Tran Quang Hai

Adelaide Ryes (Usa) & Tran Quang Hai

Barbara Smith (Usa) & Tran Quang Hai

Gisa Jähnichen (Germany), Tran Quang Hai, Minh Chau (Vietnam)

John Bailey (Uk) & Tran Quang Hai

Marianne Böcker (Germany) & Tran Quang Hai

Sheen Dae Cheol (Korea) & Tran Quang Hai

Jean Jacques Nattiez (Canada) & Tran Quang Hai

Anthony Seeger (Usa) & Tran Quang Hai

David Hughes (Uk) & Tran Quang Hai

Michael O Sulleabhain (Ireland) & Tran Quang Hai / Bach Yen

Laurent Aubert (Switzerland) & Tran Quang Hai

Oshio Satomi (Japan) & Tran Quang Hai

Raymond Ammann (Switzerland) & Tran Quang Hai

385

Um Hae-Kyung (Korea) & Tran Quang Hai

Terry Miller (Usa) & Tran Quang Hai

Yang Mu (Australia) & Tran Quang Hai

Graziano Tisato (Italy) & Tran Quang Hai

Speranta Radulescu (Rumania) & Tran Quang Hai

Susilo Hardja (Indonesia) & Tran Quang Hai

Krister Malm (Sweden) & Tran Quang Hai

Ricardo Trimillos (Usa) & Tran Quang Hai

Alexander Cannon (Usa) & Tran Quang Hai

Tran Van Khe (1921-2915) & Tran Quang Hai

Tö Ngoc Thanh (Vietnam) & Tran Quang Hai

Dang Hoanh Loan (Vietnam) & Tran Quang Hai

FRENCH ETHNOMUSICOLOGISTS FRIENDS

Bernard Lortat-Jacob & Tran Quang Hai

Gilbert Rouget (1916-2017) & Tran Quang Hai

Mireille Helffer & Tran Quang Hai

Monique Brandily

Simha Arom & Tran Quang Hai

From Left To Right: Mireille Helffer, Pribislav Pitoeff, Simha Arom,
Bernard Lortat-Jacog, Laurence Fayet, Tran Quang Hai

From Left To Right: Bernard Lortat Jacob, Francesco Giannattasio, Tran Quang Hai

Jean Lambert , Tran Quang Hai

Lucie Rault & Tran Quang Hai

Marie Barbara Le Gonidec & Tran Quang Hai

Susanne Fürniss & Tran Quang Hai

Sylvie Le Bomin & Tran Quang Hai

Alienor Anisensel & Tran Quang Hai

Dana Rappoport & Tran Quang Hai

Charles Duvelle (1937-2017) & Tran Quang Hai

SELECTION OF VIDEO CLIPS PERFORMED BY TRAN QUANG HAI

Mystères des voix du monde (VF)

https://www.youtube.com/watch?v=7Cvd2W-b840

Le chant des harmoniques - Tran Quang Hai (VF)

https://www.youtube.com/watch?v=OnXBOCBmmTU

Vietnam Musique Traditionnelle Tran Quang Hai

https://www.youtube.com/watch?v=anypfOH7mRI

GSTS Trần Quang Hải (Performance of Jew's Harps, Spoons and Overtone Singing)

https://www.youtube.com/watch?v=_NIEgVlG-_Y

Tran Quang Hai: Overtone Singing

https://www.youtube.com/watch?v=Eysu0odOips

Tran Quang Hai - "Omaggio a Demetrio Stratos '08"

https://www.youtube.com/watch?v=OkFtfPTq2cQ

Meeting of 2 Kings of Spoons: Roger Mason & Tran Quang Hai

https://www.youtube.com/watch?v=xoIZu211bE8

Tran Quang Hai & John Wright - duet in Jew's harp, Paris, January 15, 2012

https://www.youtube.com/watch?v=QalGYW7EZAw

TRAN QUANG HAI (VIETNAM), Moscow, June 9, 2012

https://www.youtube.com/watch?v=CKWAuQE9mEQ

Meeting of 2 Kings of Spoons: Roger Mason & Tran Quang Hai

https://www.youtube.com/watch?v=xoIZu211bE8

Tran Quang Hai plays the Khomus jew's harp, Yakutia, 23 june 2011

400

https://www.youtube.com/watch?v=oteRW5305DY

TRAN QUANG HAI plays the Vietnamese Jew's harp in MOSCOW, RUSSIA, 25.10.2012.

https://www.youtube.com/watch?v=sXvWinpOuUs

GS-TS Trần Quang Hải biểu diễn đàn môi (Vua muỗng) (Tran Quang Hai's demonstration of Jew's Harp)

https://www.youtube.com/watch?v=ZdkMb6959Wo

Cha con GS-TS Trần Văn Khê hòa đàn ngẫu hứng 2014 (Tran Van Khe & Tran Quang Hai in a duet of moon shaped lute and spoons)

https://www.youtube.com/watch?v=tbAuJQxkclM

"VUA MUỖNG" TRẦN QUANG HẢI biểu diễn nghệ thuật gõ muỗng, báo TUỔI TRẺ, 2011 (Tran Quang Hai's demonstration of Spoons)

https://www.youtube.com/watch?v=r5u42TM93K8

Tran Quang Hai plays ARIRANG with the Yakut Jew's harp

https://www.youtube.com/watch?v=95dnddq0qKw

Improvization with Renato, Luca and Tran Quang Hai

https://www.youtube.com/watch?v=cEQHzwqdkoY

TRAN QUANG HAI joue des cuillers, Soirée JMF, Boulogne Billancourt, 7 janvier 2012

https://www.youtube.com/watch?v=gzBlHtX_mAY

TRAN QUANG HAI on JAPANESE TELEVISION, part 2, December 26, 2012

https://www.youtube.com/watch?v=cKuT4fy84oA

TRAN QUANG HAI on JAPANESE TELEVISION , part 1, december 26,2012.wmv

https://www.youtube.com/watch?v=FD1pa45W6u4

Tran Quang Hai sings overtones in Campo Grande, BRAZIL.

https://www.youtube.com/watch?v=zhIBAKL5oII

Tran Quang Hai & Benjamin Taubkin in an improvisaton.

https://www.youtube.com/watch?v=L5HX0IUjtW8

Tran Quang Hai plays the spoons for indigenous children.

https://www.youtube.com/watch?v=jvLPPTO1Pok

TRAN QUANG HAI plays the spoons in Tokyo, Japan

https://www.youtube.com/watch?v=1GPjqrHZXLQ

NVBP: Tiếng Việt trong lòng người Việt (The Vietnamese language in the Vietnamese Heart)

https://www.youtube.com/watch?v=0vEvzywXJJY&t=1473s

Lesson proposed by TRAN QUANG HAI for learning throat singing

https://www.youtube.com/watch?v=pc9kGRvlpd0&t=29s

Lesson proposed by TRAN QUANG HAI for learning throat singing, part 2

https://www.youtube.com/watch?v=65va3GNCKvM

Tran Quang Hai sings the 7 CHAKRAS with overtones

https://www.youtube.com/watch?v=BdvlC-0DoHI

Tran Quang Hai writes the word MINIMUM with different VOICES

https://www.youtube.com/watch?v=mOtX6m9tzeI

TRAN QUANG HAI sings "The Ode to Joy" 2 times in one breath

https://www.youtube.com/watch?v=gzAIrvrro8c

Made in the USA
Lexington, KY
07 September 2019